PATTERNS
OF THOUGHT

PATTERNS OF THOUGHT

The Hidden Meaning of the Great Pavement of Westminster Abbey

Richard Foster

JONATHAN CAPE
LONDON

1 *frontispiece* The Great Pavement before the high altar of
Westminster Abbey, seen from the triforium of the north transept

First published 1991
© Richard Foster 1991
Jonathan Cape, 20 Vauxhall Bridge Road, London SW1V 2SA

Richard Foster has asserted his right under the
Copyright, Designs and Patents Act, 1988
to be identified as the author of this work

A CIP catalogue record for this book
is available from the British Library

ISBN 0–224–02910–X

Printed in Great Britain by Butler & Tanner Ltd,
Frome and London

This book is dedicated to
DOROTHY TAYLOR,
who taught me Art
and
FRED SPEKE,
who taught me Physics

Contents

1: These Porphyry Stones 1

2: King, Pope, Craftsman and Priest 8

3: The Physical Evidence 30

4: The Historical Record 48

5: The Inscription 80

6: The Art of Geometry 111

7: Images of Divine Order 131

8: Into the Labyrinth 148

Acknowledgments 167

Bibliography 168

Notes 175

Sources of Illustrations 180

Index 181

I

These Porphyry Stones

For three days in February 1989 the wraps were lifted from one of the country's greatest medieval art treasures. At Westminster Abbey, the carpet that had both protected and concealed the great marble pavement before the high altar was rolled back and, for the first time in more than a generation, the intricate patterns of its interweaving circles and squares were put on show before the public. The uncovering of the pavement was such a success that it has now become an annual event. Tour guides who had spent decades taking visitors around the Abbey were stopped in their tracks by the sight of the newly revealed pavement which they had always described but had never seen with their own eyes. In the three days more than seven thousand people filed around the edges of the pavement, occasionally complaining when they were ushered onwards more quickly than they wanted, due to the pressure of the growing queue which eventually stretched out of the Abbey itself and into the forecourt. They were spellbound by the pavement. They wanted to stay long enough for their eyes and minds to drink in the fascination of this magnificent work of art that was set in the heart of the Abbey more than seven centuries ago.

It was in 1259 that the newly-elected Abbot of Westminster, Richard de Ware, undertook the long journey to the Court of Rome for confirmation in his post by the Pope. On this trip to Italy he discovered the work of the Roman marblers, whose classically inspired designs had been the most fashionable form of church decoration there since the twelfth century. Their complex patterns made such an impression upon the Abbot that he determined to acquire craftsmen and materials to bring their work to his own Abbey at Westminster.

At that time the Abbey had become firmly associated with the monarchy, and Henry III was spending much time and money rebuilding the church in the latest French fashion. The old church had been built by Edward the Confessor, whom Henry III had adopted as his patron saint and to whose glory the construction of a sumptuous shrine and the enlargement of the Abbey were ostensibly dedicated. And so, on Abbot de Ware's instructions, craftsmen and precious marbles were brought from Italy to produce the glorious pavement before the high altar of Westminster Abbey.

The Italian craftsmen who laid the pavement belonged to a group of marblers called the *cosmati*, a name derived from Cosmatus, the paternal name of one of their leading families. The pavement is therefore often referred to as the Westminster cosmati pavement. The cosmati families were active in Italy for the best part of two centuries, producing altars, screens, ciboria, tombs, candelabra and thrones, as well as pavements. Technically, their work is not mosaic but *opus sectile*, literally meaning 'cut work'. Whereas mosaic designs are made up of tesserae all of the same size and same, roughly square, shape, cosmati designs are composed of stones of different sizes cut to particular shapes to fit the pattern, rather like patchwork. The materials they preferred for their pavements were purple and green porphyrys, rare marbles re-used from the decayed classical buildings of Rome. Their designs are entirely geometric, based on roundels and rectangular panels linked together by curving bands of pattern to give a characteristic chain effect.

The cosmati work at Westminster also includes the Shrine of Edward the Confessor, the pavement around it, and several thirteenth-century tombs, among them that of Henry III himself; these works are, however, smaller in scale and greater in their state of deterioration.

The pavement was completed in 1268, just a year before Edward the Confessor's remains were to be translated with great and holy ceremony to their resting place in the imposing new shrine. North of the Alps, the Westminster sanctuary pavement is the largest, most complete and most impressive work of the Roman marblers. Its importance may even be said to rival that of the Italian pavements, since many of them were completely relaid by restorers in the seventeenth and eighteenth centuries. The Westminster pavement also shows a far greater variety of individual patterns than its Italian cousins. This may imply either that the Italian pavements were simplified when they were restored, or that the Westminster pavement was accorded particularly rich treatment – probably the latter.

In 1802 James Peller Malcolm called the pavement 'the most glorious work in England, venerable through age, costly in its materials and invaluable for its workmanship.'[1] Today, the great pavement of Westminster Abbey remains one of the country's finest, yet little known, medieval art treasures. Little known, literally, because for the greater part of the present century this major monument has been hidden from view, covered by its protective carpet. Little known, figuratively, because the significance of a mysterious inscription, originally set in the pavement, and translated here from the original Latin, has never been completely understood:

> Four years before this Year of Our Lord 1272,
> King Henry III, the Court of Rome, Odoricus and the Abbot
> set in place these porphyry stones.
>
> If the reader wittingly reflects upon all that is laid down,
> he will discover here the measure of the primum mobile:
> the hedge stands for three years,
> add in turn dogs, and horses and men,
> stags and ravens, eagles, huge sea monsters, the world:
> each that follows triples the years of the one before.
>
> Here is the perfectly rounded sphere which reveals
> the eternal pattern of the universe.

This inscription plunges us immediately into a picture of the world quite different from our own view today. An inscription which foretells the duration of the world and claims that the abstract geometric design of a pavement can reveal the plan of the universe? To modern eyes, these notions are extraordinary. How could this elegant, but relatively straightforward, design possibly be seen to represent the complexities of the universe?

To begin to understand how the pattern of the Westminster pavement and its inscription were seen to fit together to form a cosmology we must see the world in a very different perspective from our own. For the medieval philosopher, the material universe with the earth at its centre was not reality in itself, rather it was an imperfect reflection of an absolute, divine reality which was beyond human experience. Between these two extremes was the spiritual realm of the angels which bridged the two otherwise irreconcilable worlds. But the universe was not just a physical environment, it was a metaphorical environment too. Through knowledge of the created world the philosopher might hope to come closer to knowledge of the Creator. This potential for revelation was the only valid reason for a

Christian philosopher to study the natural world in general and cosmology in particular: 'The heavens declare the glory of God; and the firmament sheweth his handywork', proclaimed Psalm 19.

Philosophy and art were, therefore, set in a rich matrix of resonances between the earthly and the heavenly. To the medieval observer no geometric pattern, natural or man-made, was neutral. Everything had its meaning in the larger scheme of things. In the search for a unified world picture, the Christian philosopher of the middle ages had to harmonise the revealed wisdom of the Scriptures and the received wisdom of the Greek writers, as it had been transmitted through Latin and Islamic channels, into a coherent pattern. In the Greek tradition, geometry and pure number acted as a kind of channel of communication between the tangible world of the senses and that divine world that could be approached by the intellect alone. The fixed rules and universality of geometry gave it an incorruptibility which enabled it to be seen as a vehicle for expressing eternal truths. The respect, reverence even, that had been accorded to number and geometry by Pythagoras and his followers was preserved in Platonic and neo-Platonic philosophy. Through the writings of the early Christian neo-Platonists and the Fathers of the Church it became absorbed into the medieval Christian world view. In his *De Civitate Dei* (*The City of God*), St Augustine discusses the perfection of the number six which 'signified the perfection of Creation'[2] and quotes the apocryphal *Wisdom of Solomon* which declares that 'by measure and number and weight Thou didst order all things'.[3]

Against this historical background, the orderly disposition of geometric figures came to play a unique and important role in expressing the interdependence of elements of natural philosophy. The relationship between the planets and the parts of the human body, the four primal Elements of Fire, Air, Water and Earth, the Seasons, the Ages of Man, the human Temperaments, and many other facets of the perceived and conceptual worlds were brought together in geometric diagrams which demonstrated the contrasts and correspondences between them.

These diagrams are often known as *schemata*, from the Greek word meaning 'shapes'. In setting out the ideas of natural science and religious philosophy, their purpose was not to analyse but to synthesise, to build towards a picture of universal harmony. To understand them, therefore, the observer had to be already familiar with many of the concepts embodied in the diagrams. In this sense, schemata were deliberately esoteric, especially where the *tituli*, or 'labels', were abbreviated or omitted altogether. They were intended more as a means of contemplating the higher order of the universe than as ways of explaining unfamiliar ideas to the uninitiated. As early as the sixth century Pope Gregory the Great had justified the painting of churches by declaring that 'a picture is introduced into a church so that those who are ignorant of letters may at least read by looking at the walls what they cannot read in books.'[4] Non-figurative, geometric design served a parallel, if more exalted, function: it provided a focus for abstract contemplation by the literate clergy. The relationships between elements of a geometric figure could be seen to reflect the nuances of theological philosophy. Such designs served as the basis for the exegesis of concepts that were not easily resolvable into figurative representation. In contrast to pictures for the illiterate, these were images for the super-literate, distilling, in the shorthand of 'sacred' geometry, ideas and ambiguities that might be only partially explained by hundreds of words.

The iconography of great churches was designed so that the whole was more than the sum of the individual parts. Like schemata, the intention of the art and architecture of a church was to reveal the world as a total construct with minimal, if any, reference to its actual physicality – to lay out a pattern of thought that pointed beyond the distortions of material existence towards the pure harmony of the sublime. Glowing with the success of his achievement, Abbot Suger described his new church of Saint-Denis as being capable of transforming 'that which is material to that which is immaterial ... I see myself dwelling in some strange region of the universe which neither exists entirely in the slime of the earth nor entirely in the purity of Heaven; and that, by the grace of God, I can be transported from this inferior to that higher world.'[5]

Today, the medieval image of the cosmos may seem at best hopelessly naive, at worst irrelevant. By the time of the Renaissance the earth had forfeited its place as the centre of the universe. In the twentieth century the divinity of the moon was compromised by Neil Armstrong's historic footprint, and our earth was seen to be a fragile blue bubble floating in the vast blackness of space. As the boundaries of the universe have receded ever further, so the idea of a Divine Being instrumental in human affairs has grown more and more remote.

But the philosophy of the middle ages should not be dismissed too easily. If we view some of the most sophisticated findings of modern science from a more symbolic perspective, strange and unexpected resonances abound. Scientists now describe the workings of the universe as being governed by a small group of basic forces: the electro-magnetic force, the strong nuclear force, the weak nuclear force, and gravity. Can it be mere coincidence that these fundamental forces are four in number, just like the four primary Elements of medieval philosophy – Fire, Air, Water and Earth? At the birth of the universe, it is thought that all four forces were equivalent to each other, just as the four Elements were undifferentiated in the unformed state of primal matter. As God's hand shaped Creation, so the four Elements became defined. In like manner, as the universe of modern science expanded and cooled, so the undifferentiated forces became resolved into the four fundamental forces observed today.

The all-pervading trinitarian theme of medieval thought finds a surprising counterpart in the equation which might be regarded as the chief rubric of twentieth-century science: $E = mc^2$. There were three levels to the medieval world: the material, the spiritual, and the divine. Einstein's equation relates together three exactly equivalent elements: energy, invisible but active and motivating like the medieval concept of spirit; mass, corresponding directly to tangible matter; and the speed of light, a universal constant analogous to the unchanging and universal character of the divine. Matter itself, according to particle physics, is triple. Sub-atomic particles are divided into electron, muon and tau families. Even the duality of matter and spirit finds its place: phenomena like light and gravity have been conceived of as being simultaneously both particles and forces, material and spiritual manifestations, as it were. The quantum theory moved towards reconciling what seemed to be opposing concepts. The latest attempt to bring particles and forces into a single unified theory, is the concept of 'super-strings'. By vibrating, rotating and making loops, super-strings account for the behaviours of both particles and forces. They exist in ten dimensions, nine of space and one of time, numbers with a sound Pythagorean and Platonic tradition. In fact, when the *New Scientist* reports that mathematicians working on the theory of Relativity have concluded that 'the universe was both born of a singularity and will one day collapse back into a singularity',[6] one might be led to suspect that mathematics and physics have been hijacked by latter-day Neo-Platonists.

The naming of the terms changes, but the patterns of thought remain much the same. We perceive and conceive our world in terms of pattern: a scientific theory is judged correct on notions of symmetry and elegance, judgments which, it could be argued, are as much aesthetic as scientific. The theories of science may be dictated more by the unchanging heritage of the structure and conditioning of our minds than by the 'reality' that they set out to describe.

It is the tradition among many ancient religions that the central holy place of a temple represents in microcosm the divine aspect of the created universe, the macrocosm. The twelfth- and thirteenth-century depiction of zodiacs on the floors of major churches in northern France and, closer to home, Canterbury Cathedral, shows that this kind of belief was current in the Christian faith. In medieval times, the symbolic significance of church floors was emphasised by the rules governing the positioning of celebrants during church services. The rituals of Old Sarum illustrate the complex variations used to mark particular festivals of the Church Calendar. One of the most important rituals of the Church, and the paramount ritual of State, was the ceremony of Coronation, enacted at Westminster Abbey by every reigning English monarch from William the Conqueror onwards. (There were two exceptions: the uncrowned Edward V, one of the two princes murdered in the Tower of London, and Edward VIII, who abdicated before his coronation.) It was upon the centre of the cosmati pavement that Church and State were brought together by the anointing of the monarch with holy oil, the ritual act that conferred divine right upon the secular ruler.

This then is the rich context in which we must seek to 'wittingly reflect upon' the esoteric cosmology of the Westminster sanctuary pavement, to unravel the parallel meanings of its geometrical design and its inscription. Unfortunately, it is no simple matter to open a door into the imagination of the thirteenth-century mind. The investigation must proceed slowly, rather like a detective story: character references must be presented, evidence examined, documents checked.

The story begins with what might be regarded as the circumstantial evidence. The inlaid brass inscription named four protagonists as being responsible for the laying of the Westminster pavement: King Henry III, the Court of Rome, Odoricus and the Abbot. From the varying information that history provides on these four main players we may hope to discover something of the circumstances which brought the pavement into being. Then there is the physical evidence of the pavement itself. What can we tell from its time-scarred stones? How much of its fabric survives from the thirteenth century? An examination of the historical record is vital if we are to base our interpretation on firm ground and not be misled by the restorations of later centuries. The key evidence is that of the inscription itself which must be carefully scrutinised in the light of the philosophical beliefs of the times.

Finally, by adding a little appropriate speculation to the careful analysis of the evidence, we may begin to unravel the delicate web of connotations that surrounds the Westminster sanctuary pavement. In doing so we may gain a wider insight into the elusive world of thirteenth-century religious philosophy and, perhaps, learn something about our unchanging patterns of thought that is still of value today.

2

King, Pope, Craftsman and Priest

The reign of Henry III stretched between two religious ceremonies of national importance. On 7th July 1220, at Canterbury Cathedral, the young king witnessed the translation of the remains of St Thomas à Becket into his newly-erected shrine. The solemn ceremony must have made a deep impression upon Henry, still hardly more than a boy. At thirteen years old, he had already been king, in name at least, for four years. His first Coronation, in 1216, had been a makeshift affair hastily arranged at Gloucester Cathedral. A simple circlet provided by his mother served as the Crown of England. The coronation regalia and Westminster Abbey, the English coronation church, were both beyond reach in London which, together with half of the shires of the country, was under the control of the English rebel barons led by Simon de Montfort. Henry had inherited a realm divided by political uncertainty during the reign of his father, King John. It was not until four years later, on 17th May 1220, that Henry had at last been crowned with full regal ritual at Westminster. The day before he had laid the foundation stone for a Lady Chapel, which was to be built to the east of the old romanesque Abbey in the fashionable gothic architectural style newly imported from France.

Almost half a century later, on 13th October 1269, Henry III presided over the ceremonial translation of the remains of Edward the Confessor into a sumptuous new shrine beyond the high altar of Westminster Abbey. The King's long reign, set between the book-ends of the translations of these two English saints, was nearly at an end. His personal veneration of Edward the

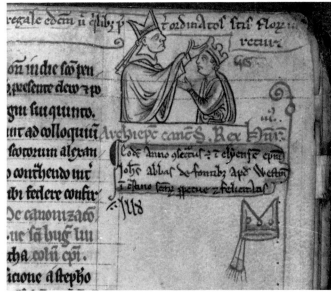

2 *left* Henry III portrayed in his tomb effigy by William Torel

3 *above* Matthew Paris' illustration of the Coronation of Henry III at Westminster Abbey

Confessor had elevated the hitherto minor Anglo-Saxon Saint to the level of a prestigious cult. The Confessor's old church and its Chapter House had been largely rebuilt, at Henry's personal initiative and his own expense, in lavish style and on impressive scale.

In economics and statesmanship, however, Henry's hand was less sure. The scar of the Barons' War ran deep across the political face of Henry's reign and never quite healed. The King's heavy reliance on papal intervention in English domestic affairs caused much resentment and left him uncomfortably indebted to the power of Rome. But when Henry died in 1272, at the age of sixty-five, he had 'got through all his troubles and left England more prosperous, more peaceful, more beautiful than it was when he was a child'.[1] An epitaph added to Henry's tomb at Westminster was recorded by John Weever in 1631 as ending with these lines:

> *Tertius Henricus est Templi conditor huius.*
> *Dulce bellum inexpertis.*

Henry the Third is the builder of this Temple.
War is sweet to those who have not tasted it.

Henry's kingship had not been distinguished by military prowess or by great statesmanship. Nor could it be claimed that he had been a philosopher king who fostered an intellectual élite, although he did show some encouragement to scholars. His reported 'simplicity' was a source of exasperation to his advisers. When Dante came to write his *Divine Comedy* at the beginning of the next century, he placed Henry in the circle of Purgatory reserved for the souls of those preoccupied and distracted from their duties.[2] The Italian poet's verdict was probably taken from the *Chronica* of Giovanni Villani who dismissed Henry as 'a simple man of good faith but of little account'.[3] In fact Henry's 'simplicity' seems to have been a kind of innocence that, in the absence of diplomatic and military skills, worked to his advantage in securing the loyalty of his subjects even when it was not completely deserved.

In military matters, reality always fell short of Henry's expectation: his futile invasion of France in 1242, intended to fulfil the cherished ambition of regaining the lands that had been lost during his father's reign, succeeded only in losing more territories. Normandy, Maine, Anjou and Poitou were all to be irrevocably surrendered to France under the Treaty of Paris which finally settled the remaining differences between the two countries in 1259. That same year, the King's Great Seal and the English gold penny were redesigned, probably by Henry's favourite goldsmith, William of Gloucester.[4] These two important icons of royalty usually depicted the monarch holding a sword, but in the new designs the sword was replaced by a sceptre. The irony of this substitution was not lost on critics of Henry's military pretensions.

Matthew Paris, whose chronicles are the most important English historical works of the thirteenth century, is hardly kinder than Villani in his assessment of Henry's abilities, despite having been befriended and publicly honoured by the King on several occasions. But, as a monk, Paris could not but respect Henry's piety, which he praised as much as he criticised the King's lack of prudence in political matters. Although the sincerity of Henry's piety has sometimes been questioned, it undoubtedly impressed his contemporaries greatly. His veneration of Edward the Confessor was especially deep. He always swore his oath by St Edward; the royal palaces and castles were decorated with scenes from the life of the Confessor, and his first-born son was named Edward in honour of the Saint.

Henry's piety was matched by an enthusiastic appreciation of the arts. The King's personal tastes found practical expression through a few trusted master-craftsmen, like William of Gloucester and Edward of Westminster, who dispensed royal patronage both at home and abroad. These twin

4 Pilgrims praying at the shrine of Edward the Confessor, from a 13th-century manuscript of the Life of St Edward

enthusiasms, patronage of the arts and veneration of the Confessor, found a natural focus in the rebuilding of Westminster Abbey which occupied the King's thoughts, and his exchequer, from the 1240s until his death, and provided the most tangible legacy of his long reign.

It is not clear whether the monks of Westminster had intended the Lady Chapel, begun in 1220, to be the beginning of a major programme of rebuilding, but Henry's intervention left them little choice. What is certain is that the Abbey could never have afforded the rebuilding without Henry's financial support. In a Papal Bull of July 1245, Pope Innocent IV appealed for contributions towards funds for the work at the Abbey 'which was very old and decayed, and which they began to repair in so sumptuous a manner that they were unable to complete it with their own resources'.[5] The King's ambitions for the Abbey were to mean decades of disruption. Royal patronage must often have seemed a mixed blessing, especially as Henry's personal interest in the day to day affairs of the Abbey sometimes bordered on interference. On occasion he even dictated the colours of vestments to be worn in the Abbey on feast days, or brought in a favourite bishop to perform the Mass. The cost of the rebuilding of the Abbey and the making of the Confessor's shrine from 'the purest, top quality gold and the most precious jewels'[6] was enormous. No other medieval monarch had ever financed the building of a church on such a scale. The King told Matthew Paris that the shrine alone had cost him more than a hundred thousand marks. It has been estimated that Henry spent a total of more than £45,000 on the project during his reign, a sum well above the annual income of the Crown that would have to be calculated in billions today.

Perhaps it is cynical to look beyond Henry's piety towards more earthly motivations for his immense investment of time and money. The extravagant rebuilding of the Abbey and the cult of his saintly predecessor may have been metaphors, conscious or not, for Henry's desire to reassert and redefine the institution of kingship in the wake of decades of political instability. The Plantagenet King was also keen to forge links between his own royal house and the ousted Saxon dynasty of England, of which Edward the Confessor had become a symbol.

Beside domestic considerations, there was a strong element of rivalry between Henry and the French King, Louis IX. Having lost to the French on the battlefield, Henry was determined to outdo France, the self-appointed cultural leader of Europe, in the field of the arts. The architecture of Westminster Abbey owes a large debt to the great French cathedrals of Reims and Amiens, and to the royal chapel of Sainte-Chapelle. It has even been suggested that the mason known as Henry of Reyns, who played an important part in the designing of the Abbey, derived his surname not from the village of Rayne in Essex, but from Reims.

Henry's rivalry with Louis in piety and patronage of the arts was hardly subtle: it was surely no coincidence that he initiated the construction of the Confessor's shrine the very year that Louis ceremoniously installed his impressive relic of the Crown of Thorns in the Sainte-Chapelle, the chapel being built next to the royal palace in Paris for the specific purpose of housing that sacred relic. The Sainte-Chapelle was raised in exquisite style, a stunning and intricate piece of gothic architecture that seemed to defy gravity. Matthew Paris graced it with his best superlatives: *incomparabilem* and *pulchritudinis*, 'incomparable' and of 'great beauty'. The English King's admiration and envy, inspired first by report and later confirmed by his own eyes, was well known and even came to be satirised in a French song: 'Paris is a fine city,' Henry is made to say, and 'in it is a chapel I long to have carried off in a rolling cart, straightaway to London'.[7]

For medieval churches the possession of awe-inspiring relics, preferably those of Christ Himself, was a vital factor in attracting prestige – and pilgrims. From time to time, a new relic was required to stimulate the lucrative pilgrimage trade. The Confessor had given Westminster an assortment of relics including a whisker from the beard of St Peter, the Abbey's patron Saint, and the maniple in which St Paul's decapitated head had been wrapped. But, by the extravagant standards of medieval relics, these were rather second-rate. In 1247, Henry rectified Westminster's relative deficiency in this respect by acquiring drops of Christ's Holy Blood from the Patriarch of Jerusalem. Matthew Paris recorded and illustrated Henry's gift of the Holy Blood 'which, with the utmost devotion, the king himself, humbly dressed, carried on foot from St Paul's at the head of a great procession, both arms and hands raised in reverence'. Within the next few years, the King presented Westminster with equally dubious relics: a nail from the Cross; the Virgin's girdle; and a stone bearing the footprint of Christ from the moment He ascended into heaven. The last of these relics may still survive. It has been suggested that the rough stone in the centre of a tomb half-buried in a recess in the south ambulatory may be the stone of the Ascension.[8]

As early as 1246, Henry expressed the desire that his own body be laid to rest in the same chapel as the remains of his patron Saint. Although his father, King John, was buried at Worcester Cathedral, by tradition the royal family had been buried at Fontevraud Abbey in France: his mother Isabella, his uncle Richard I, and his grandfather Henry II, all have fine effigies there. But Fontevraud was in Anjou, one of the territories now under the power of the French King and finally conceded to the French under the Treaty of Paris. Henry's decision to be buried at Westminster perhaps symbolised his resignation to the separation of the English royal dynasty from France, although, ironically, his heart was finally interred at Fontevraud in 1291.[9] In 1254, Henry travelled to the Abbey for the interment of his mother's body. Afterwards he obtained permission from Louis IX to extend his stay in France in order, no doubt, that he might see for himself that country's glories, including the Sainte-Chapelle in Paris. Matthew Paris records how Henry was escorted in grand style by the French King. They met first at Chartres, where Louis could be certain that Henry would be overwhelmingly impressed by the great cathedral – a gothic masterpiece of exquisite geometry and subtle symbolism that houses the famous labyrinth pavement, itself a cosmological symbol.

Under Henry's patronage, Westminster Abbey became pre-eminent in state affairs, establishing a special association with the monarchy that it still enjoys today. Westminster remains a 'royal peculiar': it owes allegiance directly to the Crown and is independent of the Archbishop of Canterbury. This is the reason why a newly-elected abbot was required to travel to the Court of Rome to receive confirmation directly from the Pope. Even in the present day, when a new Archbishop of Canterbury is appointed, he must come to Westminster and sit in the Jerusalem Chamber before the Dean of Westminster who formally explains the limits of the Archbishop's jurisdiction over the Abbey. In a single building, Westminster Abbey came to embrace the same royal functions that were performed by the three great national churches of France: like Sainte-Chapelle it was the repository of relics close to the royal palace; like Reims it was the coronation church; and like Saint-Denis it was to be the dynastic resting place of the royal family.

It was in this extraordinary context, redolent with significance, that the stones of the sanctuary pavement were laid down in 1268, ready for the drama of the translation of Edward the Confessor's body the following year. Henry's inclusion in the pavement's inscription was probably a matter of royal protocol. The Abbey often being referred to as the 'King's church', it is natural to assume that the pavement was also the King's pavement. There is nothing to suggest that the King himself played any active part in commissioning the Italian marble-workers. Henry's tastes seem to have been moulded largely by French fashions, although the workforce at the Abbey was surprisingly cosmopolitan with painters coming from Italy and Spain as well as from France. There was also the question of cost: royal finances were at a particularly low ebb. In 1267 the King had to cajole the Abbey into lending him the treasure of the Confessor's shrine, valued then at £2,500, so that he could use them as surety to raise loans to fund his army. He undertook to return the treasures within sixteen months, but in the event they were not handed back to the Abbey until February 1269, in time for the great ceremony of translation later that year.

The documentary evidence points clearly to the acquisition of the pavement being the initiative of the Abbot mentioned in its inscription, Richard de Ware, Abbot of Westminster from December 1258 to December 1283. The King's payment of £50 to the Abbot in May 1269 for services which included 'a pavement which he brought with him from the Court of Rome to the king's use, to be put in the church of Westminster before the king's great altar there . . .'[10] confirms the account recorded in *De Fundatione Ecclesiae Westmonasteriensis*, the *History of Westminster Abbey* written in 1443 by John Flete, a Westminster monk, which credits the Abbot with importing the pavement's materials and its makers. Flete writes that the Abbot 'on his return home [from Italy], brought back dealers and workmen, who brought with them the stones, those porphyries, jaspers and marble of Thasos which he purchased there at his own personal expense, from which the same workmen fashioned the pavement before the high altar of Westminster with admirable skill'.[11]

Nothing is known of Richard de Ware before he was elected Abbot, save

5 Charter with the seal of Henry III, recording the return to the Abbey of jewels borrowed from the shrine of Edward to raise money for the King's army

a note that he acted as proctor to his predecessor, Abbot Crokesley of Westminster, in June 1257. No record exists of his date of entry into the convent or of the other milestones that marked a monk's career. His election as Abbot was not auspicious: he was the Abbey's second choice. When Abbot Crokesley died in 1258, the monks unanimously elected Phillip de Lewisham as his successor. Phillip, said to have been 'very corpulent and of a highly nervous disposition',[12] was reluctant to accept election because of the arduous journey that had to be made to the Court of Rome. The monks, however, persuaded Phillip to consent to his election by suggesting that a delegation of more able monks be sent to the Pope to seek confirmation on his behalf. The monks eventually succeeded in this mission after some negotiation with the Curia – negotiations that required an outlay of 300 marks to the Papal Camera and 300 marks to the cardinals, money which the monks were forced to borrow from Italian merchants.[13] Returning to Westminster with their proxy confirmation, they were no doubt dismayed to find that Phillip de Lewisham had died during their absence and that Richard de Ware had been elected Abbot by committee in his stead.

Within months, de Ware was on his way to the Court of Rome. Once again, the Abbey was forced to borrow money to cover the expenses of

confirmation, this time 1,000 marks from Florentine merchants.[14] It was probably this trip to Italy that introduced Richard de Ware to the work of the cosmati on a significant scale. Because relations between the Papacy and the State of Rome were uncongenial at the time, the Pope, Alexander IV, and the Roman Curia were resident at their summer retreat in Anagni, a papal stronghold in the hills to the south of Rome. Alexander IV was a native of Anagni, one of four pontiffs born in the city which came to be known as the 'City of Popes'. So it was at the cathedral of Anagni, not in Rome, that Richard de Ware must have received his confirmation as Abbot of Westminster.

Anagni had been a city of religious and political importance even before the rise of the Roman Empire. Its cathedral, dedicated to the Annunciation of the Virgin Mary, was built between 1073 and 1104. Today it boasts one of the finest collections of cosmati work in Italy: pavements in both nave and crypt, paschal candelabrum, bishop's throne, ciborium, and panels surviving from a screen. The crypt is of particular interest since its central aisle provides the largest area of unrestored cosmati pavement in Italy. Both crypt and nave pavements are attributed to members of the Laurentius family, Cosmas and his two sons, Luca and Jacobo. An inscription on the top step of the main altar in the crypt reads: *MAGR* (i.e. *magister*) *COSMAS CIVIS ROMANUS CU* (*cum*) *FILIIS SUIS LUCA ET JACOBO HOC OPUS FECIT*. The crypt pavement with its central spine of eight quincunxes is particularly impressive. Both pavements were laid down during the second quarter of the thirteenth century, probably in 1231, and so would have been *in situ* at the time of de Ware's visit. The candelabrum and the episcopal throne, both the signed work of the craftsman Vassallettus, were made in 1260 and would have been the latest impressive additions to the cathedral's collection of cosmati work.

In his *History of Westminster Abbey*, Flete seems to contend that the Abbot brought the workmen and stones to make the Westminster pavement home with him to London. This seems unlikely. The date of de Ware's return from Italy is not known, but it is difficult to imagine him wanting to leave the Abbey for several years without its Abbot, especially given the 'interregnum' that had already been created by the demise of Phillip de Lewisham. Flete himself implies a sense of urgency, writing that the Abbot-elect travelled to Italy by sea in order to be there the sooner.

6 opposite Anagni Cathedral, which houses the finest collection of cosmati work in Italy, the setting for Richard de Ware's confirmation as Abbot of Westminster

The evidence of de Ware's so-called *Customary* also suggests that the newly confirmed Abbot was soon back about his business at the Abbey. The *Customary* is the last of four books dealing with the affairs of the monks of Westminster which de Ware caused to be written in an attempt, no doubt, to regularise the life of the monastery at a time when the demolition and rebuilding of the Abbey was causing much disruption.[15]

Flete says that the Abbot's post was vacant for 'two years and more' after the death of Phillip de Lewisham's predecessor, Richard Crokesley, in July 1258. But the election of Richard de Ware was approved by Henry III in December of the same year. So the two years in question might be those between the death of Crokesley and the return of de Ware from Italy, which may now be assumed to have been late in 1260 or early in 1261. If this is so, then it seems improbable that the craftsmen who, according to Flete, came back to England with the new Abbot should have waited some seven years before laying their pavement or have taken that number of years to complete the task. In fact, it seems that de Ware made a second visit to Italy in 1267–68,[16] and it was probably on this trip that he arranged for the craftsmen and marbles for the pavement to be brought to England.

Although we can only speculate upon Richard de Ware's formal education as a monk, there can be no doubt that his visit to the Papal Court for confirmation provided an excellent opportunity to deepen his philosophical knowledge in debate with some of the best theological minds of his day. Through the patronage of the Roman Curia, Anagni had become an intellectual as well as an administrative focal point. In 1256, for example, three of the Church's greatest thinkers were together there: Albertus Magnus, Thomas Aquinas and Bonaventure, each of them destined for sainthood.

The crypt of Anagni Cathedral serves as a monument to the philosophical kudos of the cathedral during the medieval period. Its walls are covered with an astonishing set of frescos, surviving from the mid-twelfth and early thirteenth centuries. They present a systematic programme of imagery quite unlike those that were normally painted in the nave and chancel, the 'public' parts of the church. The word *crypta* first appears in Italian manuscripts of the tenth century, and, like its English counterpart, is derived from the Greek word for a vault, *krupte*, the substantive feminine form of *kruptos*, meaning 'hidden', as in the English word 'cryptic'. In Latin and Italian, *crypta* retained its feminine gender: the gender, it should be noted, that the Old Testament assigns to Wisdom, the feminine principle that existed even before Creation. 'When He prepared the heavens, I was there', says Wisdom in *Proverbs* 8, verse 27, 'when He set a compass upon the face of the depth.' The crypt, then, was a place of hidden wisdom.

7&8 Frescos from Anagni Cathedral crypt: left, part of the decayed circle of zodiac signs showing Leo and Cancer, and right, the Greek philosophers Galen and Hippocrates

The crypt of Anagni Cathedral more than lives up to the overtones of the word. The scheme of its frescos represents God's progressive revelation of knowledge to humanity throughout history: beginning with the partial enlightenment of certain Greek philosophers, passing through the Hebraic world and the story of the Ark of the Covenant, and ending with the final and most mystical book of the New Testament, *The Revelation of St John the Divine*. Symbolically, the frescos also represent the personal journey undertaken by the Christian philosopher: a journey from knowledge, achieved through the human intellect, to faith, and beyond faith to the wisdom that can be attained only by Divine revelation.

The first two bays of the crypt have a cosmological theme. A zodiac circle painted on the vault of the first bay is, unfortunately, badly decayed, but several of its signs are still clearly recognisable. The second bay is more interesting still. On its wall are the two Greek philosophers, Galen and Hippocrates, painted as if in animated debate. On the face of the pillar to the left of the philosophers is a diagram showing the four Elements and the relationships between them, a schema familiar from annotations in medieval manuscripts of Plato's *Timaeus* – but unknown elsewhere in wall painting (*see illustration 105*). Above them is a representation of man as the *microcosm*, a schematic diagram relating together quaternities, like the four Seasons and the four Ages of Man, in such a way as to demonstrate the idea of man as a smaller reflection of the greater universe, the *macrocosm* (*see 106*). These images from the crypt at Anagni underline the ongoing rehabilitation of pagan philosophy through Christian theology.

Although it is not clear what the confirmation of an abbot entailed, it would be uncharitable to believe that the Papacy saw such occasions as no more than profitable formalities – though profitable they certainly were: the Papal Bull for the confirmation of Richard de Ware's successor, Walter de Wenlock, cost the Abbey the princely sum of £233.6s.8d.[17] Confirmation must surely have included some element of discussion of the more esoteric dimensions of Christian philosophy. The timing of de Ware's visit in 1260 was especially fortunate in this respect. It coincided exactly with the period during which Thomas Aquinas was writing and teaching at Anagni, the years between 1259 and 1261. The influence of Thomas Aquinas on the medieval Church cannot be overestimated: he was known as a saint even in his own day. When he was in Anagni, Aquinas had just completed one of his most important books, *De Veritate*, and was in the process of writing his next major composition, the *Summa contra Gentiles*, and commentaries on two works by Boethius. Only a very dull monk indeed would not have benefited from the intellectual atmosphere of Anagni during these years, and it is tantalising to imagine the newly-confirmed Abbot of Westminster standing with the saintly Thomas Aquinas before the frescos of the cathedral crypt – what conversations they may have had . . .

So by the time Richard de Ware officially took up his post as Abbot of Westminster, he had been exposed to the most influential thinkers of the first half of the thirteenth century, names that set the course which medieval Christianity was to follow until the Renaissance. Henry III held the Abbot in high regard, perhaps not so much for his learning as for his discipline and efficiency: the business-like instinct which had produced the *Customary*. Following a tradition which had grown up of using the Benedictine monks as 'civil servants', the King sent Abbot de Ware abroad in service to the Crown on several occasions. In the last few years of his life, the Abbot became treasurer to Henry's son, King Edward I.

By the time Richard de Ware died, in December 1283, he had become important enough for his death to be recorded in the annals of another religious house, Dunstable Priory. But he had not, it seems, greatly endeared himself to his own brethren: 'The Abbot of Westminster in London, treasurer to the King, died more or less without warning; scarcely mourned by his convent because of his severity.'[18] This explains, no doubt, the brevity of his meagre epitaph which mentioned the cosmati pavement as his sole achievement:[19]

Abbas Richardus de Wara qui requiescit
hic portat lapides quos huc portavit ab urbe.

Abbot Richard de Ware, who rests here,
    now carries the stones he carried here from Rome.

Although it is certain that Richard de Ware was responsible for bringing the cosmati pavement to Westminster Abbey, it would seem unlikely that he paid for it himself, as Flete claims in his *History*. The Abbot had already been forced to borrow 1,000 marks for his expenses in Italy and, judging by the costs of confirmation of those that went before and after him, most of this sum would have been claimed in fees to the Papal Curia. The Abbot's small change could hardly have paid for such a pavement, especially considering the complexity of its design and the value of its porphyry stones. The fifty pounds paid to de Ware by King Henry in the spring of 1269 was the payment for a number of services, and surely too small a sum, even *in toto*, to reimburse the cost of such a pavement. This payment is more likely to have been simply a reward for the Abbot's initiative. The actual cost of the pavement may well have been borne by the Pope and intended as a gift to the royal Abbey. This would justify the specific mention of the Holy City of Rome, *urbs*, in the pavement's inscription. It would not have been surprising for the Pope to make some contribution to a royal project for glorifying one of the saints of the Church. Despite the fact that the Papacy and the rulers of Europe seem to have enjoyed a relationship that varied between friction and wary tolerance, Pope Clement IV had always taken a keen interest in English affairs and had often championed Henry's cause in the Crown's darker moments.

Papal support for Henry was not without a measure of self interest. The King's reliance upon papal authority to buttress his own power over domestic matters had led him to rely heavily upon Rome, and under Henry's rule England had become 'the main source of revenue for the Popes: this revenue was obtained partly by direct taxation and partly by allowing the Popes to sell Church offices to whoever – English or foreign – would give the best price for them'.[20] However, Clement IV had been papal legate to England before becoming Pope and his personal involvement with English affairs at close quarters seems to have led him beyond regarding the country as a distant, but profitable, outpost of the Church, and engendered a genuine concern and affection for Henry III.

Of the four people named in the Westminster inscription, the craftsman, Odoricus, is by far the most elusive. The task of assigning him to any one of the documented families of marble-workers who were active in Italy during some hundred and fifty years is not an easy one. Of the four major families known to have been working during the twelfth century (the families of

Paulus, *c*.1100–80; Rainerius, *c*.1135–1209; Laurentius, *c*.1160–1235; and Vassallettus, *c*.1150–1262), only one was still productive after the middle of the thirteenth century: the family of Vassallettus, who designed the candelabrum and episcopal throne at Anagni. A fifth family, usually called the Cosmatus family, was active well into the fourteenth century, but there is no known work by this group before 1276. The laying of the Westminster pavement in 1268 fits inconveniently into this gap of uncertainty.

It seems unlikely, therefore, that Odoricus belonged to any of the well known 'cosmati' families, and it must be assumed that he was either an individual craftsman or a member of a poorly documented family. This does not necessarily belittle his importance since much of Italy's cosmati work has been lost and by far the greater part of what survives is unattributed. When cosmati work was signed, the craftsman often revealed something of family relationships. The portico of S. Maria Maggiore at Civita Castellana, for example, is inscribed *MAGISTER JACOBUS CIVIS ROMANUS CUM COSMA FILIO SUO CARISSIMO FECIT HOC OPUS*, 'Master Jacobus, citizen of Rome, made this work with his very dear son, Cosmas.' Had the Westminster pavement been signed in a similar way, more would probably have been known of Odoricus. The cosmati work of the Confessor's shrine, by contrast, was signed in the Italian fashion. This inscription, which is now lost, read:

ANNO MILLENO DOMINI CUM SEPTUAGENO ET BIS CENTENO
CUM COMPLETO QUASI DENO HOC OPUS EST FACTUM
QUOD PETRUS DUXIT IN ACTUM ROMANUS CIVIS

In the year of Our Lord, 1279,
this work was made by Peter, citizen of Rome.

Although there has been disagreement over the reading of the word *septuageno*, some commentators preferring to take it as *sexageno* which would date the shrine to 1269, the evidence of the two inscriptions at Westminster has been brought together to suggest that both pavement and shrine are the work of one craftsman, a craftsman whose family name was Odoricus and Christian name Petrus.[21]

If the identification of the maker of the pavement with the maker of the shrine is correct, then the same craftsman may be further identified with the designer of a near-contemporary piece of work in Italy: the tomb of Pope Clement IV, recorded as being made by one Petrus Oderisius.[22] The tomb's inscription, now lost, was noted in 1685 as reading *PETRUS ODERISIUS*

9 The tomb of Pope Clement IV, designed by Petrus Oderisius and now in the church of S. Francesco, Viterbo

SEPULCRI FECIT HOC OPUS. Clement IV died in 1268, by coincidence the same year that the Westminster pavement was laid, and his tomb was completed by 1271, perhaps as early as 1270. It stood originally in the church of S. Maria in Gradi, but it was dismantled in 1885 and reassembled at Viterbo in the basilica of S. Francesco. The integrity of the tomb was further compromised on 17th January 1944, when the Allies of the Second World War bombed military targets around Viterbo, reducing S. Francesco, and its monuments, to rubble. Clement IV's tomb as it stands today is a second reconstruction made in 1949 when the church was restored.

Yet, despite its chequered history, a stylistic comparison between the patterns of the tomb and those of the pavement at Westminster is still of some value. Of thirty-three different patterns examined, seven may be matched with patterns in the Westminster pavement and a further fifteen are fairly closely related. It must be admitted, however, that the matching and related patterns are predominantly the common ones to be found in the work of any of the cosmati families. Virtually all the patterns in the crypt at Anagni, for example, can be found at Westminster even though the former is firmly attributed to Cosmas and his sons.

However, there is one clear and striking exception among the matching patterns of the Pope's tomb and the Westminster pavement. The band pattern used to form an equilateral cross on the southern end of the sarcophagus that supports Clement IV's effigy (*10*) is one that I have seen nowhere other than at Westminster, where it appears as an S-shaped band pattern linking the framing roundels in the south-west corner of the pavement (*11*). The sarcophagus is the part of the tomb least likely to have been disturbed by its repeated reconstruction, and the originality of the Westminster band pattern is as certain as possible (*12*). The pattern itself is a complex one, and its appearance in these two works must be beyond coincidence.

To contemporary Italian eyes, the most striking feature of Clement IV's tomb would have been the strong influence of the new architectural style of northern Europe: gothic. The typical form of a cosmati tomb had been a classical sarcophagus, perhaps partly re-carved and decorated, surmounted by a ciborium of classical design. For Clement's tomb, however, Petrus Oderisius replaced the traditional ciborium with an unmistakably gothic canopy. If this Petrus was the same 'Odoricus' and 'Petrus Romanus civis' who worked at Westminster, then the introduction of such a feature could be readily explained by his travels between Italy and England which would have taken him through northern France, birthplace of gothic architecture. The influence might alternatively be attributed to Peter, Archbishop of Narbonne, upon whom responsibility for the erection of the tomb had fallen: a Frenchman commissioning a memorial to a French Pope might easily be expected to want to incorporate something of his homeland into the design. But even if the original inspiration for the introduction of gothic features to the tomb was that of Peter of Narbonne, who better to turn to for the realisation of his inspiration than an accomplished master-craftsman recently returned from the gothic north?

There are attractive reasons for linking the Westminster pavement with a craftsman more used to the production of tombs, screens and other church furniture rather than pavements. The patterns at Westminster are more varied and complex than those of Italian pavements. This could be the

10 The band pattern on the southern end of the sarcophagus of Clement IV's tomb

11 The same unusual design in the Westminster pavement

12 Sketch by John Talman confirming the pattern's existence in 1707

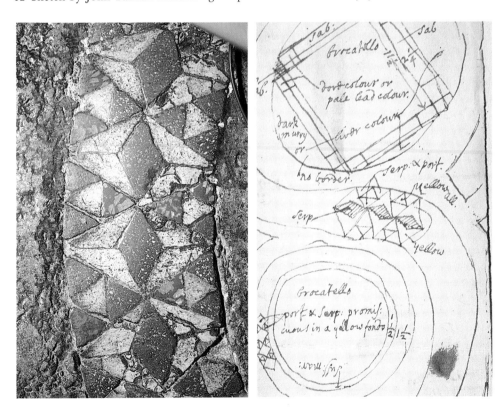

result of simplification when the latter were relaid, as most of them were, during the eighteenth and nineteenth centuries. But the evidence of the Anagni crypt, which is substantially original and no more complex than usual, would seem to argue against the proposition. Cosmati work on church furniture, by contrast, is finer in scale and more complex in design. There is usually a greater variety of patterns, and a wider range of materials can be used since the question of durability is not so important. At Westminster some areas of the pavement are set with relatively fragile vitreous materials which would have been quite adequate for a screen, but which have worn badly in the pavement.

The use of complex infill patterns within roundels is also a characteristic found more often in furniture than pavements, where roundels tend to be either plain or simply divided. The infill patterns of the large roundels on the north-east and south-east sides of the central square of the Westminster design (*see 100 and 101*) are quite commonly found on tombs and altars. Indeed, of the five patterned roundels on the tomb of Clement IV only one survives complete, and that is identical in the construction of its pattern to Westminster's north-east roundel, though made in different colours. The overall geometric design of the pavement is a further consideration. The central motif of a quincunx set within a square with circles budding from its sides is often found in tombs and screen-work but is far less common in pavements. The design is, in fact, unknown in any Italian pavement which has not been substantially relaid.[23] These factors reinforce the idea that the creator of the Westminster pavement was primarily a designer of church furniture, making what was perhaps his first excursion into pavement design, with the unusually elaborate consequence we see before us today.

The latest and most authoritative work on the cosmati by Peter Claussen, *Magistri Doctissimi Romani*, consolidates the identification of Odoricus of the Westminster pavement with the Petrus Oderisius who made the tomb of Clement IV, and assigns him to a small family of marble-workers, called the Oderisii, active for a relatively short period in the middle of the thirteenth century. Works are recorded signed by three members of this family: Oderisius Stephani, Stephanus Oderisius and Petrus Oderisius himself. Claussen speculates that Oderisius Stephani was the father of Petrus and Stephanus, but admits that the similarity of name between Oderisius Stephani and Stephanus Oderisius may mean that they were one and the same person. The sparsity of documentation, and the fact that all three craftsmen appear to have been contemporary, make it impossible to define their relationships to each other with any reliability. What is certain, however, is that Petrus Oderisius was the most outstanding member of the family – indeed Claussen goes so far as to call him 'definitely the most interesting of all the marble-workers in art-historical terms'.

The identification between the Petrus who made the Shrine of St Edward and Petrus Oderisius has not gone unquestioned. However, Claussen presents a creditable chronology that enables the same craftsmen to be the maker of all three. He accepts the *sexageno* version of the shrine's inscription and suggests that work on the shrine was carried out simultaneously with that on the pavement, between the years 1267 and 1268. The date given in the shrine's inscription, often translated as 1269 (when the *sexageno* reading is taken), is actually calculated in the Latin as 1260 and '*quasi deno*', 'almost ten'. Claussen argues that the phrase is sufficiently vague to cover the closing months of 1268, the tomb being serviceable enough by late 1269 for the translation of St Edward to have taken place. Moreover, Clement IV did not die until the end of November in 1268. A Pope's tomb was a major project which would not have been commissioned in a hurry: it is extremely unlikely, therefore, that work would have begun until 1269, allowing time enough for Petrus Oderisius to return to Italy.

Given the comparatively shadowy knowledge of Petrus Oderisius, the most surprising outcome of Claussen's work is the status which he accords to this master-craftsman. While the work of the mainstream cosmati families was essentially parochial, principally confined not just to Italy but to the Latium area around Rome, Petrus Oderisius travelled Europe and brought back with him new ideas and attitudes that resulted in the introduction of the gothic style in Italy. Claussen concludes that his tomb sculpture was a revolution in its time and that, had more of his work survived, he would perhaps have been ranked alongside Nicola Pisano and Arnolfo di Cambio as one of the greatest Italian sculptors of the thirteenth century.

This assessment inevitably increases further the importance of the Westminster Abbey sanctuary pavement. It may now be seen as the turning point in the career of a craftsman destined to become one of the most respected sculptors of his day. Indeed, from what may be deduced of the development of his career, it is quite likely that this was the only pavement to be designed by Petrus Oderisius: a superlative extension of his tomb work that was never to be repeated, giving it, in Claussen's words, those 'profound differences which make the pavement exceptional and set it above all remaining Roman examples in its substantial significance'.

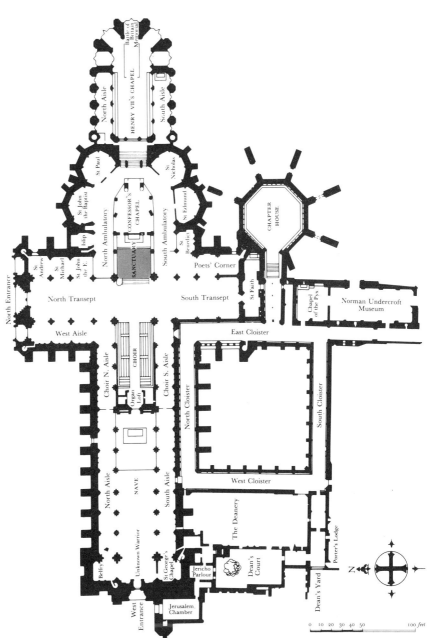

Battle of Britain Memorial

HENRY VII'S CHAPEL

North Aisle
South Aisle

St Paul
St Nicholas

St John the Baptist
St Edmund

Islip
St Benedict

North Ambulatory
CONFESSOR'S CHAPEL
South Ambulatory

St Andrew
St Michael
St John the E.
SANCTUARY

North Entrance

Poets' Corner

North Transept
South Transept
St Faith

West Aisle
CHAPTER HOUSE

East Cloister
Chapel of the Pyx
Norman Undercroft Museum

Choir N. Aisle
CHOIR
Choir S. Aisle

Organ Loft
North Cloister
South Cloister

West Cloister

North Aisle
NAVE
South Aisle

The Deanery

Belfry
Unknown Warrior
St George's Chapel
Jericho Parlour
Dean's Court
Dean's Yard
Porter's Lodge

West Entrance
Jerusalem Chamber

N

0 10 20 30 40 50   100 feet

13 The Great Pavement

14 Plan of the Abbey

3

The Physical Evidence

The opus sectile work of the pavement forms a square design measuring 11.73 metres (24 ft 10 ins) on each side. It fills almost the whole area of the sanctuary, leaving strips of incised Purbeck marble to north and south. Within this square is a border design consisting of a rectangular panel in the centre of each side linked to its neighbour by a series of ogee (S-shaped) bands enclosing five roundels. This gives the impression of a continuous chain of panels and roundels woven together by patterned bands – a major design feature of the cosmati marblers that characterises their work wherever it is found. Inside the border, a second square is set at 45 degrees to the outer square so that its corners point to the cardinal points of the compass. The bands that make the sides of this square loop outwards to form four circles, each filling the triangular space at the corner of the surrounding square. The circles circumscribe large, richly-patterned hexagons. In turn, this square with circles budding from its sides encloses a quincunx of roundels linked together by bands. The four outer roundels face towards the cardinal points of the compass, the fifth roundel marking the centre of the pavement.

The overall design of the pavement is, therefore, a most elegant example of 'natural' geometry, that is, geometry proceeding simply from the direct use of the mason's set square and compass rather than from any complex arithmetical calculation. Such design was considered more likely to reflect the universal harmonic proportions with which the Creator had underpinned His own handiwork, and was therefore considered particularly appropriate for the formulation of medieval ecclesiological design.

Although the overall design has a fourfold symmetry, the patterns of the individual elements of the design are not symmetrically disposed. For example, each of the four outer roundels of the central quincunx has a different design. In fact, nearly all the bands and roundels have their own individual patterns, often very sophisticated and only rarely repeated elsewhere in the pavement. Of the total of 60 bands, 49 quite distinctly different patterns may be observed (*see 15–18*). The 68 variously sized and shaped spaces left between the geometric elements of the design are infilled with equally complex patterns, some related in their designs to the band patterns (*see 19–22*). There is a pleasing contrast in scale and complexity between the principal geometric design and its subordinate patterns. The appeal of this combination was voiced some three centuries ago by Henry Keepe. In his guide to the Abbey he writes of the pavement's 'most artificial and delightful figures ... so laid and wrought to the Spectator's satisfaction that you are unwillingly drawn from the sight thereof'.[1] At the beginning of the nineteenth century, James Peller Malcolm's unusually detailed description gives a good flavour of the pavement's complexity:[2]

The centre of the design is a large circle, whose centre is a circular plane of porphyry, three spans and a quarter in diameter; round it stars of lapis lazuli, pea-green, red, and white, which being of most beautiful colours, have been much depredated; those enclosed by a band of alabaster; and without, a border of lozenges, red and green, the half lozenges contain triangles of the same colours ... The extreme lines of this great circle run into four smaller circles facing the cardinal points; that to the East, a centre of orange and green variegated; round it a circle of red and green wedges; without that, lozenges of the same colours; and completed by a dark border. To the North, the circle has a sexagon centre [in fact, a heptagon] of variegated grey and yellow; round it a band of porphyry, and a dark border. The West circle nearly similar, [this one really is six-sided]. The South, a black centre within a variegated octagon. A large lozenge encloses all the above circles, which is formed by a double border of olive colour; within which, on one corner only, are one hundred and thirty-eight circles intersecting each other, and each made by four oval pieces enclosing a lozenge. The other parts vary in figure, but would take many pages to describe.

The above figure has a circle on each of its sides, to the North-west, South-west, North-east, and South-east. The first contains a sexagon, divided by lozenges of green; within which are forty-one red stars. In the

15–18 Examples of band patterns from the pavement

intersections red triangles. Green triangles form a sexagon round every intersection. The second contains a sexagon; within it seven stars of red and green, forming several sexagons, containing yellow stars. The third has a sexagon, formed by intersecting lines into sexagons and triangles; within the former, stars of red and green. The latter sixteen smaller triangles of red, green, and yellow. The last a sexagon, with thirty-one within it, filled by stars of six rays, green and yellow. The spaces within the great lozenge round the circles are composed of circles, stars, squares, lozenges, and triangles, whose component parts are thousands of pieces of the above shapes. The whole of the great lozenge and circles is enclosed by a square; the sides to the cardinal points . . . The four outsides are filled by parallelograms and circles of considerable size, all divided into figures nearly similar to those described.

Malcolm's admiration of the pavement is clear: he views it with a sense of wonder and, although his description makes a few mistakes, his enthusiastic

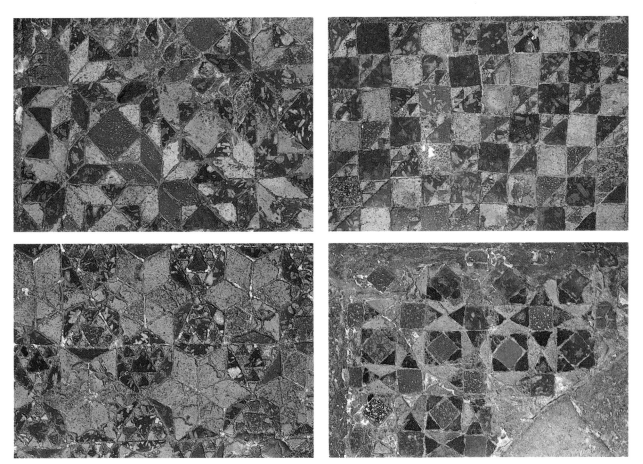

19–22 Examples of infill patterns

account is reliable enough to serve for the time being. His description is least accurate in identifying the stones which make up the pavement. He describes them as 'lapis lazuli, jasper, porphyry, alabaster, Lydian and serpentine marbles, and touchstone'. Allowance must be made for the fact that the same marble was sometimes known by different names in different places and at different times. Essentially Malcolm was following what had been given by earlier writers on the Abbey: in 1723, John Dart had described 'Porphyry, Touch, Jasper, Lydian, Alabaster and Serpentine'; in 1711, Jodocus Crull gave 'Jasper, Porphyry, Lydian, Touchstone, Alabaster and Serpentine'. All three descriptions appear to derive from the 1683 guide by Henry Keepe, who writes of 'the Jasper, the Lydian, the Touch, the Alabaster, and the Serpentine stones'. The evidence of Malcolm's detailed account of the pavement's design and his addition of 'lapis lazuli' to the list of marbles, to describe the blue material now most evident in the band pattern around the central roundel and the rectangular panel on the south side, does suggest, however, that he was writing from first-hand observation.

33

The stones that originally made up the pavement came from Italy. It is reasonable to assume, therefore, that they were typical of the materials used in contemporary Italian pavements, materials which the cosmati marblers are said to have garnered from the ruins of classical Rome. The ruins could provide a wide selection of marbles that had been brought together from every quarry within the reach of the Roman Empire. At Westminster, this diversity has been further increased by successive, and usually anonymous, restorers adding their own materials. Their choice was inevitably dictated by time and money: a piece of green bottle glass set in one roundel (immediately west of the northern rectangular panel) underlines the fact that some repair materials were less carefully chosen than others. The resulting catalogue of materials is a fascinating miscellany that gives some clues to the pavement's 700-year history.[3]

The framework into which the marble patterns are set is made of *Purbeck marble* (*see 23*). This so-called marble is, in fact, a grey-green limestone, quarried from the Isle of Purbeck on the south coast of England, but it is hard enough to take a degree of polish and so to masquerade as a marble. It is a sedimentary rock crowded with the fossilised shells of freshwater pond snails. These shells are sometimes quite large and well defined, as can be seen in several parts of the pavement. The piers of the sanctuary and the crossing are made of the same stone.

In Italy cosmati designs were always set in a matrix of white Carrara marble. Although the substitution of a local English material was obviously more convenient than transporting large amounts of white Italian marble, it did have aesthetic and practical disadvantages. Aesthetically, the grey-green Purbeck provides a poor setting for the cosmati work, its dark tone tending to dampen rather than heighten the colours of the marble patterns. Purbeck marble is also notoriously susceptible to damp. As the basis of a pavement, this weakness could have proved a disaster. However, the pavement is supported on the stumps of the piers of the sanctuary of the old church, leaving a gap between it and the earlier sanctuary floor. This gap, acting like an air brick, helped to insulate the pavement from damp, and is probably entirely responsible for its survival. When measured and photographed from above, the pavement was found to be surprisingly free from distortion. Nonetheless, the surface decay of the Purbeck matrix, leading to the loosening of the opus sectile work, does seem to have been a more destructive factor than the wearing down of the harder marbles themselves. The matrix has been repaired in several places with other types of limestone. Attempts have also been made to consolidate the crumbling Purbeck with a black tar-like substance, and elsewhere there are primitive repairs in concrete.

The most prominent of the marbles making up the actual opus sectile patterns are porphyry. Geologically, porphyry is a generic term used to describe a group of intrusive igneous rocks. These rocks were formed from volcanic magma crystallising underground. There the molten lava cooled very slowly under great pressure, encouraging the growth of relatively large and well-formed crystals. The larger crystals, known technically as *phenocysts*, stand out against a background of much finer crystals and give porphyry its characteristic speckled appearance.

Purple porphyry (*see 24*) was the most highly prized of the porphyrys, both for its colour and its rarity. There was only one source for purple porphyry: the Porphyry Mountains in the eastern desert of Egypt, some 30 miles inland from the ancient port of Myos Hormos on the Red Sea. These Roman mines were closed down in the fifth century BC and their location lost until the late nineteenth century when they were rediscovered at Gebel Dokhan. So all purple porphyry used in medieval times was antique, that is, re-used from classical Roman buildings.

'Porphyry' is derived from the Greek word for 'purple', *porphoros*, and the colour of the marble was a major factor in its status. In ancient Greece and Rome, the expensive purple dye that was used to colour the robes of kings, magistrates and generals had become a symbol of high rank. By the tenth century, the appellation *porphyrogenitus*, 'born in the purple', was given to a Byzantine Emperor born while his father was reigning. The term derives, not from clothing as might be expected, but from the room in the Emperor's Palace at Constantinople where the Empress was confined for the delivery of her child, a room clad with purple porphyry. The imperial associations of the marble were to linger on well into the fifteenth century. By the thirteenth century, purple porphyry had also acquired sepulchral overtones, becoming a popular material for the tombs of the high born. The magnificent bronze effigy on Henry III's tomb rests on a large monolith of purple porphyry. Since there was no screen behind the high altar at Westminster until the later middle ages, the sanctuary pavement originally led up to an uninterrupted view of the Confessor's shrine rising majestically beyond the altar. In this setting, purple porphyry, with its imperial and sepulchral allusions, can be seen as the most fitting and respectful of materials to use.

Second only to purple porphyry in esteem, was the *green porphyry* mined in classical times from the Spartan quarries of Greece. In Italy it was also known as *serpentino* and *marmo di Lacedermore*. It too was primarily re-used from antique buildings. The green porphyry used in the Westminster pavement (*see 25*) has more pronounced phenocysts than its purple counter-

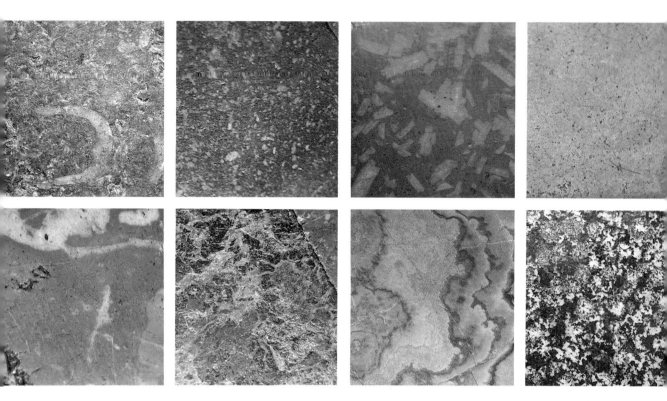

23 Purbeck marble   24 Purple porphyry   25 Green porphyry   26 Giallo antico
27 Carboniferous limestone   28 Genoise serpentine   29 Egyptian onyx marble
30 Egyptian gabbro

part, and provides an excellent example of what geologists term 'porphyritic texture'. Both purple porphyry from Egypt and green porphyry from Greece are very hard stones, and were favourites of the cosmati workers not only for pavements, but for all their decorative work.

The dark tones of the two porphyrys were usually contrasted with a golden-yellow limestone of smooth texture, called *giallo antico* (*see 26*), literally 'antique yellow', which supplied the lighter background to the figure-field patterns. This was the combination used at Westminster. Giallo antico, sometimes also known as *marmo di Numidia*, had been widely used for pavements from the second century AD onwards. The lime mortar, with which these stones were set together, seems to have been mixed to match closely the colour and tone of the giallo antico, disguising the gaps between the stones that were inevitable when a band of geometric pattern was coaxed into a curve.

The pavement contains many stones of a fine-grained *carboniferous lime-stone* (*see 27*), that is, a limestone deposited during the Carboniferous period of the Palaeozoic era, some 350 million years ago. The Palaeozoic era

36

31 Black limestone   32 Black coralite limestone   33 Devonian limestone   34 Red crinoidal limestone   35 Breccia giallo   36 Carrara marble   37 Cipollino   38 Alabaster

was the first of the geological ages; the Carboniferous period, named from the common occurrence of coal in the rock strata, was the fifth period of this era. The carboniferous limestone in the Westminster pavement is liver brown with blotches and streaks of cream and grey. Its origin is likely to be west-European rather than east-Mediterranean.

There is a roughly equal amount of *Genoise serpentine* (*see 28*) in the pavement. Serpentine is a greenish mineral of magnesium and silica, with a fibrous crystalline structure. The name came into use in the sixteenth and seventeenth centuries and derives from *serpens* the Latin word for 'serpent', apparently because the colour and texture of the stone were seen to resemble the scaly skin of a snake. The variety found at Westminster is dull green with tinges of reddish brown. Genoise serpentine, sometimes also called *rosso di Levanti*, comes, as the name implies, from northern Italy.

The stones so far described make up the greater part of the pavement. But there are still a variety of other stones to be found especially in the roundel and infill patterns. The central roundel is a rare *onyx* marble (*see 29*), almost certainly from Egypt. Onyx is a semi-precious chalcedony with

37

bands of variegated colour and is closely related to agate. The Westminster roundel has bands in various shades of yellow, orange, pink and bluish grey. Also from Egypt are a few pieces of *gabbro* (*see 30*), a coarse-grained igneous rock. The Egyptian gabbro at Westminster is speckled with white and greenish black.

Limestone is found in the pavement in various forms. There is a fine-grained *black limestone* (*see 31*), which occurs in many parts of the world. This is probably the stone referred to as 'touch' or 'touchstone' in the Westminster guides. A *black coralite limestone*, distinguished by fragments of coral trapped within the sedimentary rock, is also used (*see 32*). Once again it is of widespread occurrence: the Westminster samples may even be of native British origin.

The eastern roundel of the central quincunx is made of *Devonian limestone* (*see 33*), named from the geological period in which it was formed, the Devonian period immediately preceding the Carboniferous. Devonian limestone was quarried in Britain and on the Continent, where the deposits are traditionally known as the Old Red Sandstone. The *red crinoidal limestone* (*see 34*) used in the northern panel and one roundel has a more orange tint. This limestone is described as 'crinoidal' because it is composed largely of the fossilised remains of a small sea creature called a crinoid, a member of the echinoderm class of animals which includes sea-urchins. An indeterminate buff-coloured limestone, probably used to imitate antico giallo, crops up in diverse parts of the pavement.

Several of the roundels contain large pieces of *breccia giallo* (*see 35*). Smaller pieces also occur in some of the infill patterns. 'Breccia' means 'gravel' in Italian and is the term used to describe a stone formed of angular fragments compressed together. (When the fragments are rounded, it is referred to as a *conglomerate* instead.) The breccia giallo, 'yellow breccia', employed in the buildings of ancient Rome came from Asia Minor, but it was also mined in the Iberian Peninsula. Italy's famous fine-grained white *Carrara marble* (*see 36*) may be seen in small amounts, and there is some *cipollino* (*see 37*), a Greek marble sometimes known as *marmo di Caristo*. Cipollino has gently shaded bands of bluish or greenish grey, and takes its name from the layers of an onion, 'cipolla' in Italian. Its softly-toned dove greys earned it a more romantic appellation among the Christian masons of the middle ages who gave it the charming name of *penna dello spirito santo*; 'plumage of the Holy Spirit'.

The physical catalogue of the Westminster pavement is completed by a group of materials which are concentrated in the band around the central onyx roundel, and in panels of the border to north and south. This group consists of *alabaster* in various shades of white and cream (*see 38*), and several opaque coloured glasses. Alabaster is a soft stone also known as gypsum, chemically a sulphate of lime.

The alabaster used in the pavement is almost certainly of English origin. The accounts of the Sheriff of Nottingham for 1269 record a payment of £2. 10s. for alabaster for the 'pavement of the church of the Blessed Edward at Westminster',[4] although it does not specify which pavement. Alabaster deposits were quarried in Derbyshire, Nottinghamshire, Staffordshire and elsewhere. English alabaster carvings provided a healthy export trade during the later middle ages, and are to be found in many parts of the Continent. The pavement at Westminster provides a very early example of its decorative use. The oldest monumental use of alabaster is usually considered to be the cross-legged effigy of a knight in Hanbury Church, Staffordshire, dated around 1280. However, alabaster was employed as early as 1160 for one of the concentric orders of moulding above the Norman west doorway of Tutbury Priory in Staffordshire. Alabaster from the nearby Tutbury quarries was generally of an even white colour, but often had broad, cloudy veins of reddish brown. Such veins and blotches may also be seen in the alabaster used at Westminster, and the Tutbury quarries must be considered a likely source for the stone.

Due to its softness, alabaster was an unfortunate choice for a pavement. As a consequence, it has worn away badly. The opaque glasses have fared little better. Though hard, glass is also brittle, and in most places it fractured and the resulting fragments were easily dislodged. These strongly coloured glasses may have been used in imitation of semi-precious stones – coloured glasses had been highly prized in Egyptian times and are found among the precious jewels set in the treasure of Tutankhamun. The 'lapis lazuli' referred to by Malcolm is, in fact, a cobalt blue glass (*see 39*). There is also a turquoise blue glass (*40*), a red glass (*41*) and a white glass with a bluish tinge (*42*). No trace can now be found of the associated pea green pieces mentioned by both Malcolm and Brayley, which were presumably also vitreous. Small fragments of the glasses are also found scattered among some of the infill patterns.

Glass was regularly used by the cosmati in screens, candelabra, and other church furniture, but it is rare in pavements. The presence of opaque glasses in fair quantity in the Westminster pavement, at a date well before the heyday of the glass-makers of the island of Murano in Venice, makes them of historical curiosity. Their appearance is unlike other thirteenth-century European glass, the colours being more like those of Islamic glass produced in the Near and Middle East. Four possible origins may be considered:

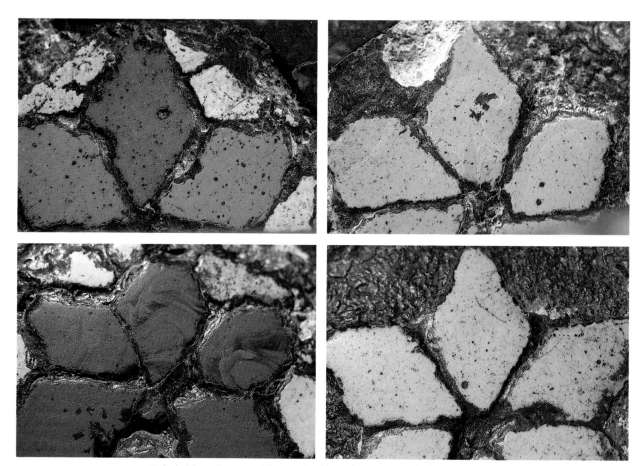

39 Cobalt blue glass   40 Turquoise blue glass   41 Red glass   42 White glass

1) The glasses are of classical Roman manufacture, scavenged from ruined buildings of Rome and re-used, in the same manner as the porphyry marbles.

2) The glasses are of Islamic manufacture, brought from some outpost of the Roman Empire to decorate the buildings of ancient Rome and subsequently re-used by the cosmati.

3) The glasses are of Islamic manufacture, contemporary with the laying of the pavement, acquired firsthand by the cosmati specifically for their own use. (A fragment of a thirteenth-century Islamic drinking vessel found on the site of the Chapter House at Westminster, now in the Museum of London, shows that materials from the Middle East were available in western Europe at this time.)

4) The glasses are of contemporary European manufacture, either Italian or English.

Because of the historical importance of these glasses, the Dean and Chapter of Westminster gave permission for samples to be taken for analysis in order to distinguish the most likely of these four hypotheses. From the rectangular panel on the southern side of the pavement samples, approximately one cubic millimetre in size, were taken of each of the four surviving colours of glass. The samples were examined at the British Museum Research Laboratory with a scanning electron microscope, and then analysed by energy dispersive X-ray techniques.[5]

All four colours of glass were shown to have a soda-lime-silica composition which was typical of Mediterranean manufacture from 2000 BC onwards. Their composition is quite distinct from the potash glasses that were being produced in north-west Europe during the thirteenth century. It appears at first sight, therefore, that the glasses cannot be of contemporary European manufacture.

Could the glasses be of classical origin? The level of magnesium is relatively high in all four glasses. Such 'high-magnesia' glasses are not associated with the classical Roman period when glasses had a low magnesia content. Furthermore, Roman glass was usually made opaque by the addition of calcium antimonate: the opacifying agent in the Westminster samples is a mixture of lead and tin oxides. These glasses were not, therefore, made in classical Roman times and re-used later by the cosmati.

In fact, soda-lime-silica glasses with high magnesia content are generally associated with Islamic manufacture. Islamic glasses also used lead and tin oxides as opacifying agents. This type of composition can be traced back to the earliest glass-making in Mesopotamia and Persia. Under the dominance of the Roman Empire, however, the traditional high-magnesia composition was displaced by the Roman low-magnesia glasses in areas around the Mediterranean. It was not until the spread of Islam in the eighth century that the high-magnesia formula was revived in these areas. Thus it appears that the origins of the Westminster pavement glasses are reduced to two possibilities: either they are of contemporary Islamic manufacture (similar opaque glasses were certainly in production in Egypt and Syria during the thirteenth century) or they were re-used from earlier, but post-Roman, buildings.

One of the most striking features of the analysis of the four glasses is the similarity between their compositions, the main differences being those elements introduced to provide the different colours: copper oxide and sulphide in the red glass; copper oxide in the turquoise glass; manganese oxide in the white glass; and almost certainly cobalt (but below detectable levels) in the blue glass. The family likeness between all four glasses seems to discount the likelihood of them being scavenged from earlier buildings. If this had been the case, a variety of compositions might be expected, reflecting a number of different dates and locations of manufacture. Instead, the close similarity indicates the converse. It is highly probable that all the glasses were produced by workshops using very similar recipes or, indeed, by a single workshop.

Despite the fact that the opaque glasses were made to a traditional Islamic formula, there are reservations in accepting that they were actually manufactured in an Islamic country. In a study of Islamic glass weights used by merchants, Judith Kolbas has produced a chromatic chronology which charts the changing tastes and technologies in Islamic glass production.[6] Glass weights were made in opaque white and turquoise, both similar to those at Westminster, but these colours seem to have fallen out of favour by around 1215, some fifty years before the laying of the pavement. No equivalent to the opaque blue glass is found among thirteenth-century Islamic glass weights. A few rare examples of red weights do exist, dating from around the eleventh to the mid-thirteenth centuries, but these are duller in colour, more brown than the brilliant red of the Westminster glass.

To square these reservations with the chemical similarity which suggests a common source for the glasses, it seems most practical to argue that the cosmati acquired their opaque glasses from a local centre of production, but one which had imported traditional Islamic manufacturing techniques. Venice, open as it was to Byzantine influence, might be considered a possible location, or perhaps Corinth, bearing in mind that several of the marbles used by the cosmati came from Greece. Until further research is available, therefore, there can be no absolute certainty about the provenance of the Westminster opaque glass tesserae.

However, these findings must call into question the accepted image of the cosmati marble-workers grubbing for their precious materials among the ruins of classical Rome. The cosmati may well have begun in this way during the early years of the twelfth century, and no doubt local availability dictated their choice of materials and exerted a permanent influence on their designs, but by the thirteenth century the popularity of their art was such that they must have had to acquire materials in a more systematic fashion and stock them on a larger scale. The widespread sources of the various stones and glasses the cosmati marble-workers employed point to an extensive network of suppliers, possibly stretching from Spain to the Middle East.

Despite the fascinating diversity of materials present in the Westminster pavement, there is a degree of order. The distribution of different materials is neither homogenous nor random: a particular type of stone nearly always

43 Band pattern showing 'primary' mix materials 44 The same band pattern restored in 'secondary' mix materials 45 The restorers were unable to make this band turn a corner without distorting its pattern 46 The original work in this pattern achieved a subtle banded effect by reversing the figure-field of purple and green porphyry shapes

appears in combination with certain other stones. Three quite distinct mixes of materials can be identified. These different stone mixes are not located in such a way as to suggest that their placing formed a deliberate part of the pavement's design. On the contrary, the mixes seem to be arbitrarily distributed, some bands of pattern beginning in one mix of stones and ending in another. It is clear, therefore, that the distribution of the various materials must reflect successive restorations.

Most cosmati pavements in Italy were partially or completely re-laid during the eighteenth and nineteenth centuries. The pavements that remain unrestored, such as those of S. Maria di Castello in Tarquinia and S. Domenico in Narni, show the pathetically fragmented state that must have been typical of many cosmati pavements before restoration. It may be suspected that many of the Italian pavements that look so impressive today owe more to the skill of the restorer than to the cosmati. It is vital, therefore, to examine the distribution of the materials in the Westminster pavement as a first step towards addressing the question of what belongs to the thirteenth century and what does not.

Two quite different mixes of stones are clearly distinguishable. The first group, the *primary mix*, consists of purple porphyry, green porphyry and giallo antico (*see 43*). This mix is the basic formula of the cosmati marblers and is found everywhere in their Italian repertoire. The second mix comprises liver-coloured carboniferous limestone, serpentine and buff limestone, and will be called the *secondary mix* (*see 44*). This mix appears to be a careful substitution for the primary mix: carboniferous limestone for purple porphyry, serpentine for green porphyry, and buff limestone for giallo antico.

There are ample reasons for assuming the secondary mix to be a replacement for the primary mix, rather than the other way round. Firstly, there is the example of contemporary cosmati pavements in Italy, all rich in purple and green porphyrys. Secondly, there is the circumstantial evidence that while the secondary mix stones could have been quarried in west Europe at any time during the pavement's history, those of the primary mix, the purple porphyry in particular, must have come from a classical Roman source. Finally, there is conclusive evidence provided by the patterns of the pavement. The band pattern which surrounds the rectangular panel in the northern border has sections in both mixes. The primary mix gives way to the secondary mix at the point where the pattern is about to turn through a right-angled corner. The paviours laying the secondary mix stones, however, were unable to take the band around the corner without turning the pattern itself through 90 degrees (*see 45*).

Elsewhere, patterns in the secondary mix are seen to be simplifications of primary mix patterns. For example, the band along the south-east side of the central square and around its roundel has a pattern with a motif of four petal-like lozenges enclosing a square. In its primary mix version, sections with purple porphyry lozenges and green porphyry squares alternate with sections having green porphyry lozenges and purple porphyry squares (*see 46 and 47*). This reversal of colours gives a subtle banded effect. The same device is used in a square section of cosmati pavement at the Badia di SS. Severo and Martirio, near Orvieto in Italy. Here the reversal of purple and green porphyrys marks out a cross within the otherwise homogeneous infill pattern. However, this pavement was restored in 1909–10, so a degree of caution must be exercised. At Westminster, the craftsmen repairing this band appear not to have noticed the subtle reversal of purple and green porphyrys in the surviving primary pattern, and made no attempt to reproduce it in their secondary mix version, using lozenges and squares of carboniferous limestone and serpentine at random (*see 48*). A close examination of several patterns shows that, while the overall impression of the original, primary mix pattern is maintained, there are errors in detail. For example, *43* and *44*, which are both sections of the same band pattern. Although the basic geometry of the secondary mix section is the same as that of the primary mix pattern, the actual placing of the triangular stones within the geometric grid does not follow the same logic as the original nor, indeed, does it follow any consistent rule of its own.

It is reasonable to conclude, therefore, that the secondary mix must represent repairs by paviours rather less skilled than those who laid the original pavement. Their work was, however, relatively carefully executed, and the considered substitution of stones approximating in colour to the primary mix preserves the spirit, if not the precise letter, of the thirteenth-century patterns.

Black limestone, breccia giallo, carboniferous limestone, cipollino and serpentine make up a third mix. The work in these materials is less considered than that in the secondary mix. In most instances, no effort was made to produce patterns even approximating to the originals. For example, compare the infill patterns between the roundels on the north side of the central square with those in the south side: there is a mismatch both in type and scale of pattern. Brayley, writing in 1823, seems to have been the only commentator struck by the inconsistency of the two areas to the south, roundly declaring them to be 'more modern than the others, in consequence of some partial repairs'.[7] It may be that the pavement had been so severely damaged that no trace of the lost patterns was left to guide the restorers. However, comparison with the surviving infill patterns alone could have inspired far more appropriate replacements. Here is work obviously carried out in a hurry. From the evidence of the infill between the west and south roundels of the central square, which appears to show just a part of a larger design, it seems quite possible that most of the tertiary mix elements came from a pavement which already existed elsewhere and was used, virtually *en bloc*, to make repairs at Westminster. There is a degree of overlap between the materials used in the secondary and tertiary mixes, but since black limestone, most prominent in the tertiary mix, is found as a repair in a few secondary mix areas, it seems most probable that the tertiary mix post-dates the secondary, though perhaps by only a relatively short period of time.

Other physical criteria may also be applied to detect restoration. In medieval times, the stones were carefully chipped to shape by hand, porphyry

47 Detail of the original band pattern in 46

48 Simplified version of the same pattern laid by restorers

being too hard to be sawn. But after the industrial revolution, power machinery was available to saw the hardest stone. A close look at the edges of the pieces of stone differentiates work of the two periods by the change in cutting technique: the hand-cut medieval stones have slightly serrated edges (49), whereas the edges of the nineteenth-century machine-cut stones are razor sharp (50). This comparison reveals that repairs were made in the nineteenth century using the original mix of materials; purple and green porphyrys. The green porphyry used at this time is also distinguished by more prominent phenocysts and a rather brighter tone.

The restorers did not always need to provide new materials: sometimes it was only necessary to re-lay stones that had become dislodged. The lime mortar which was originally used to set the stones together was mixed to match closely the colour and tone of the giallo antico, disguising the gaps between the stones that were inevitable. Close examination of the mortar reveals particles of brick dust. The addition of brick dust was a technique particularly associated with Roman masons. In his *Ten Books on Architecture*, Vitruvius, the classical Roman architect, recommends a recipe to be used for the mortar of pavements in which one third of the aggregate added to the lime consists of pounded brick. The nineteenth century brought the introduction of new types of mortar, like Portland cement (50). These are harder than medieval mortars and light grey in colour. The difference between the colours of the two mortars betrays re-laid stones in many parts of the pavement. Where particles of brick dust are visible in the lime mortar, it is likely that the mortar is original and the stones undisturbed since they were first set in place by the Roman masons in the thirteenth century.

Another factor in deciding whether stones have been re-laid or not is the

46

49&50 The contrast between medieval work with hand-chipped stones set in lime mortar, left; and 19th-century repairs with machine-cut stones in grey cement mortar, right

way in which their surfaces have been worn down by time. Both purple and green porphyry are harder than giallo antico, so the giallo antico in the pavement has eroded more quickly. Where it is set between two pieces of porphyry, the surface of the giallo antico becomes concave while its porphyry neighbours become convex. The junction between the softer and harder materials forms a smooth undulation. Where stones have been re-laid the disturbance is often made evident by the interruption of this smooth junction.

The physical evidence of the pavement's stones, then, reveals three major waves of restoration, each differing in extent and quality of workmanship: the restoration carried out in secondary mix materials, the restoration in tertiary mix materials, and the nineteenth-century restoration using the right stones but distinguished from earlier work by machine-cut edges and grey cement. Examination of the pavement alone can lead us no further: its clues are exhausted. Now, in an attempt to establish dates for the restorations and to determine how much the pavement's design and patterns were compromised by them, the investigation must turn to the written and pictorial evidence that can be found by sifting through what remains of the historical record of the pavement.

4

The Historical Record

historical records of the pavement fall into three categories: visitors' guides and descriptions in histories of the Abbey; photographs and engravings; and references among the Abbey's own muniments, the records of its affairs. The guides that have been produced over the centuries vary in the space devoted to the pavement and the quality of their accounts. The story of Abbot de Ware's import of the cosmati pavement is first told in John Flete's fifteenth-century history of the Abbey.[1] Flete was the Abbey's Receiver in 1445, and is known later as the *custos maneriorum Regis Henricii*, 'Warden of the Manors of King Henry'. His material was copied and annotated in the next history of the Abbey which was compiled in 1450 by another monk, Richard Sporley.[2] Both these early works are completely silent on the condition of the pavement, referring only to its origin, its materials and its inscription.

The first printed account of Westminster was produced in 1600 by William Camden, the Abbey's librarian and later headmaster of Westminster School. Camden, like the earlier manuscript sources, provides no hint about the condition of the pavement in his day. The first author to comment on the preservation of the pavement is Henry Keepe. Writing in 1683, he contrasts, in poetic terms, the decaying exterior of the Abbey with the apparently good condition of the pavement. 'But leaving the outward view of this ruinous building, let us see whether her entrails [the inside] be altogether as decayed and forlorn. For though she seems by her outward shape and appearance to be clothed with the disconsolate veil of Widowhood, yet if we enter . . . you there behold that noble and most glorious inlaid floor still remaining intire.'

John Dart, writing in 1742, complains of some damage to the pavement, but assures the reader that 'What is left makes a most beautiful appearance, and seems to brave all the injuries of Time.' In 1751, Richard Widmore, who was also one of the Abbey's librarians, was able to report that 'a good part is still remaining'. So it would appear that the pavement survived well into the eighteenth century, damaged, but still retaining its dignity.

The nineteenth century opens with an altogether more depressing picture: 'An admirer of the arts must view it with the deepest regret', laments James Peller Malcolm in 1802, 'since it has been the custom to show the choir for money, it is trodden, worn, and dirtied, daily by hundreds, who are unconscious of its value, and I know barely look at it. Is it not a national treasure? When it is quite destroyed, can we show such another?' The situation did not improve. In 1812, Rudolph Ackermann, whose text in the matter of the pavement follows Widmore's almost word for word, could not bring himself to state, as Widmore had, that a good part of the pavement remained, but prefers to say merely that 'some part of it still remains'. Five years later, William Dugdale admits only that 'a sufficient portion is still remaining to indicate its former beauty', and Edward Brayley was soon to describe the pavement as still of interest 'though in ruin . . . greatly injured by wanton spoilation and by accident'.

The picture that emerges from the testimony of the Abbey guides is, therefore, of a pavement which survived relatively intact until the middle of the eighteenth century. From that time onwards a gradual decay set in, encouraged by neglect and the trampling feet of visitors. By the 1820s, the pavement presented only a ruinous shadow of its former glory. This is obviously a simplified view: there are long periods of time between the guides; authors sometimes slavishly reproduced earlier descriptions; and their assessments of the pavement's condition were inevitably subjective and dependant to a degree on whether the marble work had been recently repaired.

Pictorial records may prove more reliable, being more objective and capable of comparison. The earliest representation of the interior of the Abbey still surviving is an illustration of the funeral service of Abbot Islip, who died in 1532. It appears in the *Obituary Roll of John Islip*[3] and shows the high altar and the area before it (*see 51*). Unfortunately the Abbot's impressive hearse and its attendants completely fill the sanctuary, covering the pavement and making this unique picture of the pre-Reformation interior of little use in the present context.

51 Abbot Islip's funerary cortège before the high altar in 1532

52 An early photograph by John Harrington, 1869

On the face of it, the precise detail provided by photographic records would seem to be the most useful. Unfortunately the size and position of the pavement make it extremely difficult to photograph. From ground level the view is very oblique, and wide-angle lenses have only been available in modern times, during which period the pavement has been covered by carpet. So good photographs are surprisingly rare. A typical example is that by John Harrington, taken in 1869 and the earliest in the Abbey's archive[4] (52). The view is from the altar, looking west into the choir and the nave beyond. In the foreground the uncovered pavement is seen obliquely. Although much of its overall design is clear, there is little to be seen by way of detail.

Fortunately, precise surveys have been made on a number of occasions, some resulting in scale drawings of the pavement as a whole with an indication of the details of its many patterns. The most recent, and accurate, of these surveys was made by the Royal Commission on Historical Monuments in 1924 (*53*). It is, however, schematic to a degree. Infill and band patterns are not shown in their entirety: instead each area is given a generalised geometric grid with just a part of the precise pattern filled in. This obviously limits the historical value of the plan, but what is shown does agree almost

53 The Royal Commission on Historical Monuments' plan, 1924

WESTMINSTER ABBEY. PLAN OF THE PRESBYTERY PAVEMENT

PAVEMENT OF PURBECK MARBLE INLAID WITH PATTERNS OF COLOURED MARBLE AND VITREOUS MOSAICS AND WITH REMAINS AND INDENTS OF BRASS INSCRIPTIONS

Scale of — Feet

~ South side ~

Royal Commission on Historical Monuments (England). 1924

completely with the pavement as seen today. There can have been no serious restoration since 1924. Of the few minor discrepancies in the plan, one may be put down to the later repair of a small area of damage, and the rest to mere oversight on the part of the draughtsman. The most serious of these oversights is the omission of the distinctive black centre to the octagon of the southern roundel of the central quincunx.

The Abbey's Muniment Room holds a miscellany of watercolours that divides into two groups.[5] The first group was made in 1909 on the 22nd and 23rd of October, each drawing being initialled by J. Harold Gibbons. These are life-size representations of three sections of the pavement (*see 56*). Two of them are painted on translucent brown paper, and appear to be based on a combination of tracing from the actual pavement and making a rubbing with blue crayon. The outlines were then filled in with colour. These paintings show no sign of missing or damaged pieces of stone and must be assumed to be idealised reconstructions based on the surviving stonework.

A fourth drawing belonging to this group has neither reference number nor initials, but carries the note 'Lethaby?' pencilled in a later hand. It is a rubbing of the roundel immediately to the west of the northern panel made in blue crayon with further detail added, also in blue. William Lethaby was a distinguished designer and architect who was Surveyor to the Fabric of Westminster Abbey between 1906 and 1931. Presumably, this drawing has been tentatively attributed to Lethaby because it appears as plate 133 in his *Westminster Abbey Re-examined*, which was published in 1925. However, the use of blue crayon identical to that in the other drawings raises the possibility that this too may be the work of J. Harold Gibbons. Lethaby's own description of that particular roundel as being 'so far obliterated that, without the help of sketches and a rubbing done many years ago, it is doubtful if it now could be made out', supports this possibility.

The next representation of the pavement takes us back into the nineteenth century. In 1887 a large lithograph was produced to mark Queen Victoria's Jubilee. It shows the scene at Westminster Abbey on 6th June of that year, when the Queen's anniversary was celebrated with a service of thanksgiving. The lithograph is most notable for its portraits of the royal court and of the Abbey's Dean and Chapter standing in the foreground of the picture. Unfortunately, the pavement is seen from the usual oblique

54 Lithograph commemorating Queen Victoria's Jubilee in 1887

55 Details of band patterns drawn up for George Gilbert Scott's book *Gleanings from Westminster Abbey*, 1863

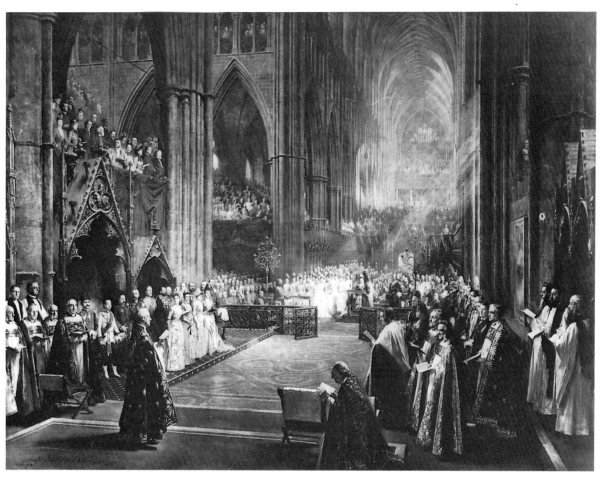

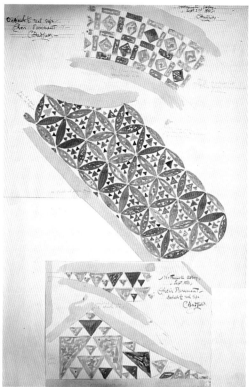

56&57 Two watercolours from the Abbey's collection: left, by J. H. Gibbons dated October 1909, and right, by C. Hadfield painted in September 1863

angle and is also partly covered by low platforms on its north and south sides. Although enough is visible to confirm the general appearance of the pavement's geometry, the lithograph is of no great value in providing details of individual patterns.

Next in chronological order is the very early photograph of 1869 by John Harrington (*see 52*). Predating this photograph by six years is a scale drawing engraved for George Gilbert Scott's book of 1863, *Gleanings from Westminster Abbey*. Like the Royal Commission on Historical Monuments' plan, the *Gleanings* engraving gives an overall representation of the pavement's geometry but shows the bands and infill patterns as basic grids with only part of each individual pattern filled in. This lack is to some extent compensated for by the enlarged details provided of 21 of the major band patterns (*see 55*). The plan is of a high order of accuracy comparable with that of the Royal Commission on Historical Monuments' record.

Also dated to 1863 are the second group of miscellaneous paintings in the Abbey's Muniment Room collection. These ten watercolours are signed by C. Hadfield and dated variously between the 2nd and 5th September. They show small sections of the pavement drawn to half real size, and are so precisely delineated in their greens and purples that, in most cases, it is possible to identify the exact part of the pavement shown (57).

Some fifty years earlier than these excellent watercolours is the aquatint of the pavement which appears in Rudolph Ackermann's *The History of the Abbey Church of St Peter's, Westminster, Its Antiquities and Monuments*, published in 1812 (58). This representation of the complete pavement is attractively tinted, and is usually cited as the earliest known. The colour helps greatly in giving a fuller picture of the pavement, but the scale of the image means that most of its individual patterns had to be reduced to simplified impressions, and this greatly limits its value as an historic record.

58 Aquatint produced for Rudolph Ackermann's history of the Abbey, published in 1812

With a little indulgent imagination, many of the patterns can be confirmed but several instances remain where the blurred distinction between artistic licence and sheer inaccuracy leads to questionable identification. A close look at the aquatint reveals a disconcerting number of definite mistakes, most of which were probably due to accidental transposition when the original drawing was transferred in reverse on to the printing plate.

Apparently even earlier than Ackermann's aquatint is a plan of the pavement which appears in William Lethaby's book, *Westminster Abbey Reexamined*, captioned as a 'Plan of Mosaic floor, 1810'. The woodcut bears a striking resemblance to Ackermann's aquatint of 1812. In fact, the two representations have a total of eleven simplifications and mistakes in common, surely too many for mere coincidence. Once again, several of these mistakes are of the kind made when an original drawing is reversed on to the plate or block from which the prints are made. So rather than suppose that both plate-makers made the same mistakes, we must assume that the woodcut was copied directly from Ackermann's aquatint or from the same original drawing. This plan cannot, therefore, be taken as providing reliable evidence of the pavement since it appears to have been made without any first-hand observation of its subject.

This dubious plan of 1810 is predated by two mysteries which, if solved, would take us first a century, then two centuries further back into the history of the pavement. The first mystery is a scale drawing of the pavement said to have been made by the antiquarian, John Talman, at the beginning of the eighteenth century.

John Dart, writing in 1723, says that 'The ingenious Mr. Talman has with indefatigable Pains measured it, a Work of long Time and close Application; a Draught of which, with other curious things, he has communicated to the Society of Antiquaries, which is now justly engraved.' Unfortunately, the Society of Antiquaries now has no record of Talman's drawing of the pavement. In fact, after Dart's remarks, nothing is heard of the drawing or the subsequent engraving apart from the laments of later authors failing to discover either at the Society of Antiquaries or elsewhere. Since the beginning of the nineteenth century, both the engraving and Talman's drawing for it have been missing, presumed lost.

The second mystery is the possible representation of the pavement as an incidental part of a large picture by Hans Holbein the Younger, painted in the year 1533. If this representation can be verified, it would provide a reference for the pavement that was not only pre-Commonwealth, but pre-Reformation too. A detailed comparison of the relationship between the Westminster pavement and this painting is, therefore, of critical importance.

59 Double portrait of Jean de Dinteville and Georges de Selve painted by Hans Holbein in 1533 and often known as *The Ambassadors*

The painting by Holbein known as *The Ambassadors* caused great excitement at the end of the nineteenth century when it arrived at the National Gallery in London. The large scale (it measures 207 x 210 cms) and bravura quality of the work were guaranteed to impress; the proud, but anonymous, sitters and their elaborately contrived 'still life' were bound to intrigue. Who were these confident sons of the Renaissance? And what significance did the meticulously painted objects hold?

Although the correct identity of one of the two men was first publicly suggested by Sir Sidney Colvin, who named the left-hand figure as Jean de Dinteville in a letter to *The Times* in September 1890, the question was completely settled ten years later by the masterly, and comprehensive, detective work of Mary F. S. Hervey. She confirmed that the left-hand figure was a portrait of Jean de Dinteville, a French nobleman, by piecing together hints provided by acutely observed details of the painting: the prominent marking of his country seat of Polisy on the terrestrial globe; the medallion of the Order of St Michael, the French equivalent of the Order of the Garter, around his neck; the age of 29 inscribed on the handle of his dagger; and the year of the painting, 1533, written beneath the artist's signature. After much diligent, almost obsessive, research Hervey's argument was finally clinched when she uncovered a seventeenth-century parchment which clearly described the painting as portraits of Jean de Dinteville, Seigneur of Polisy, Ambassador to England in 1532 and 1533, and Georges de Selve, Bishop of Lavaur. She further demonstrated that the objects of the still life – the broken lute string, the instruments for measuring time, the crucifix and the famous anamorphic skull – formed an elaborate *memento mori*, an allegory of the vanity of earthly power and learning in the face of the inevitability of human mortality. This melancholic theme had grown up among Christian philosophers during the middle ages and became a favourite allegorical subject for the painters of the Low Countries.

It was Hervey's book which first suggested that the floor of Holbein's *The Ambassadors* represented the pavement before the high altar of Westminster Abbey. Its distinctive quadripartite pattern of interlacing circles and square being unique in England, it appeared to provide the only available model for the design of Holbein's floor. The similarity was pointed out, quite independently, by William Lethaby. Furthermore, since the Latin inscription of the Westminster pavement refers to the end of the world, Lethaby declared that Holbein had intended the symbolism of the pavement to underscore the painting's complex *memento mori* theme with a cosmic dimension of mortality: 'I believe it was selected by Holbein because it symbolised Time on which death throws its recurring shadow, as in the picture the skull forms the gnomon to the dial of the pavement.'[6]

The identification between the floor of *The Ambassadors* and the Great Pavement of Westminster Abbey became universally accepted. But the convincing conjunction between the expertise of Hervey and Lethaby had eclipsed some elementary problems. Mary Hervey begins by describing the painting as an 'accurate copy' of the pavement, but a few lines later she pleads artistic licence on Holbein's behalf. Not only is the design of the pavement reversed, she admits, but 'the colouring is slightly varied' and the mosaic patterns of the interlacing circles have also been altered: 'The reduced scale and perspective has obliged Holbein to simplify some of these to a certain extent. Occasionally he has been obliged to borrow smaller patterns from the narrower strip of mosaic on either side of the central figure'.[7] In fact, two such 'borrowed' patterns are the only ones which can be matched, with any degree of conviction, to the pavement as it is seen today.

It is sometimes suggested that Holbein may have been granted only a glimpse of the pavement and was forced to rely upon some inaccurate intermediary reference, a preliminary drawing for an engraving, for example. Such a theory certainly might explain why the design is reversed. It is, however, a partial not a complete reversal. The outer figure of a square with circles on its sides is reversed: the inner quincunx is not.

In reality, Mary Hervey's 'simplifications' are major changes that cannot be comfortably dismissed. Holbein has painted his floor in shades of orange and brown: the Abbey's pavement is predominantly purple and green porphyrys set in a matrix of greenish grey Purbeck marble. Holbein's design is set in a veined white marble much more like the Carrara marble used by the cosmati workers in their native Italy. The two circles clearly visible at the ambassadors' feet should be filled with patterns of hexagons and six-pointed stars: striking designs that would have afforded the artist an irresistible opportunity to show off his superlative skill, as he does in his painting of the intricately patterned rug and elsewhere. Yet they are left blank. Not only are there obvious omissions, there is also one striking addition. The central roundel of Holbein's floor, half hidden in the shadow of the table, is inlaid with two interlocking triangles forming a Star of David.

What other model might Holbein have used for his floor? Setting aside notions of symbolism and the complication of artistic licence, the simplest explanation is that the floor beneath the ambassadors' feet was just that: the floor on which they stood when Holbein painted them, no more, no less. Two locations are most likely to have provided the setting for the picture: the royal palaces of Bridewell and Greenwich.

During Henry VIII's time, foreign ambassadors were housed at the Palace of Bridewell which stood near the northern end of what is now Blackfriars Bridge. Unfortunately, Bridewell was soon abandoned as a royal palace and its subsequent history left neither trace nor record of its floors. At

Greenwich the records of the expenses involved in the building works[8] pro vide information both about the Palace and the people employed there. Many of the decorative painters with whom Holbein worked were from Italy. The King had long nursed a passion for things Italian. His import of the sculptor, Torrigiano, and his fellow craftsmen to make the tomb of Henry VII at Westminster is generally accepted as marking the arrival of renaissance style in England. In 1511, the third year of his reign, Henry VIII had staged an Italian masque, the like of which had never been seen.[9]

The building accounts make it clear that the classical style, interpreted by the Italian Renaissance, had been extensively grafted on to the fabric of the Palace. Such features are repeatedly described as being of 'antike work'. In 1533, precisely the year *The Ambassadors* was painted, the building accounts of Greenwich Palace record that Andrew Wright and John Heythe were paid for 'devydyng of the adys of the Coundythe in th'enner courte into vj panes the grownde thereof payntyd lyke stone coloure with orbys and antyke worke'.[10] It is not unlikely that the floors of the palace were painted in similar 'antike' fashion. A closer look at the floor in Holbein's painting suggests that it was not made of stone at all, but of wood painted to look like stonework. The geometry of the design was probably set out in line first and then coloured in to imitate various marbles. This would explain the dark lines that separate the elements of Holbein's design. The mortar used to set the stones of a real pavement was generally lighter in colour than most marbles, certainly lighter than the brown and orange 'stones' of the floor of *The Ambassadors*.

Although Lethaby's symbolic notion of a cosmic dimension to the painting's *memento mori* theme adds a seductive dimension to Mary Hervey's identification of the floor of *The Ambassadors* with the sanctuary pavement of Westminster Abbey, the doubts raised by its very inaccurate representation must tip the scales against the argument. To claim that Holbein's floor is anything more than the vaguest reflection of the Westminster pavement would be to overstretch credulity. By contrast, the more practical and logical location of Greenwich may be suggested without an appeal for artistic licence. The floor of Holbein's picture is most likely not a representation of any real cosmati pavement at all but a painting of a painting: a wooden floor in Greenwich Palace painted by craftsmen, working perhaps from a pattern book, in imitation of what was to them an 'antike' work pavement – the cosmati designs of Italy. At the end of this excursion into *The Ambassadors*, it must reluctantly be concluded that the painting cannot offer any documentary contribution to the record or understanding of the Westminster pavement.

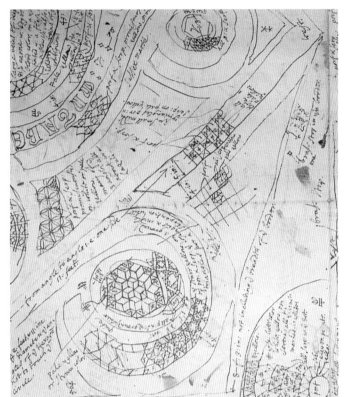

60&61 One of the meticulously detailed sketches made by John Talman in 1707, and the same section of the pavement as it appears today

The story of John Talman's lost drawing of the pavement has a more fortunate outcome. John Talman was born in 1677, the eldest son of the architect, William Talman. He spent his life studying the architecture and decoration of churches and villas in England, France, Germany and Italy. His income seems to have been mainly derived from acting as an agent for those wishing to purchase pictures and drawings by the old masters from abroad. Wherever he travelled, Talman produced meticulous drawings of whatever interested him. These were often accompanied by measurements and informative notes in a curious hybrid of abbreviated English and Italian. In 1717 he was elected first director of the Society of Antiquaries. By the time he died in 1726, Talman had amassed a huge collection of some 1,600 drawings.

The account of John Dart in 1723 provides the written evidence for the making of the drawing of the pavement. He says that Talman produced a measured drawing which was then given to the Society of Antiquaries and engraved. Unfortunately, Dart is not the most reliable of authors. In his first volume on Westminster Abbey, he says that the published verses were but a small part of the inscription on the pavement and that he would be giving the complete version in the second volume. Instead of more verses, however, the second volume brings only an apology: 'The Reader may remember, that I proposed a larger number of Verses than were ever published on it, but in the hurry of that Volume had not the leisure to examine everything that passed through my hands, and those Verses which I thought engraved on it, I find in reality were not, but in praise of it only.'

Dart's credibility is further eroded by Ackermann whose introduction to his own book on the Abbey praises the engravings and typographical beauty of Dart's work but warns that these 'gave it a reputation, to which the historical department has little claim: for a work more remarkable for negligence at least, has seldom come to pass'. Dart's own admission and Ackermann's stinging criticism may lead us to doubt whether there was any truth at all in Dart's account of Talman's drawing of the pavement.

Talman had originally intended to bequeath his large collection of drawings to Trinity College, Cambridge, but his poor financial circumstances at the time of his death meant that the drawings had to be sold to raise a pension for his wife and children. They were auctioned volume by volume over a period of six days in April 1727, and the broken collection became dispersed throughout the country. In 1940, one volume came into the possession of the Victoria and Albert Museum.[11] On its first page it is described, in an eighteenth-century hand, as 'A Portfolio with about 300 drawings of Churches etc. in Italy by Mr. Talman'. For the most part this description is quite correct, but the volume does also include some drawings made in England, among them the Crown of St Edward. More fortunate still, several drawings clearly represent sections of the Westminster pavement.[12] Talman's interest in cosmati work is attested by the many detailed examples of their designs that he recorded on his visits to Italy, drawings among which those of the Westminster pavement had become camouflaged.

The Westminster drawings, dated 1707 in Talman's own hand, are rather rudimentary sketches drawn from direct observation and clearly intended to serve only as research material for a finished work, no doubt the scale drawing of the pavement referred to by Dart. The sketches are amplified with copious notes indicating colours and types of stone, and peppered with measurements (*see 60 and 61*). Therefore they provide much more information about the pavement than could ever have been gleaned from the finished drawing. Some of these working sketches were later cut up and used on the reverse – one for drawings made in Italy, a testimony to Talman's need for economy. When the sketches are photographed, printed to the same scale, and reassembled, the picture that emerges covers a surprisingly substantial area of the pavement, including all its major design elements.

This image, though somewhat eccentric, is the most valuable of the surviving representations of the pavement, predating Ackermann's aquatint, formerly accepted as the oldest record, by more than a century. It provides a wealth of carefully observed detail that often corrects the vague impressions given by Ackermann which could lead to mistaken assumptions. It is reassuring to find that one of Talman's sketches confirms the existence in his day of that band pattern which linked the design of the Westminster pavement to the sarcophagus of Pope Clement IV's tomb (*see 12*).

It is clear that the exhaustive detail of these sketches would have given Talman all the information he needed to make a finished scale drawing of great accuracy. But was such a final drawing ever produced? Lethaby, apparently after Dart, writes that the full-scale drawing was made around 1710 and given to the Society of Antiquaries. But the drawing could not have been made as late as 1710 because it is known that Talman was in Italy by that year: a note inserted in the back of a volume of Talman's plans and elevations of Italian buildings, now in the Courtauld Institute, says that 'Mr Talman and Mr Kent set out for Italy, 1709'.[13] The fact that at least one of the Westminster sketches was cut up and its back used for drawings made during this Italian trip suggests that Talman had no further use for them – the project must either have been completed or have been abandoned. A note on one drawing suggests the former. It reads 'began at Ranworth June 17. 1707. & ended ibid: Aug: 14. cod: ano.' These dates must surely refer not to the execution of the sketches themselves, which were clearly made on the spot at Westminster, but to the finished scale plan, drawn up at leisure at Ranworth from the *in situ* sketches – the drawing that is now lost.

In fact, the completion of the final scale drawing is confirmed in the note-books of George Vertue,[14] the engraver and antiquarian who later became the official engraver to the Society of Antiquaries. Beside a rough sketch laying out the overall design of the sanctuary pavement, Vertue writes 'the Curious pavement in the Quire of the Abby Church at Westminster drawn exactly by Mr. J. Talman: being a sort of Mosaeick work inlaid with beautiful Stones of all kinds, the General form of the whole . . .'. Five smaller drawings represent attempts to sort out the problem of fitting the drawing into the engraved pages of a book: '. . . it might be Gravd in several Sheets. one the inside square two angles next it another sheet & so the other two angles then the square bordure about it each side one sheet which would make four sheets more, in all seaven sheets – or 8 sheets.' Talman's scale drawing was evidently very large and extremely detailed. Vertue's scheme for chopping the design up into nine sections spread over seven pages was far from elegant, and it may well have been the problem of reducing Talman's drawing to manageable proportions that prevented the engravings from being made.

What is so important about the Talman drawings is that they show the pavement has changed surprisingly little during the best part of three centuries. Most of the phases of restoration identified by analysis of the pavement's stonework must have happened before 1707.

Only one major restoration has been made since, and this is most evident in the eastern border of the pavement. Here the machine-cut edges of the stones and the grey cement mortar point to nineteenth-century work. This restoration was carried out by George Gilbert Scott, the most commercially successful of the architects of the Gothic Revival, who was Surveyor to the Abbey in the middle years of the nineteenth century. His major restoration of the eastern border of the pavement and, no doubt, some 'tidying up' of the rest, was made as part of a scheme to return the sanctuary to its former gothic splendour.

62 Badly decayed roundel which served as a model for George Gilbert Scott's restoration in the mid-19th century, compare 64

There had been no dividing screen between the altar and the shrine of Edward the Confessor until the late middle ages when a towering reredos was built behind the altar across the whole width of the sanctuary. This is the reredos that can be seen in the drawing of the sanctuary which appears in the *Obituary Roll of John Islip (see 51)*. The medieval reredos survived until 1706 when Christopher Wren replaced it with a grand marble altar-piece in the then fashionable classical style.

Wren was Surveyor of the Fabric during this period and, under his direction, the Abbey endured its most far-reaching building and restoration programme since the time of Henry III; largely financed by the proceeds of the coal tax which had been levied on coal coming into London to provide an income for the repair and rebuilding of churches lost in the City's Great Fire. But the classical marble altar-piece imported into the Abbey by Wren was not new: it had been made for the Palace of Whitehall where James II had built a chapel to provide a place of Catholic worship for his Queen, Mary of Modena, and the growing number of Catholics at the royal court. The chapel was lavishly decorated by the best artists of the day and the focus of the interior was the elaborate marble altar-piece, said to have been designed by Christopher Wren and executed by Grinling Gibbons and Arnold Quellin. The events of history, however, were soon to drive James II and his Catholic court out of the country. 1688 brought the so-called Bloodless Revolution when the Protestant parliament invited William of Orange, later William III, to take over the English throne. James II fled to France and the royal chapel at Whitehall was left derelict. The extravagant altarpiece was taken away and put in store at Hampton Court. But it was not forgotten. While Christopher Wren was working on his restorations at the Abbey, he evidently remembered this grand piece of work and a petition was sent to Queen Anne requesting it for the Abbey. The request was granted.

The Queen Anne altar-piece was so large that its steps spread out over the eastern edge of the cosmati pavement. An engraving of the choir in Ackermann's work on the Abbey shows the altar-piece in the distance and gives an impression of how it must have appeared in the eighteenth century *(see 63)*. The Abbey's accounts show that one John Church was paid £2. 3s. 0d. on 11th March 1707 for writing the 'inscriptions and sentences on the altarpiece'. John Dart recalls the damage inflicted on the pavement by its installation: 'The pavement, at the erecting of the Altar, was threatened by a total dissolution by the Workmen, whose mercenary and misjudging Notions destroy whatever is venerable, but by the Influence of the Lord Oxford, and the then Bishop of Rochester, it was for the most part saved; yet they broke

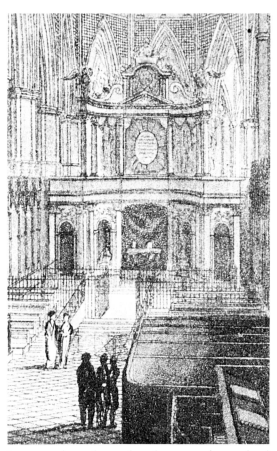

it up under where the altar stands, and where the marble slabs lie round the edges on the sides.'[15]

A note on one of Talman's sketches may suggest that this damage was, in fact, the reason which prompted the making of his detailed scale drawing of the pavement the year after the new altar-piece had been installed. The note follows a calculation and says simply, '46 – number of square feet of the pavement spoiled'. Bearing in mind the attention being paid to the Abbey by Christopher Wren, it is quite possible that Talman's survey was commissioned in order to ascertain the extent of damage to the pavement and also to provide a record for the purposes of restoration. If so, then it may be assumed that some areas of the pavement were restored during Wren's time as Surveyor. From the evidence of Talman's sketches, however, it is clear that this restoration was confined to resetting the dislodged stones that had been rescued by Lord Oxford (Robert Harley) and the Bishop of Rochester.

The Queen Anne altar-piece stood in the Abbey for more than a century. Then, in 1820, it was moved out as part of the scene-setting preparations for the Coronation of George IV. Three years later it was replaced by a new reredos designed by Benjamin Wyatt, Surveyor of the Fabric, and Francis Bernasconi. Since classicism had now fallen out of favour, washed away by the relentless tide of the Gothic Revival, the new reredos was gothic in style, allegedly a reconstruction of its medieval forerunner.

The Wyatt and Bernasconi reredos, which replaced the Queen Anne altar-piece, was not as long-lived. In 1863, the Dean and Chapter approved plans for a new altar and reredos. Here we return to George Gilbert Scott, who had become Surveyor of the Fabric in 1849. It was his designs which received the Abbey's approval, though they were not to be completely realised for some ten years. Paradoxically, Scott had been present, as a youth, in the Abbey during the construction of the Bernasconi altar-piece which he was now about to tear down. Dean Stanley, in the sermon preached on Scott's death, recalled the irony that 'when in this Abbey the first note of that revival [i.e. the Gothic Revival] was struck by the erection of Bernasconi's plaster canopies in place of the classic altar-piece given by Queen Anne, a boy of fourteen years old was in the church watching the demolition and reconstruction with a curious vigilance, which from that time never flagged for fifty years'.[16]

With the removal of the Bernasconi altar and reredos, the eastern border of the cosmati pavement once again saw the light of day. But it was badly damaged. Only the general outline of the design and sections of the band patterns had survived intact. By a stroke of good fortune, however, Scott discovered beneath the altar steps 'a concrete containing chips of glass mosaic'. These he used to refill the old matrices of the eastern border. The glasses alone would not have been sufficient, so other materials must have been added, mainly purple and green porphyrys. Some porphyry had been acquired for paving the new altar platform in a style that would complement the cosmati pavement. It was bought, at his own expense, by Dean Stanley whose 'kind, appropriate and costly gift of Porphyry for the circles in the pavement in front of the Altar' was recorded by the Chapter of the Abbey in May 1870.[17]

Since many of the porphyry pieces in the eastern section of the cosmati pavement which show machine-cut edges are also of slightly different quality from the original material – the green porphyry being of a brighter, more yellow hue, and the purple, more pink and with finer phenocysts – it may be assumed that these are restorations dating from the period during which Scott's new altar-piece was installed, that is, the late 1860s to early 1870s. Three of the roundels from the eastern border appear in the foreground of John Harrington's photograph of 1869 (*see 52*), and all three appear to be blank matrices. It is most likely, therefore, that Scott's restoration of the

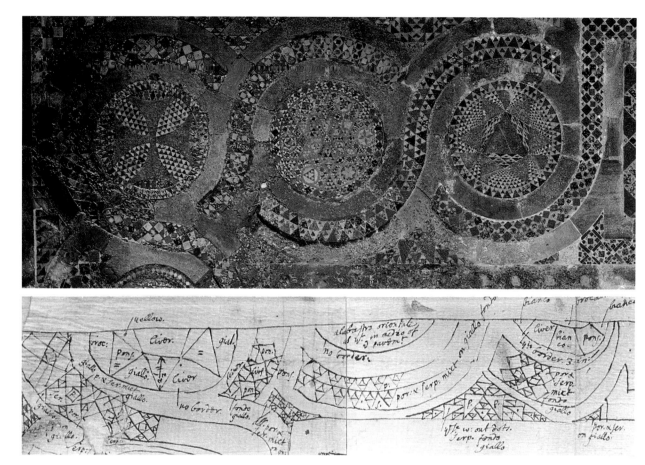

64–67 The roundels of the eastern border, restored by George Gilbert Scott, compared with John Talman's record made in 1707

eastern border was not carried out until 1870 at the earliest, shortly after Dean Stanley's gift of porphyrys. It is possible that the detailed contemporary watercolours produced by C. Hadfield in 1863 (*see 57*), were intended as a guide for Scott's restorations.

It would be wrong to assume from Scott's own description of refilling the old matrices of the pavement that he accurately reproduced the original thirteenth-century design of the eastern border. He did not. Comparison with John Talman's sketches reveals that all six roundels have brand new designs. Although Talman was handicapped by the fact that most of the eastern border was then covered by the steps of the Queen Anne altarpiece, one of his sketches records a large enough segment of each roundel to distinguish them from Scott's designs. Talman's version of these roundels is confirmed by the rather more hazy view of Ackermann. Even without the evidence of Talman, Scott's roundels would appear a little out of character

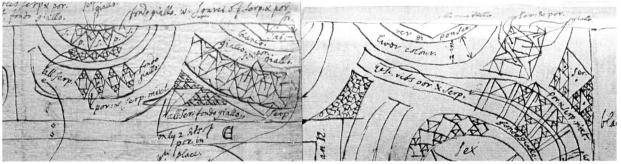

with the rest of the pavement: his designs have a degree of complexity which is generally unmatched elsewhere in the border.

Scott did not, however, indulge his imagination in some flight of fancy – such a thing would have been unthinkable for a respected architect of the Gothic Revival. The sources for his roundel designs are close at hand. The second roundel from the north in the eastern band is based on the remains of the roundel immediately to the west of the northern panel (*compare 62 with 64*). The roundel in the south-east corner derives from the roundel at the opposite corner of the pavement. The remaining four roundels are all inspired by roundels found in the cosmati pavement around the Shrine of St Edward, now permanently covered by linoleum. The roundel in the form of a Greek cross is appropriately placed at the north-east corner next to the cross which marks the beginning of the pavement's inscription.

The eastern border of the pavement constructed by George Gilbert Scott represents the last substantial restoration of the sanctuary pavement: the best documented milestone in a seven-hundred-year history of damage and repair. To reconstruct the rest of this history in precise dates and detail is an impossible task. The best that can be hoped for is to distinguish major restorations against the background of routine repair, and particular periods of damage against general wear and tear. To this must be added the history of the Abbey itself, on the tide of whose fortunes the pavement was carried.

The work begun by Henry III in the thirteenth century was carried on throughout the middle ages, culminating in the fruitful abbacy of John Islip, which saw the construction of the impressive Lady Chapel of Henry VII and the completion of the nave. After the death of Abbot Islip, in 1532, work on the Abbey came to a gentle halt, the western towers remaining unfinished until the eighteenth century when they were completed by Nicolas Hawksmoor. The guide-book to the Abbey published by T. Carnan in 1783, *An Historical Description of Westminster Abbey, its Monuments and Curiosities*, states that no repairs were made to the Abbey until the time of Christopher Wren, that is from the 1690s onwards. Keepe's description of the ruinous exterior a hundred years earlier seems to support Carnan's theory of neglect. The years between the Reformation in the sixteenth century and the end of the seventeenth century were turbulent ones in the history of English religious life, so it would hardly be surprising if no major building work had been carried out during that time. However, internal re-arrangements following the Reformation and counter-Reformation would certainly have entailed building work inside the Abbey, and it does seem unlikely that the external fabric could have survived without some attention.

The Dissolution of the Abbey in January 1540 opened the way for the systematic transfer of its assets, both lands and treasures, into the royal exchequer of Henry VIII. The Confessor's Shrine had already been stripped of its gold and jewels under the Vicar-General's order of 1536 for the removal of all shrines, relics and images from the churches and cathedrals of England – an order which effectively destroyed a major part of the country's artistic legacy of the middle ages. By the Dissolution, the Confessor's Shrine had been reduced to a stump, all but its base having been destroyed. The body of St Edward was secretly reburied elsewhere in the Abbey. In December 1540, Westminster was officially founded as a cathedral under the charge of a Dean and a Chapter of Canons, confirming the *ad hoc* regime that had been in place since shortly after the Dissolution. During this period the medieval high altar was also removed. The destructive activity of these years is unlikely to have left the sanctuary pavement untouched, but there is no evidence to suggest deliberate damage.

When Mary I, a staunch Catholic, ascended the throne in 1553, her

Coronation was preceded by a thorough cleansing of the Abbey, as if to purge it of the pestilence of the Reformation. She resolved to restore the Abbey to its former condition. Most of what had been done, could not, of course, be undone. However, the monks did return to the Abbey. The Dean was discharged and replaced, in 1556, by John de Feckenham in the revived post of Abbot. The internal arrangements of the Abbey were reset for the Catholic liturgy, and Abbot Feckenham began the work for which he is best remembered: the restoration of the shrine of the Confessor (*see 68*). Unfortunately, there was neither time nor money available to recreate the former glories of the shrine. The Saint's remains were reinterred in what was left of the base of the shrine, which was hastily patched up with new stonework and plaster, then painted and gilded in imitation of cosmati work. Where a golden feretory had once stood over the coffin, a two-tier wooden canopy was raised with a gabled roof. This period of restoration by Abbot Feckenham provides the first likely opportunity for the repair of the sanctuary pavement which must surely have been damaged by the events of preceding years.

Feckenham was to be the last Abbot of Westminster. Shortly after the Protestant Elizabeth I became Queen, the Abbey was disbanded once again. For a year it stood unused then, in 1560, it was formally constituted as a collegiate church, governed by a Dean. The relative stability of the following eighty years gave pause to look to the state of the fabric of the church. By 1603, Dean Launcelot Andrewes had begun to stockpile materials systematically for repairing the Abbey. The Chapter minutes of December 3rd instruct 'that provision be made of lead, stone, timber and other necessaries towards reparations of the fabricke of the church, yearely to the value of forty pounds, layd up in the storehouse, not to be imployed without consent of the deane'.[18] It is possible that further repairs to the sanctuary pavement may have been made during this period of consolidation. 1603 was also the year of the Coronation of James I. Such major ceremonial events often provided the opportunity, and the money, to renovate the interior of the Abbey, but they could equally be the cause of new damage. Coronations caused major upheavals at the Abbey, platforms and galleries often being built with a total disregard for the fabric of the building and its monuments.

The outbreak of Civil War and the establishment of Oliver Cromwell's Commonwealth brought a new setback in the Abbey's fortunes. In 1643, a Parliamentary Committee was set up under Sir Robert Harley with the express purpose of demolishing 'the monuments of superstition and idolatry in the Abbey Church and the windows thereof'.[19] The Abbey was subjected to a second purging of its treasures, this time motivated as much

68 George Vertue's engraving of the shrine of the Confessor as it was reconstructed by Abbot Feckenham in the 1550s

72

by fanaticism as by greed. The same year two companies of soldiers were garrisoned in the church. According to Joducus Crull, the communion table served as their dining table and the sanctuary, being used for their general recreation, fell victim to all kinds of profanation. The soldiers' occupation was the cause of further wanton destruction of the furnishings of the Abbey and, no doubt, the sanctuary pavement suffered its share of casual damage. After the initial months of anarchy, however, the Parliamentary authorities began to adopt a more responsible attitude towards the Abbey, and the Board of Governors appointed to administer its affairs did much to preserve and repair the fabric of the church during the remaining years of the Commonwealth.

With the restoration of the monarchy in 1660, the tide turned back in favour of the Abbey. The intimate relationship between Westminster and the Crown was re-established and never again estranged. The Coronation of Charles II provided the first major state occasion at the restored Abbey. The expenses incurred at the Coronation and in the succeeding two years, such as the scaffolding for the coronation platforms, are recorded in the Abbey's muniments. *An Accompt of Extraordinary Disbursements since the Restoration of the Deane and Chapter of Westminster to Michaelmass 1662*[20] shows as its third item a payment of £26 for 'Mosaic work before the Altar'. The use of the word 'mosaic' makes this the first indisputable record of repair work to the sanctuary pavement. It is confirmed in a second document: another version of the Abbey's accounts for July 1660 to October 1662, where it appears as 'Mosaique works – 026:0:0'.[21] The fact that this bill merited a separate item in both accounts to distinguish it from the more usual, and more general, entries like 'mason's works' or 'plumber's works' indicates that this was more than routine repair. It suggests that this record may well represent the systematic restoration carried out in the group of materials previously referred to as the secondary mix. If this is so, we may then better understand why Keepe, writing in 1683, could describe the pavement as 'remaining intire', despite the damage that it must have sustained during the Reformation and the Commonwealth: it had been carefully restored in the intervening years.

The entry describing the mosaic work before the altar is a happy, but unfortunately rare, exception among the accounts of the Abbey's expenditure on its fabric during the seventeenth and eighteenth centuries. More often, the accounts are of no great assistance in identifying specific restoration since the practice was to divide the expenditure into broad categories: the total sums paid in a given period to masons, plumbers, carpenters, glaziers, painters and rakers. The accounts do, however, give a rough guide to the level of activity at the Abbey. The large amount spent 'In repairs in & around the Abbey' between 1660 and 1662,'' a total of £2,153. 19s. 6d., proves that Carnan was quite wrong in believing that the fabric of the church went without repair until the time of Christopher Wren. The general lack of precise description of work carried out was probably due in part to the fact that the same craftsmen were retained by the Abbey for a good many years. George Norris, for example, was paviour to the Abbey from 1697 until 1719.

A review of the sums paid to paviours shows a great degree of fluctuation: the annual expenditure in 1697, for example, was £22. 7s. od.[23] The following year it fell to £4. 10s. od.[24] It must be cautioned that the sums recorded do not generally distinguish between paving within the church, its associated buildings and the surrounding area. However, it may not be totally unreasonable to speculate that routine repair work on the sanctuary pavement is embraced by these general figures. The first peak, in 1689, coincides with the coronation year of William and Mary and no doubt reflects the extra activity associated with that occasion. The second peak, in the years 1695 to 1697, has no immediately obvious correlation with other events at the Abbey. The third peak begins in 1702, the year of Queen Anne's Coronation, and steadily rises to £34. 8s. od. in 1705.[25] This peak must represent the surge of activity due to Christopher Wren's work at the Abbey, leading to the installation of the Queen Anne altar-piece in 1706. A fourth peak begins sharply in 1709 with the payment of £38. 3s. 6d.[26] It is tempting to imagine this total including the cost of repairing the damage caused to the sanctuary pavement by the workmen setting in the Queen Anne altar-piece, the area calculated at 46 square feet by John Talman in his drawings of 1707. By that time, we know from these sketches that the restoration in the tertiary mix materials, most obvious in the infill patterns in the southern half of the central square, had already been made. Since the earlier restoration in secondary mix materials took place in the period following Charles II's Coronation, it is logical to regard later coronations as potential dates for the tertiary mix restoration.

James II was crowned in 1685; William and Mary in 1689 and Anne in 1702. The Coronation of James II is particularly well documented thanks to the detailed record of the event published by Francis Sandford in 1687, *The History of the Coronation of James II*. The volume is well illustrated and several plates include the floor of the sanctuary. However, the pattern of the opus sectile work is not shown in any of them, and it must be assumed that the pavement was covered by some rich cloth. This appears to have been the tradition since the time of Edward I, son of Henry III. It seems more

69 The Coronation of James II

likely, therefore, that the pavement would be repaired in the aftermath of a coronation rather than in preparation for one.

Both the coronations of William and Mary, and of Anne, were followed by increases in the paviours' bills. The increase after the Coronation of William and Mary was sharp and short-lived; the increase around the time of Anne's Coronation was part of a long-term rise and fall in expenditure spread over some five years. If the restoration in tertiary mix materials has to be assigned to a particular date, then it is more likely to be associated with the sharp increase of 1689 than the later rise. The damage caused when the Queen Anne altar-piece was installed in 1706 suggests a disregard for the pavement which is inconsistent with it having been recently restored. This restoration is far inferior to the earlier restoration in secondary mix materials, and the tertiary mix materials may have been hurriedly transplanted *en bloc* from a single pavement elsewhere. An element of haste would suggest a deadline to be met. Could that deadline have been the Coronation of William and Mary, and the need to repair the damage caused four years earlier by preparations for the Coronation of James II? We know that the workmen preparing the Abbey for James II's Coronation were not as careful as they might have been. A heavy plank fell on the actual coffin of Edward

75

the Confessor, damaging it so badly that it had to be repaired.[27] In the circumstances, it is perhaps unwise to do more than suggest that the tertiary mix restoration was carried out some time in the second half of the seventeenth century, probably in the 1680s.

However, if caution is set to one side, a very speculative model and summing-up of the fortunes of the pavement may be drawn from reviewing the historical record in the light of the physical evidence of the stone work.

Throughout the three hundred years between the laying of the pavement in 1268 and the Reformation, the relative seclusion of the sanctuary meant that it was subject to only moderate wear and tear. During the medieval period, repairs would have been occasional and small scale. The first major damage to the pavement is likely to have occurred during the 1540s in the wake of the Dissolution of the Abbey. After the counter-Reformation, this damage may have been made good by Abbot Feckenham as part of his project to restore the church, in particular the Shrine of the Confessor, to its former, and Catholic, glory. The pavement was further damaged, perhaps more seriously, during the early years of the Commonwealth, partly by the systematic despoliation of the Abbey and partly by the soldiers quartered there. At some time between 1660 and 1662, following the Coronation of Charles II, the pavement received a major restoration, documented in the Abbey's archives. This is almost certainly the considered restoration carried out in the secondary mix materials. Two coronations during the 1680s were perhaps the cause of further harm to the pavement which was repaired, less carefully than the previous restoration, in tertiary mix materials. In 1706, the installation of the Queen Anne altar-piece caused damage to 46 square feet of the pavement. This was later repaired, perhaps around 1709, using the stones which had been dislodged and possibly some new materials. As the Abbey came to serve more and more as a mausoleum for national heroes, the routine wear and tear on the sanctuary pavement grew in proportion to the number of visitors touring the tombs of the famous. In the mid-nineteenth century, George Gilbert Scott replaced the eastern border, which had been hidden beneath the Queen Anne altar-piece, and generally repaired the rest of the pavement. Since this last restoration, there have been only minor repairs, mainly to the Purbeck matrix of the design which has been crudely patched in the present century with black and brown tar-like materials.

Certain sections of the pavement merit more detailed discussion. Some authorities have doubted the authenticity of the critical focus of the pavement's design, the central roundel of Egyptian onyx marble. In George Gilbert Scott's *Gleanings* of 1863, William Burges remarks sceptically that the central roundel has 'a very modern look' and suggests that the position was originally occupied by an engraved brass plate – an unlikely suggestion that would find no parallel in cosmati work elsewhere. Apart from one very much smaller piece of onyx of a different type this is the only onyx now to be found in the pavement. Talman's sketches reveal that onyx marble, 'alabastre orientale' as he called it, was also originally used for one of the roundels in the eastern border. Burges's remark about the 'modern look' of the central roundel was almost certainly prompted by the fact that the onyx stone rises above its surrounding level. This is not, however, the result of the stone having been inserted in modern times: it is a consequence of the fact that onyx is a very hard and durable stone. The more fragile, opaque, coloured glasses that made up the surrounding band, on the other hand, have fractured and been more easily eroded over the centuries, leaving the onyx proud of its setting. The same stone was certainly in place in 1707, when John Talman described it as being '2′2½″ in diameter. Large veins of deep red: . . . carne with edges of blood colour on a yellow tinted . . . with flesh colour and bluish, also veins of giallo' – a description which comfortably fits what is to be seen today. Furthermore, as early as the mid-fifteenth century, Richard Sporley described the centre of the pavement as '*unius lapidis rotundi*', 'a single round stone'. His further description, that the stone contained in itself the colours of the four Elements, agrees well enough with the present roundel of multi-coloured, veined onyx.

There is circumstantial evidence supporting the use of onyx to dignify particular stations in a church. Certain positions within the medieval basilica of St Peter's in Rome were specially marked out by four marble roundels set in the floor. The roundels were considered of such importance that the area around St Peter's was known as '*ad quatuor rotas*'.[28] Pavino, an early sixteenth-century writer,[29] describes two of the roundels as being made of porphyry and the other two of a veined Egyptian marble that sounds very like that to be seen at Westminster. There are, therefore, no strong reasons for doubting the authenticity of the central roundel, and some good ones for supporting it. It seems quite appropriate that the most exotic marble in the pavement should be reserved for this special position.

The infill pattern of the area bounded by the southern border, the southeast side of the central square and the large south-east roundel, presents an interesting problem. Although this relatively simple pattern is found elsewhere in cosmati work (for instance, on the base of the ciborium in the cathedral of Anagni), and is also confirmed in the Westminster pavement by John Talman in 1707, its context in the overall design raises some doubts. There seems to have been a deliberate distinction between the infill patterns

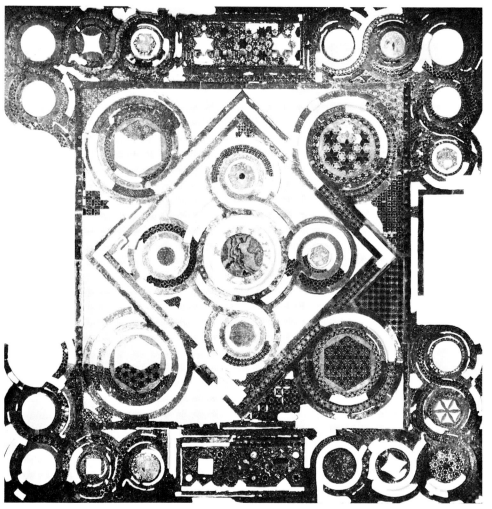

70 An estimation of the extent of the pavement's fabric surviving undisturbed from the medieval period

of the pavement's inner square and those of the surrounding square. Those in the centre show six-fold symmetries, while those in the larger square have four-fold symmetries – with the exception of this star pattern infill. This division of the pavement into areas of six- and four-fold symmetries appears to have been a conscious design decision, and one which is later given some philosophical justification. Not only does the star pattern infill go against this convention, it is also laid entirely in materials from the tertiary mix. On balance, it must be counted as a part of the late eighteenth-century restoration rather than the original cosmati work of the thirteenth century.

When all such questionable sections of the marble work and areas of known restoration are discounted, it seems at first that a distressingly small proportion of the original pavement is left. Given the age and location of the work, this is to be expected. But the picture is not a depressing one. On the contrary, the authenticity of the overall design is certain, and a large number of its individual patterns are confirmed by the partial survival, however small, of original work. Furthermore, the evidence of what does survive suggests that much of the 1660–62 restoration presents a reasonably faithful recreation of the lost thirteenth-century work. Thus it may be concluded that by far the greater part of the pavement today is, in spirit if not in substance, the same as that laid down in 1268, and may legitimately serve as the foundation for an exegesis of the inscription placed upon it.

5

The Inscription

+ *XPI:MILLENO:BIS:CENTENO:DUODENO:*
CUM:SEXAGENO:SUBDUCTIS:QUATUOR:ANNO:
TERTIUS:HENRICUS:REX:URBS:ODORICUS:ET:ABBAS:
HOS:COMPEGERE:PORPHYREOS:LAPIDES:

SI:LECTOR:POSITA:PRUDENTER:CUNCTA:REVOLVAT:
HIC:FINEM:PRIMI:MOBILIS:INVENIET:
SEPES:TRIMA:CANES:ET:EQUOS:HOMINESQUE:SUBADDAS:
CERVOS:ET:CORVOS:AQUILAS:IMMANIA:CETE:
MUNDUM:QUODQUE:SEQUENS:PREEUNTIS:TRIPLICAT:ANNOS:

SPERICUS:ARCHETIPUM:GLOBUS:HIC:MONSTRAT:MACROCOSMUM:

The Westminster sanctuary pavement is distinguished from all other known examples of the cosmati's work by its long Latin inscription set in letters of brass. Instead of the normal, usually brief, acknowledgment of the craftsman responsible for the work and the year in which it was completed, the Westminster inscription is ten lines long and set firmly in the literary rather than the monumental tradition. The author of these sophisticated verses indicated what the reader might expect to find revealed in the pavement's design, or at least he pointed out the right direction. Today, alas, the inscription is only partial, but what can be reconstructed of the original, shown above, is intriguingly enigmatic. Since it shapes any initial response to the symbolic meaning of the pavement, an accurate translation

71 The surviving brass letters of the word *monstrat* set around the central roundel

of the inscription and an understanding of its philosophical context are obviously crucial: as with the earlier analysis of the opus sectile work, it is vital to know what can be relied upon and what cannot.

The inscription is an unusual and difficult one, so a careful examination must be undertaken in which the physical witness of the surviving elements of the inscription is coupled with the circumstantial evidence of related documentary material. This detective work produces the nearest reconstruction now possible of the verses that were considered an appropriate accompaniment to the pavement's design and opens a first window into the mind of the thirteenth-century Christian philosopher who wrote them, allowing us to begin to see how patterns of thought might be reflected in patterns of stone.

Although it is the unique association between a lengthy inscription and a cosmati pavement that is the primary concern here, the inscription is important in its own right. It provides the earliest known example of brass lettering on a monument. The letters were set one by one directly into the Purbeck marble that forms the matrix of the pavement's design. Letters engraved on continuous strips of brass did not come into fashion until almost a century later. This earlier technique of setting letters separately was not widespread until the closing years of the thirteenth century, so the appearance of such letters as early as the end of the 1260s is quite remarkable – and another indication of the high status accorded at the time to the pavement project. The apparent lack of a comparable tradition in cosmati work in Italy suggests that the inscription should be regarded as a local imposition, English both in its crafting and its authorship, and therefore not necessarily exactly contemporary with the laying of the pavement.

Unhappily, history has taken its toll, and little of the inscription now remains: just eleven letters, three pairs of the diamond-shaped colons used to separate words, and two half-pairs. The eleven letters that survive *in situ* provide the forms of seven different letters: A, E, M, N, O, R and T. The most distinctive is the letter A which has a comparatively unusual V-shaped horizontal stroke. Since the letters were set singly, the forms of many missing letters can be inferred from the indents they have left behind in the Purbeck matrix. The extant letters and indents reveal that the letters were very standardised both in shape and size, suggesting that they were either cast from moulds or cut from sheets using templates.

The flat sheets of metal from which medieval monumental brasses were made was called *latten* or *laton* and was mainly imported from the Low Countries. Latten was one of several grades of brass manufactured in medieval times. Bartholomeus Anglicanus, an English theologian who studied and taught in France, compiled a text book some time between 1235 and 1250 called *De Proprietatibus Rerum* which included information on the making of alloys. Typically of writers before the eighteenth century, he makes no clear distinction between brass and bronze, but he does allow a separate entry for latten: 'Laton is called aurichalcum, and has that name, for though it be brass and copper, of tinne, and of auripigmentum, and other mettals, it is brought in the fire to the colour of golde'.[1]

Bartholomeus' description might readily be applied to the brass letters of

72–78 The seven letter forms still to be seen in the pavement

the Westminster pavement. The Muniment Room at the Abbey houses a single brass letter E which, according to tradition, comes from the inscription in the sanctuary pavement. The letter does indeed conform exactly in shape and size with those Es still *in situ*, and would fit comfortably into several E-shaped indents, but it is suspiciously free from signs of wear. The letter was analysed by the British Museum Research Laboratory with a view to establishing its date of manufacture.

Preliminary inspection by microscope of the underside and edges of the letter revealed a surface texture and tooling marks which suggest that the letter was cast from a mould rather than cut from metal sheet. Also visible were tiny specks of a dark material which might be the remains of the resin or mortar used to set the letter in its matrix.

The letter was subjected to analysis by X-ray fluorescence. This non-destructive test involves bombarding the surface of an object with a beam of X-rays. Excited by the energy of the beam, the molecules of the object diffract the X-ray particles into patterns that are different for each chemical element. When analysed by computer, the resulting dispersion of the X-ray beam reveals a qualitative description of the alloy and gives some indication of the relative proportions of its constituent elements. This test showed the Westminster letter to be an alloy predominantly of copper and tin with much smaller amounts of silver, lead and iron. Silver is found as an impurity in copper produced before the industrial age, after which improved methods of smelting enabled the silver to be separated from the less valuable copper. Its presence in the Westminster letter suggests that it was made in medieval times. A trace of calcium was also detected, but was considered to be a surface contamination. This finding was of some interest since such contamination could be interpreted as confirming the letter's intimate

contact with the Purbeck marble of the pavement, calcium being a major element in the chemical make-up of limestone.

A small sample was then drilled from the back of the letter for analysis by atomic absorption spectrophotometry to yield accurate quantitative results. This sophisticated technique relies upon the fact that when an element becomes incandescent it emits light at a series of specific wavelengths, or bands, of the spectrum. Each element has its own characteristic pattern of bands, an individual 'signature'. When the light emitted from a pure element is passed through the vapourised sample of a compound, the compound absorbs the band pattern of the pure element in proportion to the amount of that element contained in it. So by vapourising very small amounts of the sample and measuring how much they absorb of the emitted light 'signatures' of a series of elements the relative proportions of those elements in the sample compound may be deduced.

The results of this analysis showed that the letter is made of *latten*, a quaternary brass alloy of copper, tin, lead and zinc.[2] This composition is very similar to that of late thirteenth-century memorial brasses, as might have been expected, but there is another less obvious and more interesting comparison to be made.

The composition of the Westminster letter is surprisingly close to that of a group of steelyard weights.[3] Steelyard weights were standards issued by the Crown for use by the Hansa merchants of the London steelyard. The steelyard was their main trading place in England. Its name derives not from the metal but from '*stahl*', a word simply meaning a place where goods are sold. The Hansa merchants were a well established association of German and Baltic traders who carried out their business activities all over Europe, a kind of thirteenth-century multi-national corporation. A large part of their business in London seems to have been the import of wax and export of wool. The steelyard weights that closely match the composition of the West-minster letters are decorated with heraldic devices, which suggest that they were manufactured centrally under the authority of Richard, Earl of Corn-wall on behalf of the Crown, his brother King Henry III. The decoration includes the double-headed eagle of the Hansa merchants, the arms of Poitou, associated with the Earl of Cornwall, and the English royal arms. Since the steelyard was granted trading rights in 1260, this group of decorated steelyard weights can be dated reliably to the second half of the thirteenth century.

The results of the analysis, therefore, show there is no doubt about the authenticity of the Westminster letter and the inscription can confidently be dated to the second half of the thirteenth century. In fact, the close

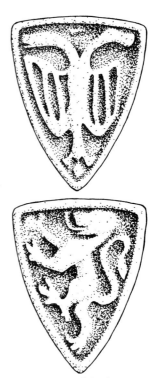

79 Steelyard weight discovered at Oswestry, cast in brass of a composition strikingly similar to that of the Westminster letters

similarity between the alloy of the letters and the steelyard weights makes it tempting to conjecture that the latten for both came from the same source and was cast in the same royal workshop. Documentary evidence shows that copper was among the goods imported by the Hansa merchants from the beginning of the fourteenth century, and there is no reason not to suppose it had been imported earlier.[4] Cornwall's prosperity was built on tin mining. Copper and tin are two of the four main elements of latten.

In their general character the pavement's letters correspond to the style of monumental lettering that was common in England from the later 1290s to the middle of the fourteenth century.[5] This style is often described as *Lombardic lettering*, despite the fact that the Lombardic script of northern Italy was very varied in form and lacked the coherent character necessary to delineate a specific style. Uncial script is perhaps a more accurate description. Uncial had been the usual letter form from the fourth to the ninth century, so Brayley's description, in 1823, of the pavement's 'Saxon capitals' is not wide of the mark. The script takes its name from the Latin word for an inch, *uncia*, since, according to tradition, St Jerome had condemned the vanity of over-rich manuscripts with their inch-high letters. It was these letter forms that were first used for brass lettering on monuments and which provided the basic models for the Westminster inscription. By the

1350s, the uncial form was replaced by the more angular and condensed style generally associated with gothic lettering and, instead of individually set letters, inscriptions were engraved on brass strips or fillets. The Westminster pavement does, however, exhibit a little inconsistency in the shapes of its letters: surviving indents show that at least one M and a U were Roman in form rather than uncial.

Although they conform in many ways to the standard form for monumental lettering from the 1290s until the middle of the next century, the Westminster pavement letters have a distinctive character of their own which led John Blair to consider them to mark the beginning of the technique in England and to suggest that they were the product of a London workshop closely associated with the royal works.[6] This suggestion is strengthened by the compositional link between the Westminster letters and the steelyard weights manufactured under the authority of Richard, Earl of Cornwall.

Identical letter forms appear on one of a pair of badly worn grave slabs in the floor of the Confessor's Chapel. The lower parts of the slabs had been hidden under the steps to Henry V's chantry until they were revealed by George Gilbert Scott in the mid-nineteenth century. So protected, they escaped the wear that virtually destroyed the rest of the slabs. The earliest guide-books ascribe the tombs to John and Margaret de Valence, the children of Henry III's brother, William. Despite some eighteenth- and nineteenth-century doubts about its validity, this ascription is upheld today. The slab thought to be that of John de Valence retains eight of its letters and some of the mosaic work that filled the background between the central brass cross and the lettering set around the edge of the slab. A watercolour by Miss E. M. Vincent records the appearance of the lettering and mosaic in 1898.[7] Lethaby dates the burial of John de Valence to 1277, so it is just possible that these letters were cast from the very same moulds as those of the sanctuary pavement. A further group of letter forms which Blair conjectures to be related to the Westminster Abbey letters is attested by the indents in the slab tomb of William de Lessington in Lincoln Cathedral, dated 1272. Both these groups of comparable letter forms are of relevance when considering the date at which the inscription may have been added to the pavement.

We turn now from the brass letters themselves to the message that they spell out. The earliest record of the complete wording of the inscription appears in Flete's *History of Westminster Abbey* compiled in 1443. Only 16 of a probable 56 folia of the original manuscript survive, at Trinity College in Dublin,[8] but these do not include the story of the pavement. Fortunately a copy made in the latter part of the fifteenth century, and kept among the

80 The Westminster Abbey copy of John Flete's transcription of the pavement's verses

muniments of Westminster Abbey, preserves the lost account of the pavement, and this provides the starting point for any reconstruction of its verses. The Westminster manuscript of Flete's history gives the inscription as follows:[9]

> *Si lector posita prudent~ cu~cta revolvat*
> *hic fine~ primi mobilis inveniet*
> *Sepes trina canes et equos ho~nesque subaddas,*
> *cervos & corvos aquilas immania cete*
> *mundu~ qdque sequens preuntis triplicat Annos*
> *Spericus Archetipu~ globus hic monstrat macrocosmu~*
> *Crsti milleno bis centeno duodeno*
> *cum sexageno subductis quatuor uno*
> *Tertius Henricus Rex urbis Odoric~ & Abbas*
> *hos compigere porphyeos lapides*

> (~ indicates a contraction sign in the manuscript hand)

The Westminster manuscript is not, however, a perfect copy of Flete's history: comparison with the existing folia of the original exposes both mistakes and omissions on the part of the copyist. It would, therefore, be

87

81 Richard Sporley's version of the inscription, dated to 1450

unwise to accept this transcription of the pavement's verses as conclusive without further corroboration.

At this point a second manuscript provides valuable evidence: Richard Sporley's *History of the Abbots of Westminster* in the British Library.[10] His history is composed almost entirely of verbatim extracts from Flete's work. Since Sporley's account was written in 1450, it predates the Westminster copy of Flete's history and is likely to have been copied directly from the original manuscript, of which only the Dublin fragment now remains. So Sporley's text provides a critical check when considering difficulties of translation caused by contractions and possible slips of the pen in the Westminster copy. As a monk at Westminster, Sporley also had the opportunity to compare Flete's words with the pavement, before which he knelt in prayer every day.

The pavement itself is the second control. The few remaining letters and the greater number of legible indents confirm or question a surprising proportion of Flete's transcription. Indents which are no longer identifiable may still be used to count missing letters, and even where no indents exist, due to replacement of the original stone matrix, the reasonably consistent spacing between letters within each line allows some estimate of the number of lost letters to be made. The general distribution of the indents in the design of the pavement shows that the inscription was divided into three parts. The first five lines, as recorded by Flete, lay around the four outer circles of the central quincunx; the sixth line circled the central roundel; and the last four lines were set in along the four sides of the outer square.

It is almost certain that no letters have been lost during the last three centuries. James Peller Malcolm, in 1802, records the same eleven letters that may be seen today: R, E, M, N, T and A around the central circle of the pavement; O and E on the eastern side of the large enclosing square; N and O along the south side; and E to the north. The preparatory notes and sketches made by John Talman almost a century earlier, in 1707, show exactly the same letters around the central circle,[11] the O and E remaining on the eastern side and the E on the northern.[12] Talman's sketches include no other letters so it is likely that none have been lost since his day.

Writing in 1683, Henry Keepe is rather vague: 'round the Squares and great Circles, in Letters of Brass, are some of the Verses still remaining, which when entire were thus to be read . . .' How many of the letters remained in Keepe's day is therefore open to question, but his description does seem to suggest that the verses, though they may have been more complete than today, were still not so complete that they could be read easily.

By contrast, John Weever's guide to the Abbey, written in 1631, mentions nothing of lost letters and describes the inscription in the present tense: 'in which are circularly written in letters of brass these ten verses following . . .' William Camden, author of the first printed guide in 1600, also makes no reference to any missing letters: 'in which marble circles these verses are spelt out in capital letters of bronze'.[13] Weever's phrase 'circularly written' and Camden's 'in which marble circles' both confirm that some of the lines were set around the pavement's central quincunx.

Since the loss of letters specifically noted by Henry Keepe in 1683 is not mentioned, or even implied, by the authors of 1600 and 1631, it is reasonable to suppose that most of the damage to the inscription occurred in the intervening years. The fact that no letters have been lost in the best part of the last three hundred years testifies to the durability of their setting and suggests that the missing letters are the result of deliberate vandalism rather than everyday wear and tear – an action which might be attributed to the iconoclasm of 1643 and 1644 when the Abbey was systematically plundered and purged of 'popery'. At that time any use of Latin on a monument might be construed as the unwelcome legacy of Rome, and the profit of melted-down brass could be counted upon to tempt any pilferer.

The following attempt to produce a reconstruction of the pavement's inscription, as accurately as is now possible, is based on a comparison between the fifteenth-century manuscripts of John Flete and Richard Sporley, and the pavement itself. Where further evidence is needed, clarification is sought from other medieval sources and consideration of the pavement's historical context. When doubt remains, the guide for discriminating between interpretations of word-forms and grammar must be sought in the structure and intrinsic meaning of the verses. Inscriptions on medieval monuments tend to be economical in their use of words, sometimes deliberately exploiting contractions and double meanings. Even by the fifteenth century Sporley felt the verses were esoteric enough to require some further explanation and provided a lengthy annotation at this point in his quotation of Flete's text. This is a thicket through which many have tried to pick their way. The varying versions of the inscription which appear in the historical guide-books are sometimes useful in highlighting alternative readings, though just as often they mislead by errors in typesetting and by perpetuating misunderstandings.

As a rule, guide-books give the lines of the inscription in the same order as in the manuscripts of Flete and Sporley, an order which does not, however, reflect their position within the layout of the pavement. The exception to this rule is William Lethaby who starts at the edge of the pavement and works inwards to the centre. Although Flete and Sporley provide the textual basis for this reconstruction of the inscription, Lethaby's lead is followed in the order of its verses. Not only does progression from the edge of the pavement to its centre appeal to common sense, but, as will become clear, it also begins the inscription at the level of the mundane and moves towards the sublime. Furthermore, there is the practical advantage of starting with the part of the inscription which has the highest proportion of identifiable indents.

Adopting Lethaby's order, the first section of the inscription begins at the north-east corner of the great square which encloses the major part of the pavement's design. The point is marked by an indent in the shape of a cross, very like the consecration crosses often found on church walls and medieval altars. Immediately to the south are the indents for the abbreviated name of Christ, *XPI*. From here, the inscription followed along the four sides of the square in a clockwise direction. The indents and the four surviving letters show that Flete's division of this section into four lines corresponds to the four sides of the square. The first two lines date the pavement:

Crsti milleno bis centeno duodeno
cum sexageno subductis quatuor uno

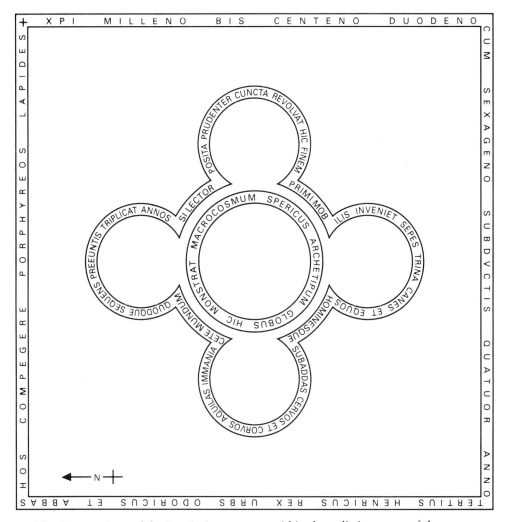

The outer frame inscription reads:

+ XPI MILLENO BIS CENTENO DUODENO · CUM SEXAGENO SUBDVCTIS QUATUOR ANNO · TERTIUS HENRICUS REX URBS ODORICUS ET ABBAS · HOS COMPEGERE PORPHYREOS LAPIDES

The inner circular inscriptions read:

POSITA PRUDENTER CUNCTA REVOLVAT HIC FINEM · PRIMI MOBILIS INVENIET SEPES TRINA CANES ET EQUOS HOMINESQUE · SUBADDAS CERVOS ET CORVOS AQUILAS IMMANIA CETE MUNDUM · MONSTRAT HIC GLOBUS ARCHETIPUM MACROCOSMUM SPERICUS · SI LECTOR PREEUNTIS TRIPLICAT ANNOS QUODQUE SEQUENS

82 The three sections of the inscription were set within three distinct areas of the pavement's design

Sporley's version of these lines keeps the more customary abbreviation of Christ's name, *Xpi*, and corrects *uno* to *anno*; a correction that makes good sense and is confirmed by the indents in the pavement which clearly show a final word of four letters.

The historical guides offer no serious variations in these two lines: their differences seem to be inadvertent mistakes rather than deliberate alternatives.[14] The literal translation of the lines is straightforward enough: 'in the year of Christ one thousand, two hundred, twelve, plus sixty, minus four' – a mixture of addition and subtraction that produces the year 1268. For no immediately obvious reason this formula replaces the more usual Latin practice of pure addition, exemplified in Sporley's annotation where he gives the meaning of this line as '*anno domini millesimo ducentesimo sexagesimo*

91

octavo' (1000+200+60+8). The formula is not expressed in a cryptic enough manner to suggest that the author of the inscription was deliberately trying to conceal the year which would, in any case, be a rather pointless exercise. But it was confusing enough for half a dozen writers from Camden to Malcolm to be misled into dating the pavement variously to 1260 and 1272. Even Richard Widmore, who did get the year right, was moved to complain that 'the poet seems to have been under some difficulty to express the time'. The sophistication of the rest of the inscription, however, makes it certain that the author was quite capable of giving a conventional account of the year if he had so wished. It may be argued that the deliberate introduction of subtraction was a matter of poetic licence or metrical convenience, but the limited space on monuments normally tends to produce abbreviated rather than extended inscriptions, although it must be remembered that the Westminster pavement inscription is more in the literary tradition than the monumental.

Ackermann writes: 'the lines express the time the work occupied', the intention being to indicate the period between 1268 and 1272. The Westminster pavement is significantly more complicated than most Italian cosmati pavements, but four years still seems an improbably long time for its construction. However, Ackermann was on the right lines in spotting the implied duality of the dating formula, an aspect all other commentators have missed. It is more likely that the period of four years refers to the time taken to produce all the cosmati work associated with the Confessor's Shrine, that is the shrine itself, the pavement of the Confessor's Chapel and the sanctuary.

A second explanation is possible – one of numerical significance. The unusual formula for the year 1268 might reflect a preference in symbolic terms for the numbers 60, 12 and 4, rather than 60 and 8. The former group all have strong cosmological overtones: 60 having represented the idea of time since the Babylonians divided the hour into sixty minutes; 12 being the number of months in the year and signs of the zodiac; and 4, the division of the year into seasons. The notion of numerical symbolism in this context may seem a little improbable at first but numbers and their interpretation were of considerable interest to the Christian philosopher. The presence of implicit mathematical formulae here and elsewhere in the pavement's inscription suggests that a numerical dimension to its meaning should not be too easily discounted.

As is common in monumental inscriptions, the date is coupled with the names of those responsible for the work. Flete completes this first section with the following lines:

The Inscription

Tertius Henricus Rex urbis Odoric~ & Abbas
hos compegere porphyeos lapides

Since King Henry III (*Tertius Henricus Rex*) and the Abbot (*Abbas*) are listed in the nominative case, it is reasonable to assume that the contraction sign indicates a likewise nominative ending for the third capitalised name, *Odoricus*. Flete's transcription, then, attributes the pavement to Henry III, the Abbot, that is Richard de Ware, and Odoricus, identified earlier with Petrus Oderisius, the master craftsman from Italy who actually designed and laid the pavement. In the first printed guide to the Abbey, Camden gives the craftsman's name as Odericus, and thereafter the guides opt for Odoricus or Odericus seemingly at random. The correct spelling, with an 'o' is still verifiable from the indent.

In Flete's manuscript the word *'urbis'*, the Latin word for 'city' in the genitive case, makes the line translate 'King Henry III of the city, Odoricus and the Abbot', or 'King Henry III, Odoricus of the city, and the Abbot'. The latter translation is still sometimes given. However, it is mistaken. Sporley corrects the Westminster Abbey manuscript of Flete, using *'urbs'* instead, nominative like the rest of the list and enabling the line to scan as a hexameter. This correction is almost certainly confirmed by the surviving indents which show a four- rather than a five-letter word. Sporley's annotation says that *'urbs'* refers to the City of Rome. This reading is corroborated by contemporary usage elsewhere, most appropriately by the inscription formerly to be read around the tomb of Abbot Richard de Ware. The mention of Rome in the pavement's inscription may simply refer to the geographic origin of the marbles but it could also acknowledge them as a gift from the Court of Rome, a personal gesture from Pope Clement IV.

In the final line of this section of the inscription, *'hos compegere porphyeos lapides'*, Flete uses one strange spelling and one unfamiliar word. The pavement itself gives us virtually no help with this line since only the letter E of *lapides* survives on the northern side of the great square, and the remains of the indents are insufficient even to estimate the number of symbols it formerly contained. Flete describes the stones (*lapides*) as *'porphyeos'*. Clearly he means porphyry and all the historical guides amend his spelling to *'porphyreos'*. The unfamiliar word *compegere* is elucidated by Sporley who takes it to mean *composerunt*: 'they put together, composed or constructed', from the verb *compono*. In fact, the word derives from *compingo* (the '-ere' ending being the standard alternative form of the more familiar '-erunt' ending, that is, third person plural, perfect indicative, active). *Compingo* is compounded from *com* and *pango*, and does have the same primary meanings as *compono* but is even more appropriate in the context of the making of an opus sectile pavement, since it combines the idea of joining and fixing. *Compingo* also has two apposite supplementary meanings: to compose (poetry, etc.) and to mark out the ground or set boundaries.

On the next section of the inscription the pavement's silence is almost total: neither letters nor indents remain. The only record of the five lines that followed the date and attribution is provided by the medieval manuscripts, according to Flete:

> *Si lector posita prudent~ cu~cta revolvat*
> *hic fine~ primi mobilis inveniet*
> *Sepes trina canes et equos ho~nesque subaddas*
> *cervos & corvos aquilas immania cete*
> *mundu~ qdque sequens preuntis triplicat Annos*

It is known that these lines were set around the four outer circles of the central quincunx from the partial remains of a shallow wide groove in the Purbeck marble of their circumferences, and from Camden's and Weever's observation of the pavement's circularly written letters. Lethaby concludes that this middle verse was engraved upon a continuous brass strip let into the stone groove and following its curves. If this were so, the section would have to be regarded as a significantly later addition to the pavement, since this method of adding lettering to monuments was not common until well into the fourteenth century. However, the chance survival of one colon shows that this was not the case. Its two diamond-shaped dots are set in a dark brown resin-like compound that fills the width of the groove.

So the letters of these lines were indeed set individually, like the rest of the inscription, but into a bed of resin instead of directly into the stone. There is no obvious reason for setting this part of the inscription differently and the change in technique must leave open the possibility of a later date or a different hand. There is also a practical problem with the setting of this section: five lines of Flete's transcription have to be fitted into a space less than two thirds the length of that occupied by the four lines around the great square. Using the most closely set extant letters and indents as a guide, the groove that ran around the four circles of the quincunx might be expected to have accommodated an estimated 156 symbols, well below the 212 symbols indicated by Flete. The letters here must have been set very much closer together, and at first sight this is worrying since the surviving parts of the inscription are fairly standard in their spacing. That spacing is, however, rather generous and in fact the letters may be arranged around the quincunx without undue crowding. Although the two diamonds of the single surviving colon are nearly identical in shape and size to the colons in the other lines they are set closer together. The average space between the upper and lower diamonds of the colons in the rest of the inscription is just under 21 mm: the colon in the quincunx has a space of 9 mm. This compressing of the height of the colon may suggest that the letters here were smaller than elsewhere in the pavement. The relatively fragile setting of this section of the inscription almost guaranteed its total loss, and so we must put our faith in the manuscripts of Flete and Sporley which are, fortunately, in complete agreement here, varying only in their use of contractions. The verse begins with an address to the reader:

Si lector posita prudent~ cu~cta revolvat

The first two words immediately state the instructive intent of the pavement: 'If the reader . . .' The purpose of the pavement is evidently to be read, both in inscription and in design. This literary metaphor is continued by the use of the verb *revolvo* which literally means to roll something back to where it came from, especially a scroll, in order to read it from the beginning. Figuratively, it means to go back over past events or re-enact, and carries the overtone of a circular journey which returns to its start. All these meanings are singularly appropriate to the cyclic design of the pavement and to Christian philosophical speculation of the time.

Flete's Westminster copyist writes two words of this line with contractions: *prudenter*, which the thirteenth century understood as 'purposely' or 'wittingly' and which still carried its classical sense, 'sagaciously' or 'wisely'; and *cuncta*, meaning the 'totality of' or simply 'all'. The object to which the reader is directed is that 'set down', *posita*, derived from the verb *ponere*. The verb carried the meaning 'to set' in both literal and figurative senses. While *ponere* could refer specifically to the laying of stones and the setting of jewels, it could also convey the ordaining of laws or rules, expressing in visual terms, or setting out a hypothesis. So *posita* here plainly implies something set out rationally to a plan or purpose. We are alerted to the idea that just as a word may carry literal and figurative meanings, so may the design of the pavement 'if the reader wittingly reflects upon all that is laid down'. In classical Latin *finem ponere* meant to fix boundaries or limits, both in space and time, and an echo of this expression is caught in the second line of this verse:

hic fine~ primi mobilis inveniet

95

'Here', the inscription tells the reader, 'he will discover (*inveniet*) the end (*finem*) of the *primum mobile*'. The *primum mobile*, literally the 'first moved', provided the motive power of the universe.

The medieval model of the universe was a series of concentric spheres with the habitable world at its centre. The sun, moon and the five known planets each had its own heavenly sphere which carried it on its course around the earth. These were enclosed by an eighth sphere for the fixed stars, the background against which the planets were seen to move. Beyond this was a ninth and invisible heavenly sphere, the *primum mobile*.

The name *primum mobile* reflects the hierarchy of the spheres presented in the neo-Platonic writings that had become absorbed into Christian cosmology and theology. The Divine nature was one of unity, immutability and stillness, the 'One and Unchanging'. The multiplicity, mutability and restless activity of earthly life were the marks of its material imperfection. The further the heavenly spheres were from the earth, the nearer they approached the ideal nature of the Divine. The outermost sphere, being the closest to that ideal, revolved with perfect precision, turning on the spot being the nearest approximation in the material universe to Divine stillness. This motion was initiated by God, though whether directly or through spiritual intermediaries was a matter of intense theological debate. It was this rotation of the *primum mobile*, inspired by the divine Unmoved Mover, that powered the movements of the visible heavens, hence the name, the 'first moved'. Its motion was transmitted down through the hierarchy of heavenly spheres but, since the universe was a material creation, the transmission between spheres could not be perfect. Each sphere received its motion in an increasingly degraded form, which explained why the planets, named from the Greek word for 'wanderers', pursued varied and sometimes apparently erratic paths across the sky. This progressive 'corruption' of divine perfection is summarised by a passage from the pseudo-Aristotelian text of the first century AD, *de Mundo*: 'his power is experienced most of all by the body that is closest to him, less by the next, and so on down to the regions inhabited by us. So earth and the things that are on earth, being at the farthest remove from the help of God, seem feeble and discordant and full of confusion and diversity'.[15]

What would 'the end' of the *primum mobile* have signified to the thirteenth-century reader? *Finis*, like its English counterpart, carries more than one sense. It can mean the limit or boundary of an area; the completion of a sequence of events; the destruction of something; even the goal to which an action may be directed. Where 'end' in the sense of spatial limit is intended the plural form, *fines*, is most often used. However, since the Flete manuscript uses a contraction symbol at the end of this word, there can be no certainty as to whether he is recording a singular or plural noun. Sporley adopts the singular form *finem* in his transcription and in his annotation maintains that it was the temporal end of the *primum mobile* that the author of the inscription had in mind. This is indeed the most likely primary interpretation, not only because of a certain implied tautology in applying a spatial limit to the *primum mobile* which, as the sphere enclosing all others, was of itself the physical limit of the universe, but also because the chronology of the world was a vital contemporary issue.

Due to the growing influence of Aristotelian philosophy, the question of whether the universe was of finite or infinite duration was one of the major theological debates of the thirteenth century, the eternity of the world being one of the least palatable of Aristotle's teachings for Christians reared on the Creation narrative of Genesis. This does not mean, however, that the implication of the spatial limit must be ruled out. It may be taken as a secondary meaning since '*primi mobilis*' is in the genitive case which may be used in an appositional sense in Latin, making the line read, 'the end which is the *primum mobile*'.

In the wider context of the pavement none of the meanings discussed need be seen as excluding the others. It was the tradition in medieval Christian thinking to interpret biblical texts at four levels of concurrently valid meaning: the literal, the symbolic, the analogical and the anagogical. Such concurrence and multiplicity of meanings were the building blocks of theological exegesis.

Sporley's annotation makes it clear that he takes '*finem primi mobilis*' to mean the temporal end not only of the outermost heavenly sphere but of the whole universe contained within it: 'Si lector posita etc: note that primum mobile is strictly applied, rather than as might seem from the words themselves, to that world around you, whose duration or end the writer presents as a calculation by triple mathematical increments, according to his own particular fancy.'

Returning to the inscription itself, the lines that follow present the mathematical calculation to which Sporley refers, couched in the most surprising terms:

> *Sepes trina canes et equos ho~nesque subaddas,*
> *cervos & corvos aquilas immania cete*
> *mundu~ qdque sequens preuntis triplicat Annos*

The contractions here are most likely to indicate *hominesque* and

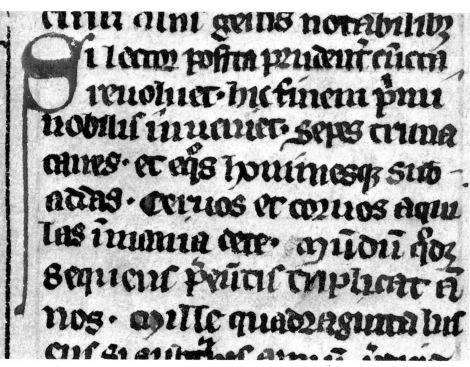

83 Part of the *Chronicle* of William Rishanger, 1310, showing the same verse for dating the end of the *primum mobile* that appears in the pavement's inscription

mundum; '*qdque*' is an abbreviation of *quodque*. Minor variations of Flete's spelling are given in the historical guides which are likely to be even less reliable here than usual, since this section of the inscription was probably the first to be lost. The lines give a list of creatures each of which is said to live for three times as long as its predecessor. The final tripling gives the age at which the world will come to its end, 19,683. This rather compacted formula of multiplied life-spans is well explained by Sporley's annotation: 'Sepes: that is a hedge, once built, will last for three years. A dog will live as long as three hedges, i.e. 9 years. A horse will live as long as three dogs, i.e. 27 years. A man will live as long as three horses, i.e. 81 years. A stag will live as long as three men, i.e. 243 years. A raven will live as long as three stags, i.e. 729 years. An eagle will live as long as three ravens, i.e. 2,187 years. A huge sea monster will live as long as three eagles, i.e. 6,561 years. The world will last as long as three huge sea monsters, i.e. 19,683. And so, according to the particular fancy of this writer, there will be this number of years from the world's beginning to its very end.'

It comes as a surprise to discover that this rather odd verse is not unique. Other examples are found in two manuscripts which are significantly closer in date to the pavement than either Flete or Sporley.[16] The first appears in three folia appended to the *Rishanger Chronicle*, written in 1310 by William

98

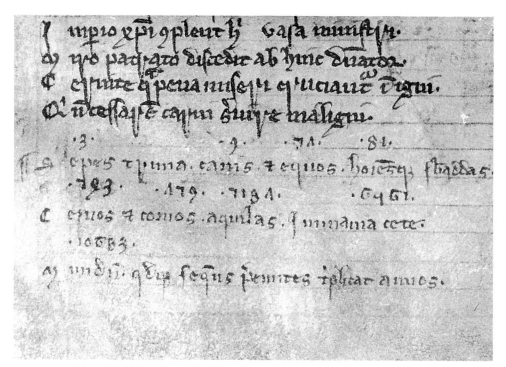

84 The same formula as it appears in the *Miscellany of John de Everisden*

de Rishanger, a monk at the monastery of St Albans.[17] The second is among a collection of miscellanea and original works ascribed to John de Everisden, a monk in the Abbey of St Edmund at Bury, and dated between the late thirteenth and the early fourteenth centuries.[18] The *Rishanger Chronicle* reproduces all five lines of the Westminster verse; the *Miscellany of John de Everisden*, just the last three. The John de Everisden version, catalogued simply as 'three technical verses',[19] adds a number above the name of each creature to indicate the cumulative total of years. By virtue of their early date these two manuscripts provide valuable corroborative evidence for this section of the Westminster inscription.

There is only one difference between the manuscripts of Flete and Sporley in these three lines. Flete's version ends the first line with '*sub-addas*'; Sporley writes '*sup addas*'. The historical guides that followed have either understood Sporley's version to be a contraction of *superaddas* and have substituted that word, or have maintained Flete's reading of *subaddas*.[20] Whereas the verb *subaddo* means simply 'to add to', *superaddo* suggests a further addition or sequence of additions and, at face value, seems to be a better choice. However, both the earlier manuscripts of William de Rishanger and John Everisden use the word *subaddas*, so in this matter the decision goes in favour of Flete. The shorter word is also preferable on literary grounds since it allows the line to scan as a hexameter. As Sporley writes '*sup addas*' with no indication of a contraction, and given the close phonetic similarity of *sub* and *sup*, it is quite possible that both scribes did, in fact, intend the same word.

One other word of this verse has also been questioned: some commentators amend the word *trina* to *trima* on the grounds that this is the word that appears in both the *Rishanger Chronicle* and the *Miscellany of John de Everisden*. *Trimus* generally means 'three years old': *trinus* implies 'threefold' or 'triple'. *Trinus* would, therefore, suggest a hedge of triple thickness. Although it requires a little grammatical sleight of hand, *trima* is obviously preferable in the context of the life-spans that follow. On balance, the evidence of the *Rishanger Chronicle*, the *Miscellany of John de Everisden*, and Richard Sporley's explanatory note, must outweigh quibbles over grammar. It requires an 'understood' verb, by no means unusual, to enable *sepes* to be regarded as nominative singular. Instead of the traditional verb, 'lives', however, the verb 'stands' will be used here since 'the hedge stands for three years' implies an appropriately figurative as well as literal meaning.

Expressing a calculation of the duration of the world in terms of the multiplied life-spans of various creatures would not have seemed as bizarre in the middle ages and late antiquity as it does today. In the Platonic tradition, the created Universe was itself imagined to be a living creature, animated by a World Soul. So a metaphor, placing the world as the oldest of animals, was quite appropriate. In this cosmological context, it is also worth remembering that the word 'zodiac', like 'zoo', comes from the Greek root for 'living', a diminutive of the word for animal.

The zoological metaphor clothes a simple mathematical formula: three raised to the power nine. In a numerological sense this is a most fitting number for the end of the *primum mobile*. From Pythagoras onwards, three was seen as the number of completion – in its simplest sense representing beginning, middle and end. Theon of Smyrna wrote that 'the number three is called perfect since it is the first number which has a beginning and middle and end . . . It is the first bond and power of the solid; for in three dimensions is the solid conceived.'[21] Aristotle begins his book on the heavens, *De Caelo*, by declaring that 'the Pythagoreans say the world and all that is in it is determined by the number three.'[22] In neo-Platonic thought, three came to express the proceeding of the individual human soul from the World Soul, its abiding in earthly life, and its final re-integration with the World Soul. This concept of the threefold movement of the soul survived throughout the medieval period. At the Renaissance it became elaborated into what the Christian Florentine philosopher, Marsilio Ficino, described as the *emanatio*, *raptio*, and *remeatio* of the human soul, its passage 'from the Good to the Good'.[23] For medieval and renaissance neo-Platonists alike it was this third stage, the return of the soul to God, that was the goal of earthly life, the *finem*, both in time and in aspiration. So it is completely appropriate that three is the numerical brick from which the pavement's calculation of 'the end' is built up. Significantly, the final sum is three raised to the power nine, the number of the *primum mobile*, the ninth heavenly sphere whose end is the subject of the verse. So the number 19,683, three raised to the power nine, can be seen as a direct numerical counterpart to the words '*finem primi mobilis*'.

The connection between the manuscripts of William de Rishanger and John de Everisden, and the verses of the Westminster pavement inscription is not known. It may be more than coincidence that the section of the *Rishanger Chronicle* immediately preceding the lines on the end of the *primum mobile* concerns the funeral of Edward I at Westminster in 1307, just three years before the chronicle was written. Since Rishanger gives the whole verse, it is tempting to hope that he recorded what he had seen in the pavement of the Abbey, but there is no concrete evidence to this effect. However, the texts of both these early versions are so close to those of Flete and Sporley that if they were not copied from the pavement, then the pavement and the manuscripts must derive from the same model, a common 'ancestor'. William Lethaby pointed out the remarkable similarity between the form of the Westminster calculation of the world's duration and a traditional Irish poem, said to date from the ninth century, in a fifteenth-century compilation known as the *Book of Lismore*, edited and translated by Whitley Stokes in 1890. Whitley Stokes gives the following translation of the poem:

> A year for the stake. Three years for the field.
> Three lifetimes of the field for the hound.
> Three lifetimes of the hound for the horse.
> Three lifetimes of the horse for the human being.
> Three lifetimes of the human being for the stag.
> Three lifetimes of the stag for the ousel.
> Three lifetimes of the ousel for the eagle.
> Three lifetimes of the eagle for the salmon.
> Three lifetimes of the salmon for the yew.
> Three lifetimes of the yew for the world
>   from its beginning to its end, *ut dixit poeta*.

It is worth noting that Sporley's annotation on the pavement's inscription closes with the very similar phrase 'from the beginning of the world to its very end', especially since both manuscripts are roughly contemporary. Although their final totals do not agree, the Westminster Abbey inscription evidently represents a much compressed version of the same tradition preserved in this Irish poem. Whitley Stokes mentions two other Irish manuscripts containing similar poems. Both are in the British Library[24] and both, unlike the *Book of Lismore* poem, produce the same formula as the Westminster verse: three to the power nine. Stokes also gives an example of a parallel Welsh tradition, *Yr Oed* by Ap Gwilym, and Lethaby suggests, but without further elaboration, that such zoological chronologies were a part of the folklore of most countries from Italy to Ireland.[25] In *The White Goddess*, Robert Graves quotes this English folk-saying, unfortunately without attribution:

> The lives of three wattles, the life of a hound;
> The lives of three hounds, the life of a steed;
> The lives of three steeds, the life of a man;
> The lives of three men, the life of an eagle;
> The lives of three eagles, the life of a yew;
> The life of a yew, the length of a ridge;
> Seven ridges from Creation to Doom.

A wattle can be taken as a version of the *sepes*, the hedge, of the Westminster verse. Graves maintains that the picturesque image of mountain ridges receding to the crack of Doom is an error caused by the miscopying of the Latin *aevum*, 'age', as *arvum*, 'ridge', the ages in question being the Seven Ages of the World according to Nennius, the ninth-century Bishop of Bangor.[26] However, Nennius says that the Day of Judgement will usher in the Seventh Age, the Sixth Age having begun with John the Baptist. So there are only six Ages, not seven, from Creation to Doom, reflecting the six days in which God created the world. Stokes suggests that this evidently widespread literary motif of multiplied life-spans can be traced back as far as the eighth century BC in the work of the Greek poet, Hesiod. A surviving fragment of his writings reads: 'A chattering crow lives out nine generations of aged men, but a stag's life is four times a crow's, and a raven's life makes three stags old, while the phoenix outlives nine ravens. But we, the rich-haired Nymphs, daughters of Zeus the aegis-holder, outlive ten phoenixes.'[27]

The five lines of the Westminster pavement inscription represent, therefore, an elegantly condensed reflection of a long and intriguing tradition. If the folklore origin of the verse was known to Sporley, we may better understand the rather disparaging reference in his annotation to the writer's 'own particular fancy'. But it would be wrong to dismiss such folklore simply as a quaint, but foolish, tradition. Often folk-poems and sayings preserve vestiges of otherwise lost ancient systems of ideas. Christianity and much classical learning survived in Ireland during the so-called Dark Ages in England. The final phrase of the *Book of Lismore* poem, '*ut dixit poeta*', 'so says the poet', could be taken as a reference back to a more ancient source, perhaps even to Hesiod himself.

The cosmological theme of the Westminster inscription reaches its climax in the short line that surrounds the central roundel of the pavement's design. Flete records it as:

Spericus Archetipu~ globus hic monstrat macrocosmu~

Here the inscription's Platonic undercurrent is made explicit by the use of Latin transliterations of three Greek words: *spericus, macrocosmum* and *archetipum*, the last being the Platonic term given to the ideal Forms or patterns that were believed to exist in the Divine Mind, the universal spiritual 'moulds' from which the imperfect copies of material creation were cast. A contemporary definition of *archetypus* is given by Robertus Anglicus in his *Commentary on the Sphere of Sacrobosco* where he derives the word from *archi*, 'chief', and *tipos*, 'figure'.[28]

Although this last line is written in a complete circle, the starting point for a linear transcription can be deduced from the scansion. If the line begins with *spericus* it may be scanned as a dactylic hexameter. Any other starting point produces a line that will not scan. All commentators have followed Flete in beginning at this point, although their spelling of *spericus* varies.[29] Some, however, have also taken the liberty of altering the order of the words. In 1751, for example, Richard Widmore gives:

Sphaericus archetypum monstrat globus hic microcosmum

Fortunately, enough of this section of the inscription survives to confirm the order of words given by Flete. Like the first section, these letters were set directly into the stone matrix: six letters and three colons survive intact, together with ten indents of which five are readily identifiable. Indents which have since been lost were noted by John Talman in his sketches of the pavement made in 1707. One drawing[30] indicates that there were places for eight letters in what is now the badly eroded space between the E of *archetipum* and the last three indents of *globus*. On the other side of the circle Talman dots in twelve indents, presumably for the word *macrocosmum* and a colon.

Richard Widmore's version of this line not only alters the order of the words but also departs from Flete's text in a more crucial matter: '*macrocosmum*' is replaced by '*microcosmum*'. The word *microcosmum* first appears some seventy years earlier in Henry Keepe's guide of 1683, most probably as the result of an error of typesetting. With the exception of William Dugdale (1817), this mistake was slavishly copied by all writers until Steven Wander pointed out the error in 1978. In Sporley's fifteenth-century manuscript *macrocosmum* is plainly written, and his understanding of the word is made quite clear in his annotation. Confusion between the microcosm and the macrocosm may have already arisen in his day because he is at pains to distinguish between the two: 'the lesser world, meaning man, is spoken of as the microcosm; the greater world, namely this same one in which we live, is spoken of as the macrocosm'. The substitution of *microcosm* for *macrocosm* obviously introduced a major corruption of the text and misled many of those readers trying to 'wittingly reflect upon' the inscription's meaning.

The ready acceptance of critical printing errors and of the rearrangement of its words is a telling measure of the difficulties presented by this line, difficulties due in large part to an apparent tautology. Since the case ending of '*spericus*' agrees with '*globus*', and '*archetipum*' with '*macrocosmum*', the line has usually been translated as 'the spherical globe shows the archetypal macrocosm'. But the phrase 'spherical globe' has an obvious redundancy to modern ears, and it has been suggested that the tautology should be avoided by an 'understood' repetition of the verb *monstrat*: 'the sphere shows the archetype, this globe shows the macrocosm'. Those earlier commentators who took the liberty of rearranging the words to read '*Sphaericus archetypum monstrat globus hic microcosmum*' obviously had a similar intention in mind. However *spericus* is indisputably adjectival in form and its agreement with *globus* cannot simply be ignored. In his annotation, Sporley takes *spericus globus* to refer to the central roundel of the pavement's design, and he seems unconcerned by the apparent tautology of the phrase, making no attempt to distinguish between the two words: 'Spericus globus: or rather, that same round stone, having in itself the four colours of the Elements of this world, namely fire, air, water and earth.' The variegated colours of the central roundel seemed to Sporley to be the reason why it was chosen to illustrate the archetype, the '*figurativum principalem*' as he explained it.

Before examining possible resolutions of the tautology of this 'spherical globe', if such resolution proves necessary, it is profitable to investigate how the apparent tautology may have arisen. To modern minds, it sometimes seems that medieval writers were somewhat casual in their descriptions of geometrical forms. Even a writer like Isidore of Seville, noted for his fastidiousness, can follow a clearly recognisable definition of a sphere ('a round figure alike in all its parts') with a description of a cylinder that seems impossible to envisage, 'a square figure which has a semicircle on top'.[31] However, such ambiguities should not too readily be put down to carelessness or ignorance on the part of the author. Obscurity is sometimes in the eye of the beholder: when it is realised that Isidore is describing a lengthwise section of a cylinder, his logic becomes quite clear. What seems to be confusion may, in fact, represent an unfamiliar set of priorities. The numerical aspects of a geometric form were often considered more important than dimensional or spatial factors. The change of emphasis between quantitative and qualitative elements of a form means that the 'accuracy' of any description is always a subjective assessment, coloured by the perspectives of history. What seems confused or deliberately cryptic today may have been crystal clear to readers at the time.

In the thirteenth century the philosophical view of both cosmology and cosmogony was derived ultimately from Plato's *Timaeus*. Although the writings of this pagan Greek philosopher of the fourth century BC conflicted in many ways with the strictly theological view drawn from the Scriptures, the two systems had become successfully amalgamated over several centuries through the works of Christian neo-Platonists from Plotinus onwards, and many of the images and rationalisations of Plato's world picture were engrained in everyone's ways of thinking. The *Timaeus* sets out Plato's image of the universe as a sphere and explains why the Creator chose this as the most appropriate form:[32]

And these were His intentions: first, that it might be, so far as possible, a Living Creature, perfect and whole, with all its parts perfect; and next, that it might be One, inasmuch as there was nothing left over out of which another like Creature might come into existence . . . Wherefore, because of this reasoning, He fashioned it to be One single Whole, compounded of all wholes, perfect and ageless and incorruptible. And he bestowed on it the shape which was befitting and akin. Now for that Living Creature which is designed to embrace within itself all the shapes there are: wherefore He wrought it into a round, in the shape of a sphere, equidistant in all directions from the centre to the extremities, which of all shapes is the most perfect and the most self-similar, since He deemed that the similar is infinitely fairer than the dissimilar.

A degree of tautology is already evident in the translation into English:

'He wrought it into a **round**, in the shape of a **sphere**'. In the original Greek text the two operative words are *sphairocides*, 'spherical', and *kukloteres*, 'rounded'. Since Greek was not widely known in the Latin-speaking world of the middle ages, the *Timaeus* was only accessible to most philosophers and theologians through Latin translations and commentaries. The most well read of these was the commentary by Calcidius. Equating *sphairoeides* with *globosus*, and *kukloteres* with *rotundus*, Calcidius gives the crucial part of Plato's description as:[33]

> . . . *formamque dedit congruam, quippe animali cuncta intra suum ambitum animalia et omnes eorum formas regesturo:* **globosam et rotundam.**

> . . . and the form He gave it was fitting, because all living creatures and all their forms are assimilated by the Living Creature within its compass: *spherical and round.*

The acknowledged model for the translation of Greek words into Latin, and for Latin style in general, was the work of Cicero, the Roman author of the first century BC. In his *Republic*, Cicero uses the same phrase to describe the planets and stars. The last section of the *Republic* was known to the middle ages as a self-contained work called *The Dream of Scipio (Somnium Scipionis)*, popularised by a commentary of Macrobius. The spirit of Scipio the Elder addresses the younger Scipio in a dream:[34]

> *Homines enim sunt hac lege generati, qui tuerentur illum globum, quem in hoc templo medium vides, quae terra dicitur hisque animus datus est ex illus sempiternis ignibus, quae sidera et stellas vocatis, quae* **globosae et rotundae,** *divinis animatae mentibus, circulos suos orbesque conficiunt celeritate mirabili.*

> You men were created under this law: that you should guard this sphere called earth, which, you see, is placed in the centre of the temple, and were endowed with a soul from those eternal fires, which you call planets and stars; they are **spherical and round**, animated with divine minds, and perform their circles and orbits with wonderful celerity.

In the attempt to unravel the tautology of 'spherical globe' we seem merely to have uncovered another: 'spherical and round'. But it must be assumed that for Cicero, as the arbiter of style, the phrase '*globosae et rotundae*' was not an objectionable tautology, that there was a distinction between the two terms, or that two words were used to reinforce the meaning. Since he uses *globum* earlier in the same sentence to describe the earth, it is likely that he too intends the word *globosae* to mean 'spherical'. This is confirmed by Cicero's own version of the critical passage of the *Timaeus*, where he spells out the connection: '. . . *et globosum est factus, quod sphairoeides Graeci vocant*':[35] '. . . and it was made spherical, which the Greeks call *sphairoeides*'.

Now how might 'round' be differentiated here from 'spherical'? There are three possibilities: 'round' may be used in the two dimensional sense whereas 'spherical' must describe three dimensions; it might imply the circular motion of 'going round'; or it might imply the smoothness of being 'rounded'. In the light of the rest of Cicero's version of this passage from the *Timaeus*, the last appears the most plausible possibility. After describing the spherical form of the Living Creature that is the universe, Cicero continues:

> . . . *idque ita tornavit ut nihil efficere posset **rotundius**, nihil asperitatis ut haberet nihil offensionis, nihil incisum angulis nihil anfractibus, nihil eminens, nihil lacunosum – omnesque partes simillaimae omnium, quod eius iudicio praestabet dissimilutidini similitudo.*

> . . . and He rounded it off in such a way that He could make nothing more rounded, so that it would have no unevenness, no imperfections, no sharp corners, no bends, no projections, no holes – and every part similar to every other.

There is some evidence to suggest that the distinction between 'spherical' and 'round' was already unclear even in the thirteenth century. In the first pages of his commentary on *The Sphere of Sacrobosco*, written in 1271, Robertus Anglicus is at pains to define the precise meanings of the terms he uses. In particular he clarifies 'spherical' and 'round' by this analogy: 'Also note that there is a difference between "spherical" and "round", since anything spherical is round and not *vice versa*; for something may be round like an egg, yet it is not spherical unless it is completely so.'[36]

Although the tautology of 'spherical and rounded' is therefore at least partly resolved, the original tautology of the 'spherical globe' is, if anything, tightened since it has been shown that both *spericus* and *globus* have been used by Latin authors as the translation of the Greek word *sphairoeides*. However, it may be from the 'grey areas' of early translations that the redundancy of the thirteenth-century expression ultimately derives. Calcidius' version of the *Timaeus*, the most readily available at that time, follows Cicero in using *globosum* to interpret *sphairoeides* in the actual translation of Plato's words, but in his commentary on the text he uses both *sphaera* and *globus* in close proximity:[37]

> . . . *est porro longe excelsa et eminens sphaera qua aplanes dicitur, subter quam sunt positae sphaerae planetum ita, ut supra demonstavimus, ordinatae, perspicuum est lunae globum, quae est infimus proximusque terra.*

The so-called sphere of the fixed stars is next, very high up and noble, beneath which the planetary spheres are set in place, ordered, as shown above, so the globe of the moon, the humblest and nearest to earth, is the most evident.

This passage at first holds out hope of discriminating between *globus* and *sphaera* by taking 'globe' to be the round solid of a planet, and 'sphere' to be the hollow shell that contained its circular movements. The universe would then be a nest of concentric spheres each carrying its own particular globe. Unfortunately this neat distinction soon breaks down: at a later point Calcidius writes that the heavenly bodies must have souls and knowledge of God because '*planetes quoque in globos proprios redacti*', which must mean 'the planets too are held within their own spheres'. Evidently it has to be concluded that there was no sharply defined distinction in the usage of the two terms *globus* and *sphaera*.

The two words occur in close proximity again in the writings of Martianus Capella, in a phrase that is strikingly relevant to the Westminster inscription:[38] '*mundus igitur ex quatuor elementis isdenque totis in spaerae modum globatur*': 'The world is rounded into the form of a sphere composed entirely of the four Elements'. The phrase comes from Martianus' book on Astronomy, which was one of the most popular books used in the teaching of the quadrivium during the middle ages, and, together with Calcidius' commentary on Plato's *Timaeus*, must be seen as a possible source of the ideas encapsulated in the final words of the Westminster inscription.

It can now be seen that although 'this spherical globe shows the archetypal universe' is an uncomfortable translation to modern ears, the grammar and the words themselves leave little room for manoeuvre. *Spericus*, *archetypum* and *macrocosmum* all have well-defined and specific meanings. *Globus* alone offers some degree of latitude: in classical Latin its meanings include a 'mass' or 'cluster'; in medieval Latin it can be found used in the sense of a 'clique', or to imply a totality, rather like the modern usage of 'global'. This latitude of meaning might allow the tautology to be eased by a translation such as 'this spherical cluster shows the archetype of the universe', but it is an unlikely reading and one which does nothing to further the meaning.

Another approach to this line is to regard the agreement between *spericus* and *globus*, and between *archetypum* and *macrocosmum*, as being not adjectival but comparative and, by repeating the verb *monstrat*, make the sentence read: 'As the sphere [of the cosmos] reveals the archetype [i.e. is a theophany of its Creator], so this globe shows the Universe.' This makes excellent sense in terms of religious philosophy, but does so at the expense of ignoring, yet again, the patently adjectival form of *spericus*, although it could conceivably be argued that it is used to replace the usual feminine form *spaera* in order to strengthen the parallel with the masculine *globus*.

As has been shown to be the case with *globosus* and *rotundus*, it is quite possible that the phrase was not considered a discordant tautology at the time and that *spericus* was used in true adjectival fashion to qualify *globus*, emphasising its spherical qualities in order to build up a literary counterpart of the perfect sphericity of the archetypal model of the universe. However, in the light of the close parallel provided by Martianus Capella, and the fact that both *spericus* and *globus* have been used by Latin authors to translate the Greek word *sphairoeides*, the translation 'rounded sphere', perhaps even 'perfectly rounded sphere', might be considered more accessible and more true to its Platonic origins.

The free translation of the inscription offered below is designed to express, where possible, some of the apposite overtones of the Latin words employed. The Latinised Greek word '*archetipum*', for example, is translated as 'the eternal pattern' for two reasons: 'pattern', because of the inscription's setting in an elaborate design, and 'eternal' because it hints at the compromise which was found to be acceptable to Christian theologians between the eternal world of Aristotelian philosophy and the finite world of the Bible. *Finem* is translated as the 'measure' of the *primum mobile* so that it reflects both the spatial–temporal ambiguity of the Latin word, especially when used in conjunction with the genitive, and its context within a mathematical calculation. This reconstruction and its translation form the basis for all later consideration of the pavement's symbolism:

> In the four years before this Year of Our Lord 1272,
> King Henry III, the Court of Rome, Odoricus and the Abbot
> set in place these porphyry stones.

If the reader wittingly reflects upon all that is laid down,
he will discover here the measure of the *primum mobile*:
the hedge stands for three years,
add in turn dogs, and horses and men,
stags and ravens, eagles, huge sea monsters, the world:
each that follows triples the years of the one before.

Here is the perfectly rounded sphere which reveals
the eternal pattern of the universe.

The division of the verses into three sections is not arbitrary: each has its own time scale. The first relates to the everyday calendar of human endeavour. The second deals in world ages, the astronomical time scale on the borders of human comprehension. The final section, transcending the natural world altogether, crosses the threshold of time into the realm of archetypes, the Divine and time-less scale of eternity. The placing of the three sections of the inscription within the pavement's design is exactly analogous. It will be remembered that the journey from earthly materialism to heavenly spirituality was seen as a progression from multiplicity and diversity towards unity and uniformity, the 'One and Unchanging'. As the three sections of the inscription ascend in time scales towards the Divine, so the design of the pavement makes a parallel transition. At the pavement's edges the roundels are greatest in number and in variety of pattern – the level of earthly life. As the *lector* moves inwards, the roundels become fewer and their patterns are simplified to plain, regular polygons, images of pure number which was seen as the 'go-between' linking created forms to their ideal archetypes. Finally, the zone of the eternal archetype, the centre, is marked by a single round stone, the purest of shapes.

In broad terms then, the pavement may already be seen as a mapping-out of three levels of existence. The sensible, the intelligible and the spiritual worlds are represented both in space, by the pavement's design, and in time, by its inscription, thus fulfilling its promise of setting out the ambiguous '*finem primi mobilis*'. Now, against the background of the full meaning of the Latin inscription, something of this unique thirteenth-century monument's philosophical dimension begins to make itself known. Like the pale outline of a great building approached through a mist, the patterns of thought that bound design and inscription together begin to emerge. To further appreciate the sophisticated philosophy embedded in its design, we turn now to examine something of the role that geometry played in medieval thinking.

6

The Art of Geometry

he design and patterns of the Westminster pavement were based on tried and tested geometric constructions. During the medieval period geometry was not just a subsection of mathematics, confined to the narrow meaning it tends to have today. The thirteenth century used geometry in three quite distinct ways. There was the 'practical geometry' of scholars, derived from Euclid, concerned with theoretical proofs and rejuvenated by the introduction of Arab learning; the 'speculative geometry' of philosophers and theologians, centring on symbolic and transcendental views of geometry, that can be traced back in an unbroken line through the writings of the Fathers of the Church to the ancient Greek philosophers; and there was what has been called 'constructive' geometry, that is the 'technical knowledge and skill received through oral transmission of the craft traditions'.[1] Though he was undoubtedly aware of some of the symbolic overtones of the products of his set square and compass, the chief concern of the practising mason was with constructive geometry.

The work of the various families and generations of the cosmati represents an unusually homogenous and ubiquitous taste in geometric surface decoration, particularly pavement design, that dominated the churches of Rome and the surrounding region from the early twelfth to the later thirteenth centuries. Although well-defined and tenacious, the style of cosmati work did not, of course, spring fully-formed from a cultural vacuum. The relatively sudden revival of interest in opus sectile pavement design was born of a general resurgence of artistic activity in Italy during the calm which followed the political conflicts between successive Popes and Holy Roman Emperors, a storm which had begun in 1075 and continued until 1122.[2] This conflict, usually known as the Investiture Controversy, had been brought to a head in 1076 when Pope Gregory VII excommunicated Emperor Henry IV. Henry had opposed a papal decree forbidding lay investiture: the practice whereby lay monarchs could invest a bishop or abbot. Although this practice, an extension of the monarch's feudal rights, was technically the subject of the controversy, in fact the dispute was over the wider political question of whether spiritual or secular authority should be supreme within the Holy Roman Empire.

During the rule of the classical Roman Empire, opus sectile pavements had been common throughout the Mediterranean area. By the middle of the ninth century, however, interest in such pavements seems to have waned in Italy. The south aisle of SS. Quatro Coronati in Rome, *c.* 850, can be seen as a last echo of the geometric opus sectile pavements that had flourished in and around the city during the Carolingian age.[3] It was to be some two and a half centuries before Italian interest in opus sectile work was completely reawakened, to dazzling effect, at the beginning of the twelfth century. Since the technique continued to be practised in the eastern Mediterranean while it was out of fashion in Italy, its revival has traditionally been attributed to the Byzantine marble-workers who were brought by Abbot Desiderius to the abbey of Monte Cassino to construct the pavement there around 1070. But the absence in this pavement of the most distinctive of the cosmati design devices, the chains of roundels and band patterns, shows this to be but part of the story. Alessandra Guiglia Guidobaldi has demonstrated that the reality was a subtle interaction of classical revival and local survival, tempered by Byzantine influences. She prefers to regard the Monte Cassino pavement as a non-isolated case which 'affirms the moment of convergence between the two artistic traditions'.[4] Elements from both these traditions, the Roman and the Byzantine, became drawn together in the cosmati style.

The roundel and band pattern clearly derives from the *guilloche*. By the sixth century, this plait-like motif, surviving from the classical period, had become a platitude of design throughout the Mediterranean region in textiles, painting and architecture, as well as in mosaics. During the centuries that followed it was absorbed differently into the Roman and Byzantine traditions. In Italy, the motif was less popular in general, and excluded altogether from pavements which, even in antiquity, had not used the

85 *opposite* The opus sectile pavement laid at the abbey of Monte Cassino by Byzantine craftsmen around 1070

VI

PAVIMENTUM ECCLESIAE CASINENSIS
DIVERSORUM LAPIDUM VARIETATE
CONSTRUCTUM

Andreas Mulier sculp
Neap. an 1813

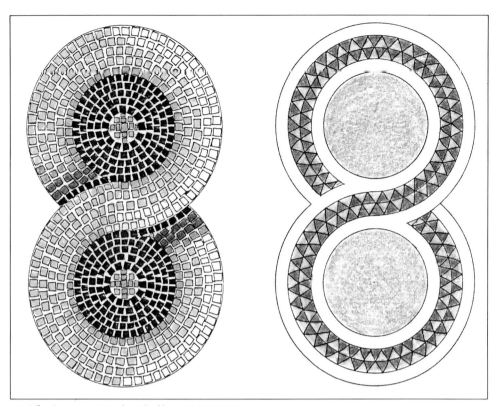

86 The interweaving band effect of the guilloche motif was expressed by tone in mosaic work, left, but by geometry in opus sectile, right

interweaving guilloche in opus sectile work. By contrast, in the eastern Mediterranean the guilloche of mosaic pavements was successfully translated into an opus sectile version. The basic geometry of the pattern remained the same, but its artistic treatment changed. In mosaic pavements the interweaving bands were formed of tesserae whose tones were graded to produce an impression of shadow where two bands crossed. This chiaroscuro method of investing a three dimensional quality to the design was not available to craftsmen working in opus sectile. Their medium dictated a more two-dimensional approach. Instead, they achieved something of the third dimension by a geometric device: cutting off the patterned band of marble that ran along the centre of each interweaving band in such a way as to suggest that it was disappearing under the margins of the band that 'overlapped' it. The artist in opus sectile, therefore, relied more heavily on the use of geometry than his counterpart working in mosaic, the visual movement of his pavement being governed by subtle adjustments to its geometric structure.

The spaces between the loops of the bands also became more important. What had been merely a row of central points in the guilloche, grew outwards into strings of roundels which came to dominate the bands which embraced them. There was probably a very practical dimension to this development: the circular monoliths may have been cross-sections of antique columns, sawn off and re-used for paving.

In the eastern Mediterranean, opus sectile work grew in popularity and, by the sixth century, had ousted the ancient mosaic tradition almost completely. Paradoxically, the Byzantine craftsmen who laid the opus sectile pavement at Monte Cassino failed to reproduce the chains of roundel and band patterns which had been the main Eastern innovation, and which were to become the most distinctive hallmark of the cosmati. The paradox deepens when it is considered that the pavement they did produce consists largely of rectangular panels filled with regular geometric patterns, a decorative unit which had been common in classical opus sectile pavements but which had not been used in the eastern Mediterranean since the beginning of the seventh century. In the Byzantine style, rectangular panels were usually single slabs surrounded by a band. In Italy, however, rectangular panels in the classical tradition, with geometric patterns, were still being laid as late as the seventh century, and it seems that these provided the models for revival in the eleventh century. So, although crafted by Byzantine marblers, the Monte Cassino pavement does not represent the straightforward import of a Byzantine style. Rather, Guidobaldi asserts, it is one surviving example of the confluence of two styles, the Roman and the Byzantine, both having a common classical root.

Cosmati patterns divide into those based on four-fold symmetry and those based on six-fold symmetry. The triangular patterns are composed either of

87&88 Band patterns from Westminster showing four-fold symmetry and using the geometric technique of 'doubling of the square'

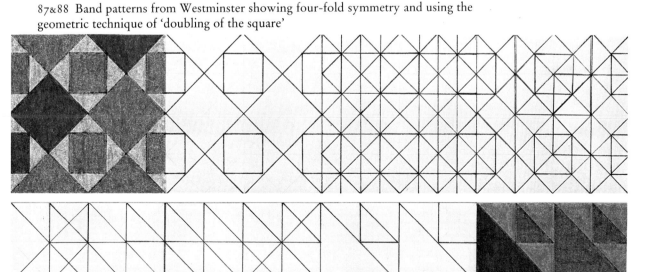

89&90 Band patterns from Westminster showing six-fold symmetry, based on the hexagon

right-angled triangles, which may be classed as belonging to the four-fold symmetry group since they are half-squares, or of equilateral triangles, counted among the six-fold symmetry group as they are sixth-hexagons. All the four-fold patterns rely, sometimes obviously and sometimes more subtly, on a geometric operation often known as the *doubling of the square*.

The doubling of the square can be traced back at least as far as Plato's dialogue, the *Meno*, written in the fifth century BC. There it appears in an argument put forward by Socrates to prove that the soul has knowledge of the ideal world of Forms prior to its incarnation in the human body. As a result of incarnation this divine knowledge becomes masked by the material nature of the body and 'forgotten'. Socrates' thesis is that human knowledge is not learned but recollected from the soul's experiences before earthly birth. Visiting the house of a young aristocrat called Meno, the philosopher picks one of his slaves and shows how the boy, despite his lack of education, is capable of solving a complex geometric problem. The problem Socrates sets is the doubling of the square: given a square of any dimension, how may a second square be constructed from it having twice the area of the first? By a skilful sequence of leading questions, Socrates guides the slave to the solution of the problem: the second square is built on the diagonal of the first (*see 91*). Thus, Socrates concludes, 'Either then he has at some time acquired the knowledge which he now has, or he has always possessed it. If he always possessed it, he must always have known; if on the other hand he acquired it at some previous time, it cannot have been in this life.'[5] This conclusion leads the philosopher to a moving defence of the spirit of human enquiry: 'one thing I am ready to fight for as long as I can, in word and act: that is, that we shall be better, braver and more active men if we believe it right to look for what we don't know than if we believe there is no point in looking because what we don't know we can never discover.'

Plato's geometric operation of the doubling of the square was handed down to the masons of the later middle ages through the writings of the Roman architect, Vitruvius. In *De Architectura*, his ten books on architecture, Vitruvius describes the doubling of the square in detail:[6]

If there is a place or a field being square and of equal sides be required to be doubled and still be of equal sides, this, which cannot be done by numbers, may be accurately performed by lines, and it is thus demonstrated:

The square place being in length and breadth ten feet, contains an area of an hundred [square] feet; if therefore the space is required to be doubled, and to contain two hundred [square] feet, and still be of equal sides, it is demanded how large each side of this square to contain two hundred [square] feet, answering to the double of the given area, must be made. This cannot be solved by numbers; for if 14 be taken and multiplied into itself, it produces 196 [square] feet, if 15, 225 [square] feet: as therefore it cannot be found by numbers, in the square which is in length and breadth ten feet, the line that extends from angle to angle diagonally, is to be drawn, so that it may divide the square into two triangles of equal magnitude; the area of each being fifty [square] feet: then with the length of this diagonal line another square of equal sides is described. Thus as the two triangles formed by the diagonal line in the lesser square contain fifty [square] feet each, the same magnitude, and same number of [square] feet, will each of the four triangles of the greater square contain.

Essentially the same geometrical operation that Socrates had prised from Meno's slave boy may be used to construct a square half the area of a given square. Instead of building a square on the diagonal, the square is constructed by joining the mid-points of the four sides of the first square. It was more usually in this guise that the doubling of the square appeared as one of the routine techniques of medieval masons. This technique of manipulating squares is often known as *quadrature*. It underpins much medieval art and design, and is sometimes considered to have been one of the hidden masonic 'mysteries', or secrets.

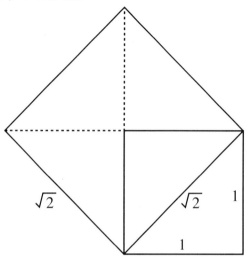

91 Plato's method of constructing a square with an area twice that of a given square, as described in his 'Meno'

The famous sketchbook of Villard de Honnecourt[7] represents the surviving pages of what probably came to be used as a masons' lodge-book during the period that the Westminster pavement was laid. This book of annotated drawings was begun by Villard during the 1220s and 1230s. It has been generally assumed that Villard was himself a master-mason, but there is no direct evidence to support this supposition. It has been suggested instead that he might have been a sculptor, a metal-worker, or perhaps not a craftsman at all but a clerk with a keen eye for drawing.[8] Initially, Villard's drawings seem to have been made entirely for his own record and amusement, but the collection was subsequently bound into a book together with additional drawings and notes added by a second hand. The more systematic nature of these additions suggests that the intentions of the second author were overtly didactic and that he may have been a practising mason. Soon after, the book was further elaborated by a third writer. A study of its pages reinforces the image of medieval craftsmen as well-travelled people of great ingenuity and curiosity.

The book contains elevations and plans of the churches Villard visited; drawings of sculpture, animals and insects, some of them apparently drawn

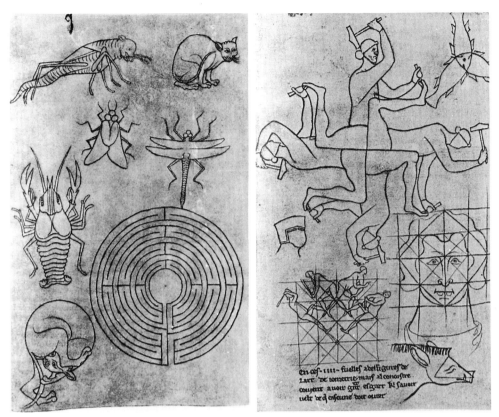

92&93 Drawings from the 13th-century notebook of Villard de Honnecourt, including the geometric construction of faces and figures

from life; practical measuring techniques to determine, for example, the width of a river, or the diameter of a circular pillar of which only a part is visible; and a number of mechanical devices, including the earliest known representation of a water-powered saw. Several illustrations show how to draw natural forms based on geometric grids.

The importance of geometry to the medieval designer is underlined in the preface to Villard's sketchbook, in which he appeals directly to the reader:[9] 'Villard de Honnecourt greets you and bids all those who make use of the devices found in this book to pray for his soul and remember him. For in this book you may find sound advice on the proper skill of masonry and the devices of carpentry. You will also find the skill of drawing forms just as the art of geometry requires and teaches it.'

In the present context it is interesting to note not only how many of the plans and designs in Villard's book are underpinned by the $1:\sqrt{2}$ proportion generated by the doubling of the square, but also the veiled demonstration of this geometric operation tucked away among the illustrations of mechanical devices and measuring techniques on folio 20, a page added by

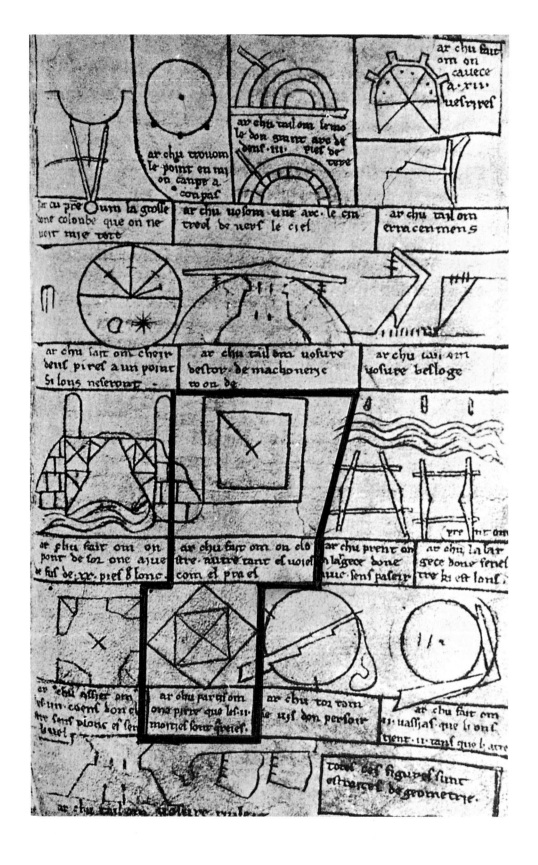

ar chu trouom
le point en mi
on camps a.
compas

ar cu pre Oum la grolle
vne coloube que on ne
voit mie vert

ar chu uolom une arc le cin
treol de nevf le ciel

ar chu tailom lirmo
le don gratit arc de
dens iii pies de
vve

ar chu tail om
om on
cauece
a xii
uertres

ar chu tail om
erra cen mens

ar chu fait om chon
deul pires a un point
Si lons neleront

ar chu tail om uofure
bestor de machonerye
vo on de

ar chu tail om
uofure bestoge

or chu fait om on
pont de for one ajueue
e tus de xx. pies s lone

ar chu fait om on elo
itre nautre tant el uoiel
com el pra el

ar chu prent om
la gece done
auc sens paleir

ar chu la lar
gece done fenel
tre ki est lons

ar chu aster om
vt un caent don el
tre fent pione et fen
vue f

ar chu partist om
one pirre que les ii
mortiel sont sinrel.

ar chu tor rom
ie uil don persour

ar chu fait om
ii uasias que si ont
tient ii tant que li arre

toret les figures sunt
estraret de geometrie.

ar chu tail om uofure rrale

the more didactic hand of the second author (*see 94*). He shows the method of cutting a stone in quadrature proportions by joining the mid-points of each side to form an inscribed square, half the area of the original square. Immediately above this, the correct way of planning a cloister is illustrated. The width of the walk-way is the difference between the outer square and an inner square of half its area, determined as in the first drawing and rotated through 45 degrees to bring its sides parallel to the outer square. The area of the walk-way and the central courtyard are, therefore, equal.

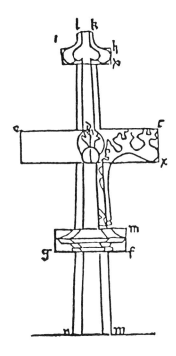

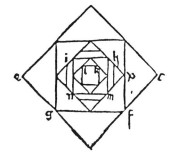

94 *facing page* A page from Honnecourt's notebook added by the second author showing useful measuring techniques, among them the 'doubling of the square'

95 Matthias Roriczer's method of constructing a pinnacle using the quadrature technique

Evidently, Villard himself was also familiar with the method of quadrature since he uses it extensively, though perhaps rather arbitrarily, in his imaginative designs, for example, in the amusing drawing of a wheel of masons each carving the foot of his predecessor in the wheel (*see 93*). The quadrature technique for producing harmonious proportions between the constituent parts of a building or architectural feature, using only the traditional masonic tools of set-square and compass, persisted throughout the medieval period. As late as 1486, the German master-mason, Matthias Roriczer, describes precisely the proportioning of the diminishing stages of a gothic pinnacle in terms of the progressive 'halving of the square'. The step by step process illustrated in Roriczer's *Booklet on the Correct Design of Pinnacles*[10] contrasts sharply with the tentative and disorderly approach of

Villard's sketchbook, and makes it clear that the practical geometric technique of quadrature was no longer protected by the secrecy of the masons' lodge by the late fifteenth century, if indeed it ever had been.

In his detailed work on the measurement and proportions of medieval architecture, Peter Kidson[11] stresses the importance of the ratio of $1:\sqrt{2}$ in medieval building and suggests that it was the chief *modus operandi* of the masons, tracing the use of the proportion back from medieval times through Roman and Greek antiquity to ancient Egypt and Mesopotamia. In practice it seems that masons achieved the $1:\sqrt{2}$ ratio either by the geometric method described in Plato's *Meno*, Vitruvius and Villard de Honnecourt, or by measuring out the proportion 17:12, a means of approximating the $\sqrt{2}$ proportion which had survived from classical into medieval times ($\sqrt{2}$ = 1.414213; 17/12 = 1.41666). *Perticas*, literally 'poles' and used in the same sense as the English measurement, of 12 and 17 roman feet appear to have been standard measurements.

Quadrature not only ensured aesthetically successful designs, it also made economical use of materials. Frederico Guidobaldi has shown[12] how the pieces for a simple opus sectile quadrature pattern in two colours can be cut from square blocks of stone in two straightforward operations. The pieces made by cutting the squared stone diagonally into two triangles, and twice diagonally into four triangles, may be arranged with the uncut square piece to form two variations of the same pattern without any stone being wasted. As a basic design and construction technique, quadrature became engrained in the medieval craftsman's way of thinking. So it is not surprising to find that the overall design of the Westminster sanctuary pavement is virtually a text-book exposition of the doubling of the square (*see 98*).

The most obvious quadrature element is the central diagonal square, ABCD, set within the larger square, EFGH, of twice its area. This may be compared directly to diagrams in Villard de Honnecourt's sketchbook and in the writings of Matthias Roriczer. Doubling the EFGH square produces approximately the dimension of the square which contains the whole of the design, in just the same manner that the second author of Villard's sketchbook demonstrates the correct way of proportioning a cloister (*see 94*). The dimension is not precisely that of the doubled square because, unlike the lines of a geometric diagram, the bands of Purbeck marble which describe the figures of the design have a substantial width (generally between 4 and 5 inches) which repeatedly introduces a second factor and gives a slight distortion to the pure geometry of the construction.

It is possible that the square ABCD provided the starting point for the mason's setting out of the pavement. All the squares of the pavement are

96&97 The use of quadrature to cut stone for two different patterns (after F. Guidobaldi), and an example of one such pattern in the Westminster pavement

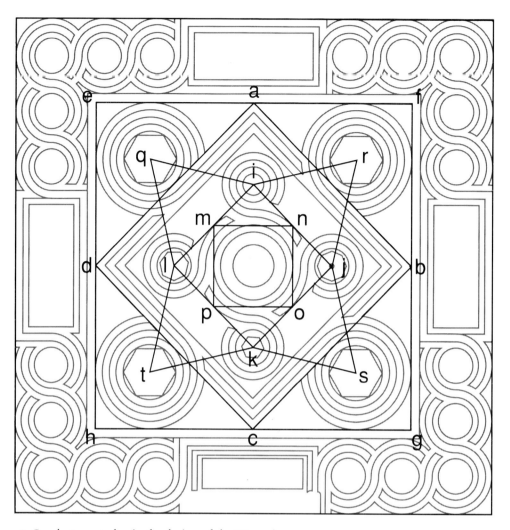

98 Quadrature at play in the design of the Westminster pavement

still surprisingly true, the length of their sides never varying by more than $\frac{3}{4}$ of an inch, but the sides of the inset square, ABCD, are exactly equal, each being 11 feet $8\frac{1}{2}$ inches. Moreover, what seems to be an arbitrary measurement is, in fact, equivalent to 12 roman feet, a roman foot being equal to 29.6 cms. or just over $11\frac{1}{2}$ ins. Although the 'modern' foot was already in use in England during the thirteenth century, in Italy masons were still working to the traditional foot of the Roman Empire. The craftsmen imported by Abbot de Ware seem to have stuck to their native foot. None of the dimensions of the·Westminster pavement are rational numbers in modern feet, but two are in roman feet: the square already mentioned, ABCD, and its doubled square, EFGH, which measures 17 roman feet (16 feet 7 inches). The discovery of these two measurements is particularly

124

important as they correspond precisely to the two standard roman poles, the *perticas*, identified by Peter Kidson in his research on the systems of proportion used by masons in early medieval building. It was with these two measurements that the Roman marblers began to set out the great $1:\sqrt{2}$ motif of the Westminster pavement. The square formed around EFGH by the addition of the Purbeck marble bands measures just under 18 roman feet square on each side.

The principles of quadrature also dictated the proportions of the design within the diagonally inset square. The imaginary square, MNOP, which contains the external diameter of the second band around the central roundel, when 'doubled up' generates the square, IJKL, whose corners are the centres of the four outer roundels of the central quincunx. The sides of this square determine, in turn, the positions of the next set of four roundels, the large roundels on the sides of the inner square, their centres being at the apexes of equilateral triangles built on the sides of the square IJKL, that is triangles IJR, JKS, KLT and LIQ.

Among the individual patterns of the pavement, the quadrature technique is seen in the design of both band and infill patterns (*see 88 and 96*). The same technique underlies other patterns in a more disguised form. The cosmati's joy in the fragmentation of the basic design units, usually by 'breaking off' tiny triangles and re-setting them in the background spaces, sometimes almost completely obscures the simplicity of the basic geometry. It is impossible not to admire the geometric dexterity of the cosmati craftsmen, especially when it is remembered that the overall design of their pavements meant that the intricate geometry of individual band patterns had to

99 Band pattern from the northern corner of the pavement's central square

be shaped into circles or round ogee curves, and turned through right-angled corners.

The patterns based on six-fold symmetry are even more impressive, and in them we may catch something of the Byzantine influence. Particularly rich are the patterns of the band which runs around the northern corner of the central square and the large north-west roundel (*see 99*), and of the infills of the four larger roundels (*see 100, 101, 102 and 103*). The south-east roundel exhibits a delightful refinement: within a honeycomb of hexagons formed by thin strips of purple porphyry, stars are built of lozenges of green porphyry and giallo antico and set in rows which not only alternately reverse their figure-fields (green stars on a yellow background in one row, yellow stars on a green background in the next), but also rotate the stars through an angle of 30 degrees to produce a pattern that ceaselessly fascinates the eye (*see 100*).

In using their geometric methods, it should not be assumed that the craftsmen were consciously exploiting any of the symbolic overtones that would have been second nature to Pythagorean or neo-Platonic philosophers, or that they were aware of the systematic mathematical ideas expounded in the many commentaries on Euclid. The compendium of Villard de Honnecourt demonstrates that the interest of practising masons was in the constructive aspects of geometry rather than the speculative. It shows little concern either for the traditional geometry of Euclid which was mostly involved with theoretical proofs and surveying – the literal meaning of geometry being 'earth measuring'. The newly-invented astrolabe and the surveyor's quadrant, which had come to Europe via Islamic Spain, were landmarks for scholars of practical Euclidian geometry. But neither of these innovations finds a place in Villard's sketchbook, which must, in this sense at least, be considered old-fashioned even in its own day.

Constructive geometry, practical geometry and speculative geometry can be seen as a triangle within which the function of any particular geometric construction or design may be plotted. Although in practice the majority of craft designers stayed firmly at home in the corner of constructive geometry, few could have been unaware of the more commonplace symbolism of geometry, and some must have ventured further afield. In his introduction to his book on the proper construction of pinnacles, Matthias Roriczer recounts that he discussed the art of geometry on many occasions with his

100–103 *previous pages* Infill patterns of the hexagons in the pavement's four major roundels

patron Wilhelm von Reichenau, Bishop of Eichstatt, to whom the book was dedicated. Such discussions between craftsmen and their Church patrons must have drawn together the constructive and speculative aspects of geometry.

Of all the arts, it was in church architecture and, perhaps to a lesser degree, manuscript illumination that constructive and speculative geometries were fused. A great church had to be planned in such a way that its structure would be sound, both literally and figuratively: the same geometry had to satisfy the rules of construction and the dictates of theological philosophy. Which came first remains uncertain, but the greater flexibility of symbolic imagery enabled almost any constructional advance to be given an appropriate interpretation.

Their mastery of constructive geometry enabled the masons of the gothic era to free architecture from the weighty material limitations that had constrained their predecessors. With the benefit of post-Jungian hindsight, we might also argue that their use of pure geometric forms infused their work with the language of archetypal imagery, tapping directly into the emotional reservoir of the collective unconscious that Jung saw as the universal heritage of all humankind. Even today, who can look upon the intricate geometry of a great rose window without a deepening of the breath? Something of this emotional response seems to be at work in a story about Galla Placidia, the devout daughter of Emperor Theodosius, who died in AD 450. At her command four roundels of red marble were laid down as a pavement. The marble was probably purple porphyry since the narrator of the story describes it as '*quae sunt ante nominatas regias*' – 'which was already known as royal'. At the potent point between the four roundels she lay herself down in prayer. There she remained all night until she was found, soaked by her tears, the following morning.[13] From this story it may be inferred that this arrangement of roundels, like that at the centre of the Westminster pavement, was already of considerable symbolic importance in the fifth century.

Petrus Oderisius' primary concern in laying the stones of the Westminster sanctuary pavement was to produce a design that worked in its own right. But, over and above this consideration, the pavement also had to be worthy of its critical location and to appeal to the more esoteric eye of his patron, Abbot Richard de Ware. Although he may not have been able to put together a detailed exegesis to fit the image he had created, Oderisius must surely have been aware of the more obvious symbolism of the geometric shapes he had employed. The circle, with its endless circumference, had long been recognised as a symbol of the eternal, even of God Himself: the square was seen as matter or the created world. Since the inscription tells us that the subject of the pavement is 'the measure of the *primum mobile*', that is the ninth sphere which represented the boundary between the created universe and the divine realm beyond, the interplay of squares and circles within the design can readily be seen as an appropriate metaphor for this interface between temporal matter (squares) and eternal divinity (circles).

Though more of a master to architecture, geometry was a willing servant to philosophy, enabling it to map out and relate together a whole world of harmonious concepts. Using geometry as a tool, the phenomenal chaos surrounding the philosopher could be forged into a decorous order – a cosmos. Pattern-making is the basic activity of intelligent existence. Arranging lines and colours to please the eye, sounds to please the ear, or concepts to please the mind are all essentially the same process. Without the mental grid of orderly pattern that is geometry, there would be no net to cast upon the waters of perceptual chaos, and, therefore, no understanding of the world around us. Robert Grosseteste, as the first known Chancellor of Oxford University and later as Bishop of Lincoln, was one of the most influential minds of his day. In the first half of the thirteenth century he wrote:[14]

> There is an immense usefulness in the consideration of lines, angles and figures, because without them natural philosophy cannot be understood. They are applicable in the universe as a whole and in its parts, without restriction, and their validity extends to related properties, such as circular and rectilinear motion, nor does it stop at action and passion, whether as applied to matter or sense . . . For all causes of natural effects can be discovered by lines, angles and figures, and in no other way can the reason for their action possibly be known.

Pattern-making allows the mind to move, by analogy and extrapolation, beyond the understanding of things directly perceived to conceptions of matters as yet unknown. To Christian thinkers of the thirteenth century, the order of the universe was a manifestation of eternal truths, communicated by the Creator to the created through the medium of number and geometry. The contemplation of this order through geometric concepts was, therefore, not only theologically justifiable, but might even lead to revelation of those divine things hidden from the direct experience of the senses. Having exhausted the physical and circumstantial evidence of the Westminster sanctuary pavement, we must now look for a motive – and it is precisely in this area of speculative geometry that we may hope to find it.

7

Images of Divine Order

Geometric diagrams had been used for expressing and exploring philosophical ideas since classical times. Plato's story of Socrates demonstrating the doubling of the square by tracing figures in the sand at his feet probably illustrates the normal teaching method of the ancient Greek philosophers, their students committing the lesson to memory before the image in the sand was brushed away. In their most elementary form medieval schemata, as such geometric diagrams are often known, appear as didactic annotations in the margins of manuscripts. They were usually added by a later hand and served to explain further or to summarise points already made in the text. These are simple diagrams without any pretension whatever to art, often no more than abbreviated labels linked by lines.

Gradually schemata grew more sophisticated and became integrated with the text as equal partners. In some instances, the ability of a schema to express concepts more concisely than the written word enabled them to achieve greater importance, to become works of art in their own right and with their own conventions. Once such conventions had been established, it was possible for the intellectual content of geometric schemata to be smuggled into forms of manuscript illustration which were not overtly diagrammatic, adding an esoteric dimension to what might at first sight appear to be purely figurative decoration. From this vantage point, schemata were poised to escape from the folia of manuscripts and colonise other media: wall painting, stained glass, carving, in fact any of the arts and crafts associated with religion.

Schemata then ranged from simple didactic annotations to esoteric designs meant to provide a focus for contemplation in much the same way as the mandalas of Eastern religions. Generally cosmic in intention, they sought to help the initiated observer to an apprehension of the divine order of the universe through the language of number and 'sacred' geometry.

The transition from incidental explanatory sketches to works of such artistry that their philosophical significance may easily pass unnoticed may be well illustrated by a selection of schemata designed to express the concept of the four primary Elements. The relationships between Fire, Air, Water and Earth were a popular theme among the devisers of schemata, and provided the intellectual scaffolding upon which more comprehensive concepts were built.

Empedocles, the Greek philosopher of the early fifth century BC, is usually credited as the originator of the theory of four Elements which come together under the influence of 'love' and disintegrate under the influence of 'enmity' in a cycle that forms the material diversity of the created world. The four are related together by two pairs of opposing qualities: Fire is Dry and Hot; Air is Hot and Moist; Water is Moist and Cold; Earth is Cold and Dry. Each Element, therefore, shares a quality with two of the others. Elements with a common quality are obviously more capable of combination, thus Earth and Water may be more readily combined than Fire and Water. Elements sharing a quality may also be transmuted one into the other by the replacing of the quality which differs between them. Thus Water (Moist and Cold) may become Air (Moist and Hot) by replacing Cold with Hot, that is heating it so that it becomes vapour. The primary purpose of any schema of the four Elements was to demonstrate this double set of reconciled opposites.

The reconciliation of opposites was a dominating principle that lay at the heart of medieval philosophical speculation. The opening sentence of Abbot Suger's description of the rebuilding of his church of Saint-Denis during the twelfth century presents a resounding verbal image of the harmonising of opposites as the paramount act of Divine creation:[1]

> The awesome power of one sole and supreme Reason reconciles the disparity between all things of Heaven and Earth by due proportion: this same sweet concord, itself alone, unites what seem to oppose each other, because of their base origins and contrary natures, into a single exalted and well-tuned Harmony.

This short but triumphant passage, redolent with the neo-Platonic imagery that had long been absorbed into Christian philosophy, conjures up the breadth and majesty of the Divine order that the designers of schemata sought to encapsulate in their work.

In the process of harmonising neo-Platonic teaching with that of the Bible, the Church Fathers had identified the *caelum et terram* created by God in the opening words of Genesis with the Elements of Fire and Earth: 'In the beginning God created the heaven and the earth.' In the *Timaeus*, Plato describes Fire and Earth as the first two Elements to be created, an opposing pair which were then reconciled by the creation of two intermediary Elements, Air and Water.[2] The reconciliation of the four Elements was achieved not only by the qualities of Hot, Cold, Dry and Moist, but also quantitatively by giving them numerical values.

The numerical treatment of the theme of the four Elements plaited together strands from both the Pythagorean and the Platonic traditions. Being primal, the Elements must be represented by, or derive from, the simplest numbers. Since 1 was reserved for the divine unity of God, the first two numbers that could possibly be used to represent the first two Elements to be created, Fire and Earth, were 2 and 3. However, these numbers were not considered adequate in themselves. A simple number can represent only one dimension, in visual terms, a line. By analogy, a square number, for example 4 (2 × 2), may represent a surface area, that is, a plane figure. But for material and spatial existence, three dimensions are necessary. Theon of Smyrna, the Greek mathematician, wrote that 3 'is the first bond and power of the solid; for in three dimensions is the solid conceived'.[3] Thus the appropriate numbers for the first two Elements had to be the cubes of the first two available numbers, 2 and 3. So Fire was assigned the number 8 and Earth the number 27.

The extremes of Fire and Earth, 8 and 27, then had to be reconciled by bonds which were sufficiently strong, in the numerical sense, to hold together the whole of the created world. Between two square numbers (those representing plane figures) a single mean is sufficient, but for cube numbers (solid figures) two means are needed. These means are 12 (2 × 2 × 3) and 18 (2 × 3 × 3). So the intermediary Elements of Air and Water received the mean numbers of 12 and 18 respectively. The numbers of the Elements, therefore, form a progression in which each individual Element is bound to its neighbour by the ratio of 2:3, one of the favourite harmonic ratios of the Pythagoreans, known as the sesquialter, the sixth of the proportions described by Nicomachus of Gerasa in his *Introduction to Arithmetic*,[4] c. AD 100. In this way the Elements that 'seem to oppose each other' were united into a stable and 'well-tuned harmony'.

As Plato summarised it in his *Timaeus*:[5]

> Having bestowed upon them so far as possible a like ratio one towards another – air being to water as fire to air, and water being to earth as air to water – he joined them together and constructed a Heaven visible and tangible. For these reasons and out of these materials such in kind and four in numbers, the body of the Cosmos was harmonised by proportion and brought into existence.

As well as assigning numbers to the four Elements, in the Pythagorean and Platonic traditions each had its own regular geometric solid. Pythagoras is generally credited with having discovered the five regular solids: the cube, with square faces; the tetrahedron, octahedron and icosahedron, with triangular faces; and the dodecahedron, with pentagonal faces. The tetrahedron was associated with Fire, the octahedron with Air, the icosahedron with Water, and the cube with Earth. The fifth solid, the dodecahedron, was taken to represent the heavens as a totality.

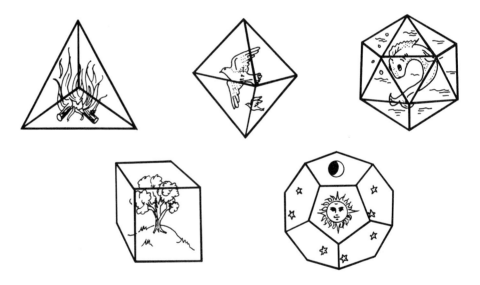

104 The five regular solids, sometimes known as the Platonic solids

To the primary qualities of Hot, Cold, Dry and Moist six more subtle secondary qualities were added: Fire is sharp, tenuous and mobile; Air is sharp, mobile and weighty; Water is mobile, blunt and weighty; Earth is blunt, weighty and immobile.

In the attempt to harmonise all aspects of the world around them, the philosophers also related the four Elements to the four human Temperaments. Four bodily fluids, or 'humours', were believed to govern the constitution of the body and mind: blood, phlegm, black bile and yellow bile. An excess of one humour gave an individual a particular temperament. Blood made a man sanguine; phlegm, phlegmatic; black bile, melancholic; and yellow bile, choleric. This theory had been suggested first by Hippocrates, the 'Father of Medicine'. The fiery choleric temperament became associated with Fire, the breezy sanguine with Air, the dissipated phlegmatic with Water, and the heavy melancholic with Earth.

These then were the 'facts' of the four Elements that the geometry of schemata was called upon to summarise. There were two basic approaches: a linear diagram which tended to emphasise the numerical relationship between the Elements, and a square or circular diagram which was more useful for showing their qualitative connections and also had the advantage of expressing their cyclic nature.

Both these forms are to be found at Anagni Cathedral among the wall paintings in the bay of the crypt devoted to the Greek philosophers Galen and Hippocrates (*see 105*). The linear schema is arranged vertically with Fire, the lightest Element, at the top and Earth, the heaviest, at the bottom. The numbers assigned to the Elements are the reverse of the normal sequence, Fire being given the number 27 and Earth, 8. It is not clear whether this apparent mistake was made in the original painting or if it is the result of inaccurate restoration. The names of the Elements are written in discs and related by arcs and straight lines to their six secondary qualities which are also set in discs. The circular version is to be seen in the vault of the same bay (*see 106*). Here the four Elements are grouped around the outer edge of the circle together with their primary Qualities. They are related immediately to a second circle divided into the four Seasons, and to the centre of the design which shows *homo*, man, surrounded by the four Ages of Man and the four human Temperaments. Although still predominantly diagrammatic, aesthetic considerations begin to make themselves apparent in both these schemata.

The description of the four Elements in the early twelfth-century *Tractus de Quaternario*[6] is followed by a lively foliate interlace filling the bottom third of the page (*see 107*). At first it seems nothing more than an incidental embellishment of the text in the form of a scrolling vine, but the medieval eye would have spotted immediately that the interlace forms four interlocking circles. Each circle surrounds a short list: the name of an Element and its three secondary qualities. These *tituli* are evenly written, matching the text above, and subservient to the schema. The interlocking of the circles

105 & 106 The crypt frescos at Anagni Cathedral: left, a linear schema of the Four Elements, and above, a circular schema with Man at its centre

illustrates the link between those Elements which combine more readily. Moreover, the qualities listed are linked together by leafy tendrils which make it a more pleasing design and, paradoxically, add more information to the schema at the same time as further disguising its function.

There could be no mistaking the cosmological diagram from a manual of around the same date in the manuscript collection of St John's College, Oxford[7] (*see 108*). Here the four Elements are set at the four corners of a lozenge. The lozenge serves as the 'scaffolding' for a whole panoply of correspondences, more complex than the circular schema at Anagni. Within it are earthly quaternities: the Qualities, the Points of the Compass, the Seasons, the Winds, the Ages of Man. Around it is the super-terrestrial dimension: the Signs of the Zodiac and the Months of the Year. Although completely non-figurative, the elements of the schema are built up, by variation of line and weight of lettering, into an elegant visual composition that is at the same time a working tool summarising concepts of Nature and Time.

A *Glossarium* by Solomon of Constance illustrates the relationship between Man (the microcosm) and the Universe (the macrocosm) in a more literal and figurative way. A graceful representation of the human form is set in a square with the four Elements at its corners[8] (*see 110*). The human body, like the rest of creation, is formed by the four Elements. In this

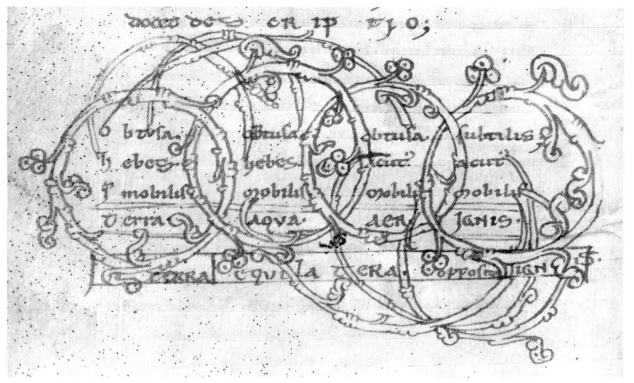

107 Interlacing foliage used to form a schema of the Four Elements in the early 12th-century *Tractus de Quaternario*

schema bands carrying *tituli* link the Elements to parts of the body with which they have a special affinity: Fire gives man his vision; Water, his taste; Earth, his sense of touch; and Air his hearing and sense of smell. The seven openings of the head are shown as corresponding to the seven planets, arranged like the radiating lines of a halo. This drawing was made in Regensburg in the middle of the twelfth century and is a good example of the school of schematic drawing that flourished there.

The next example of the four Elements schemata is perhaps the most accomplished of all in its artistry. It is an illuminated monogram (*see 109*), formed of I and N, the two letters of the first word of the opening sentence of Genesis: '*In principio creavit deus caelum et terram*', 'In the beginning God created heaven and earth.' The monogram appears in the Bible from St Hubert dated to around 1070 and now in the Bibliothèque Royale in Brussels.[9] Its schematic significance was first discussed at length by Harry Bober.[10]

The letter I bisects the letter N vertically to produce a symmetrical design which is woven together by a foliated interlace. The intersection of the I and the cross-bar of the N is covered by a roundel containing a half-length image of Christ flanked by the Greek letters *alpha* and *omega*, signifying His divine role as the beginning and ending of all things.[11] Around this central

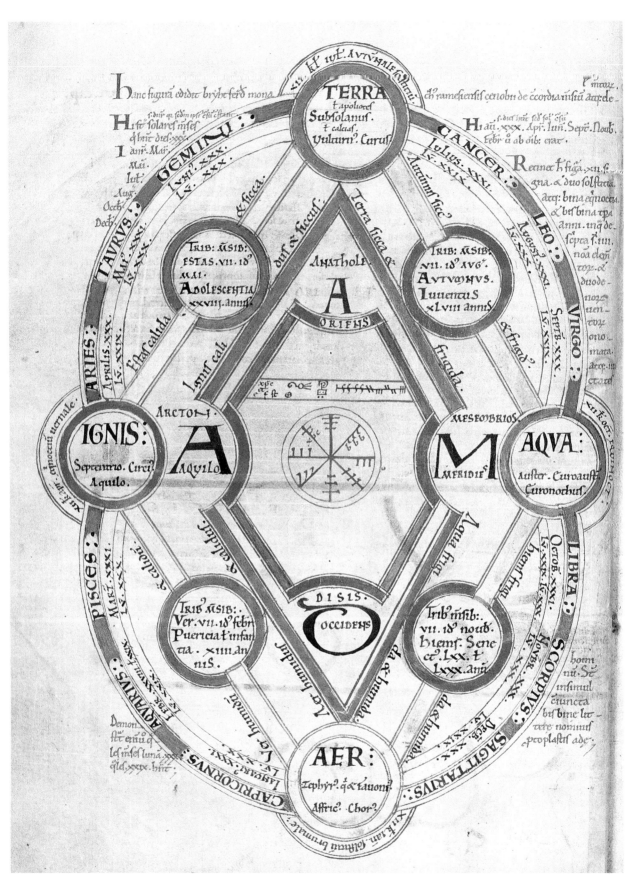

108 *opposite* A complex 12th-century schema built around the Four Elements and summarising concepts of Time and Nature

109 The Four Elements, and their numerical formulae, woven into a richly illuminated monogram of the first two letters of the Book of Genesis, from the 13th-century St Hubert Bible

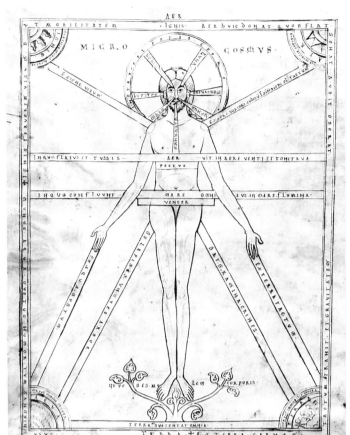

110 Man and the Universe, a 12th-century manuscript illumination from the Regensburg school of schematic drawing   111 Central panel of a Rhenish triptych, *c.*1150, showing the influence of manuscript schemata

roundel are four others, each bearing a full-length figure ringed with an inscription. The figures carry attributes which identify them as the four Elements, confirmed in three cases by written identification, and in all four by the mathematical formulae which produced their particular numbers. Thus, the roundel above Christ shows a figure bearing the sun and moon, the chief 'fires' of the heavens, and is inscribed with the number eight in Roman numerals and the formula by which it is derived: '*BIS.BINA.BIS*', (twice two twice). The roundel beneath Christ carries a spade and a plant. Two discernible letters, '*TE*', confirm that this is '*TERRA*', the figure of Earth. The inscription gives the number twenty-seven and the formula '*TER.TRIA.TER*', (thrice three thrice). Climbing on the interlacing foliage above it is a rodent-like animal. To the left of the centre, the roundel has a figure with a horn and is labelled '*AER*'. It is given the number twelve and the formula '*BIS.BINA.TER*', (twice two thrice). Nearby, a bird flaps its wings through the interlace. The right-hand roundel carries a spoon and pours out a pitcher of water. He is labelled '*AQUA*', numbered eighteen and given the formula '*TER.TRIA.BIS*', (thrice three twice). The circle of the interlace beneath him traps a swimming fish.

In this way, the artist who illuminated the Genesis monogram of the St Hubert Bible managed to convey a great deal of information about the philosophical concept of the four Elements without compromising either his artistic integrity or the religious context of his work. In fact, the sublime blend of figurative and schematic representation demonstrated so convincingly by this miniature masterpiece is an exact counterpart of the fusion of the Scriptures and neo-Platonic philosophy that had been achieved by medieval theology. It also underlines the complexity of the medieval mind which never took the world at face value, but always sought to see co-existent and equally valid layers of meaning in everything.

Although the art of drawing in line had been practised throughout Europe during the Carolingian Age, by the late eleventh and early twelfth centuries brighter and more opaque colour began to become the fashion in manuscript illumination, miniature painting overshadowing the use of elegant line and subtle washes of colour. But the older technique survived in two areas: England, where the skill and exhilaration of manuscript drawing that had blossomed during the Anglo-Saxon period was perpetuated in the work of illuminators like Matthew Paris, and the area of southern Germany and Austria centred on the city of Regensburg.[12] In both these areas line drawing continued to be the dominant technique for manuscript illustrations. Since this technique was particularly suited to schematic illustrations, it is likely that the readers of these regions were more finely attuned to the philosophical implications of geometric figures.

The schemata produced by the Regensburg school seem to have been especially influential. A small Rhenish triptych of around 1150 in the Victoria and Albert Museum collection appears to have been directly inspired by the geometry of Regensburg schemata (*see 110*). Typological subjects, those linking themes from the Old to the New Testaments, are incorporated within an inscribed geometric framework of interlinking squares and circles which has a degree of affinity with the overall design of the Westminster pavement. This triptych provides an illustration of the way in which conventions of manuscript schemata, and the philosophical concepts their geometry embodied, found their way into a variety of other media. The range of this infiltration into other art forms may be demonstrated by two quite disparate examples: the spectacular rose window of Lausanne Cathedral, near Lake Geneva, and a humble wooden bench-end in an East Anglian parish church.

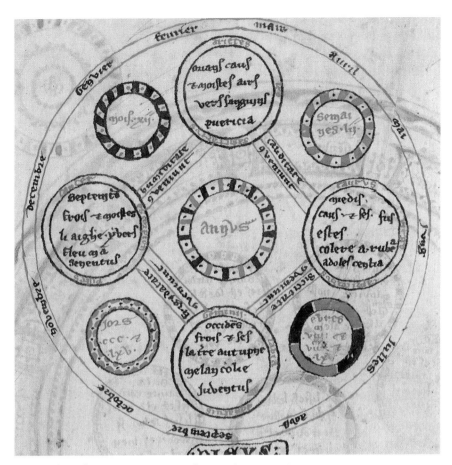

114 Manuscript schema, *c.*1240, centred around Annus, the Year

The wooden bench-ends at the Church of the Holy Trinity in Blythburgh were carved in the fifteenth century and are famous for their personifications of the Seven Deadly Sins. Among the lesser-known images is that of an angel bearing a shield with the 'arms' of the Holy Trinity, to whom the church is dedicated (see *115*). The arms of the Trinity is, in fact, a schema: a graphic representation of the mystic paradox of the individuality of the Father, Son and Holy Spirit within the unity of God: the Father is not the Son, the Son is not the Holy Spirit, the Holy Spirit is not the Father, yet all three are God. The carving has no *tituli*, the observer being left to supply them from his own knowledge of theology (see *116*). The same elegantly simple triangular schema continued to appear in alchemical texts[13] where it was often used to express other parallel 'three-in-one' concepts, such as the triplet of Body, Spirit and Soul that is united in Man.

112&113 The cosmological rose window of Lausanne Cathedral, *c.*1230, made up of 61 figurative stained-glass panels. A falconer represents the month of May

143

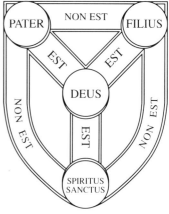

115&116 A bench-end carved with an angel bearing the arms of the Trinity, Blythburgh Church, Suffolk

By contrast, the rose window of Lausanne Cathedral is a *tour de force* in the quantity and complexity of the information it displays. Its tracery has a design of interpenetrating squares and circles that recalls the geometry of the Westminster sanctuary pavement (*see 112*). Constructed around 1230, it is also close in date. The imagery of the sixty-one figurative glass panels set within the geometric framework is drawn from a wide range of sources from classical Greece to contemporary legend. Together they add up to a comprehensive world view, a cosmology.

The central square depicts the Creation, but all five of its panels are late nineteenth-century replacements. The circles around this square have the four Seasons at their centres and the Months of the Year with their appropriate activities grouped around them (*see 113*). Four more circles grow from the intersection of the inner circles. These have personifications of the four Elements at their centres, each ringed by three of the Signs of the Zodiac. The Air circle also contains a representation of the Aeromancy, foretelling the future by the flight of doves. The Fire circle has its comparable image of Pyromancy, but the other two Elements have the Sun and Moon. These have probably been wrongly re-set, logic dictating that they should have represented Hydromancy and Geomancy, prediction by water and earth. The four Elemental circles are joined through their diameters by a square frame. In the corners of the square are the four Rivers of Paradise, each flanked by two of the fanciful mythological creatures supposed to inhabit that corner of the world. This composition touches the encompassing circle of the window leaving eight segments, each with a panel showing one of the eight Winds of the Cosmos.

This remarkably comprehensive image of the order of the cosmos is further refined if the replacements made by Eduoard Hosch at the end of the last century are discarded and the reconstruction suggested by Ellen Beer accepted.[14] The central square as it stands today has God the Father surrounded by Light and Dark, Land and Sea, Fish and Birds, and Animals and Man – rather too literal an illustration of the day by day story of Creation for the thirteenth-century mind, it might be thought. Beer suggests that these were originally a representation of the Year surrounded by images of Dark, Light, the Sun and the Moon, the last two being those panels now found grouped together less appropriately with two of the Elements. The spaces they vacated could then be filled by the more logical images of Hydromancy and Geomancy. This rearrangement would make the composition more consistent and bring the window in line with manuscript schemata, for example a near contemporary French manuscript,[15] which shows *Annus*, the Year, at its centre surrounded by the Seasons, Signs of the Zodiac, Elements, Qualities, Ages of Man, Temperaments and Months of the Year (*see 114*). With its banded roundels this manuscript schema once again echoes the design of the Westminster pavement. By analogy with this schema, it seems likely that Hosch also replaced the Signs of the Zodiac in the wrong positions. Today they run around the window in their yearly order: the manuscript schema breaks them down into four groups of three, and sets each group around its appropriate Element. Thus, the water signs Cancer, Scorpio and Pisces surround Water, and the fire signs Leo, Sagittarius and Aries are grouped with Fire, etc. It is almost certain that this arrangement would have been followed in the original layout of the window. The original central image personifying the Year may also be compared with the mosaic pavement in the cathedral of Aosta in Italy (*see 117*). There the seated figure of *Annus* holds the sun in his right hand and the moon in his left. The Labours of the Months are shown in a circle around him, and in the four corners of an enclosing rectangle are the four Rivers of Paradise.

The iconography of the Lausanne rose window may have been inspired by the west rose window of Chartres Cathedral and the teaching of the famous school of theological philosophy based there. It is known that priests from Lausanne travelled to Paris between 1222 and 1224, and are likely to have passed through Chartres at the time when the cathedral's impressive

117 Mosaic pavement at Aosta Cathedral with the figure of the Year surrounded by the Labours of the Months

windows were being designed and built. The great circle of the west rose window of Chartres is complemented, in content and geometry, by the circular labyrinth set in the floor beneath it. Keith Critchlow has demonstrated that the labyrinth is laid out at a distance from the west end of the nave such that if the west wall were to be 'hinged down' the rose window would fit almost exactly over the labyrinth.[16] The window portrays the awesome scenes of the Last Judgement with the souls of the damned condemned to Hell and those of the blessed conducted to the Heavenly Jerusalem. The labyrinth symbolised the earthly path of the soul in its search for salvation. Medieval pilgrims followed the twists and turns of the labyrinth on their knees, not only as a substitute for pilgrimage to the earthly Jerusalem but also as an enactment of this metaphorical journey of the soul. Bringing the images of window and labyrinth together adds a cosmic dimension to the journey, the concentric circles of the labyrinth becoming a cosmology like that of Dante's *Divine Comedy*.

146

From the example of the figure of *Annus* in the cathedral of Aosta we know that the pavements of great churches shared the same iconographic tasks as stained-glass windows and wall painting and that their concern was often with the cosmological dimension. Closer to home, the roundels of the Trinity Chapel pavement at Canterbury Cathedral, probably laid at some time between 1213 and 1220, carry designs of the Signs of the Zodiac and the Labours of the Months. There were also zodiac pavements in northern France at the Abbey of St-Bertin, at the church of St-Remi in Reims and at the Abbey of St-Denis – one of the churches which had served as Henry III's inspiration for Westminster Abbey.

The pavement which formerly existed at St-Remi in Reims is of particular interest. It is known only from descriptions recorded in the seventeenth century.[17] The pavement was divided into panels of mosaic with figurative schemata representing not only the Zodiac but also the four Rivers of Paradise, personifications of Earth and Water, the Four Seasons, the Seven Liberal Arts, the Four Cardinal Virtues and the Apostles of the New Testament opposed with the Prophets of the Old Testament. Its didactic purpose is unmistakable. Together these images must have provided a compendium of Christian philosophy that rivalled, if not surpassed, the 'Platonic cosmology' of the crypt of Anagni Cathedral.

The few examples given above illustrate the range and prevalence of schemata and their influence upon all aspects of ecclesiastical design, not least the pavements of great churches. They also show the extent to which the properties of geometric figures conditioned medieval thinking. The philosophical allusions and resonances of geometry had become so acceptable to Christianity that when William of Malmesbury gazed upon the geometric pavement of the old church at Glastonbury, where he stayed between 1125 and 1130, he observed that it was 'artfully interlaced in the forms of triangles or squares', and mused that 'I do no harm to religion if I believe some sacred mystery is contained beneath them'.[18] With no lesser authority behind us, we are now prepared to venture into the labyrinth of meaning that surrounds the Westminster sanctuary pavement.

8

Into the Labyrinth

St Thomas Aquinas wrote that 'it is the mark of the poetic arts to indicate the truth of things by means of invented similitudes'.[1] The veiling of concepts in the writings of philosophers, which usually took the form of a narrative acted out by mythological characters, was given the name *integumentum* by Martianus Cappella who considered it to be the secular counterpart of allegory in the Scriptures.[2] The Bible had traditionally been expounded at four levels of meaning: *historia*, the literal description of a story or event; *allegoria*, which gave the significance of the story in terms of Christian faith; *tropologia*, which provided a moral explanation for the guidance of the individual; and *anagogia*, the transcendental function which raised the thoughts of the reader from this tangible world to the hidden truths of the invisible world, Suger's realm 'which neither exists entirely in the slime of the earth nor entirely in the purity of Heaven'. The four levels of exegesis were long established, going back to Cassian in the fourth century, who had in turn amplified the three levels of meaning propounded by Origen. This multiple function of the written word was applied with equal enthusiasm to the natural world, which was seen as a book in which the qualities of the Divine might be revealed to those who could read them. The language that was the key to understanding this world was number. So number, and geometry too as we have seen, became subject to interpretation at several levels. They became keys to the anagogical meaning of the physical world.

The Four Elements schemata illustrated the philosophical allusions and significances that geometric design might be expected to provoke in the mind of the medieval observer. However, all concepts were subject to appropriate interpretations in particular contexts – interpretations that were not always mutually consistent. For example, odd numbers were generally considered to be superior to even numbers. This was because even numbers were 'feminine' and capable of being split into two equal parts while 'masculine' odd numbers could not be equally divided, there always being an extra one. Therefore odd numbers manifested the monad, the divine unity which was the source of all numbers. Yet the number six was seen as a perfect number because it was both the sum and the product of its factors. In this context, the 'imperfections' of its even and feminine character were completely overlooked. Such inconsistency was not the hurdle it is to the modern mind. Meaning was subject both to context and to level. There was no single or absolute interpretation, and it is this ability to shift and shimmer through layers of meaning that endowed medieval symbolism with its rich vitality. We should not expect, therefore, to find any simple, one dimensional answer to the riddle of the design of the Westminster sanctuary pavement.

Faced with the intricate geometric pattern that Petrus Oderisius had produced for him, Abbot Richard de Ware would have been unlikely to resist the urge to see in it echoes of the schemata which had long been used to summarise the basic elements of Christian philosophical belief. For a man who was familiar with the teachings of the great Robert Grosseteste and had, perhaps, discussed the schemata of the crypt frescos at Anagni Cathedral with no lesser luminary than St Thomas Aquinas, the design would have conjured up multiple resonances. Moreover, it was precisely this potential for multiple exegesis, a labyrinth of significances, that gave the pavement its value as an object of contemplation.

No more is attempted here than to follow a single strand of the cord that threads this labyrinth. The path is illuminated by the metaphorical light of the rose window of Lausanne, and there are two chief literary guides: the *Bible* and Plato's *Timaeus* as it had been presented to the Christian reader by Calcidius. The *Bible*, at whatever level of interpretation, was the ultimate authority for Christian philosophy. Calcidius' commentary on the *Timaeus* of Plato was the main source of cosmological theory during the thirteenth century and had long been so. It had the added virtue of having been commissioned specifically to explain the pagan philosopher's ideas in a Christian context. Calcidius wrote the work during the first half of the fourth century for Bishop Ossius, an influential churchman who played a major role in the deliberations of the Council of Nicea in 325.[3]

118 *opposite* The figure of St Peter from the Westminster retable, contemporary with the pavement, which has strong artistic affinities with the Douce Apocalypse

119 *above* St John the Divine's vision of the end of the world from the Douce Apocalypse

Even without the evidence of its inscription, the position of the Westminster pavement within the church would hint at a cosmological significance. The central liturgical area of a temple or great church had always had cosmic overtones. The Latin word *templum* comes from the Etruscan vocabulary. Originally, it described an area of the sky which was used for divination by a priest who interpreted the omens he saw there. Later the word came to mean an earthly sanctuary devoted to the gods and representing a projection on the ground of the sacred area of the heavens.[4] This symbolism was absorbed into Christianity, the church becoming a gateway to heaven by imitating the cosmos. The nave was seen as earthly life, and the chancel or sanctuary as heaven. The chancel arch of even the smallest church was often painted with the scene of the Last Judgement, marking in symbolic terms the division between the temporal life of the nave and the eternal life hereafter of the sanctuary. The nave was, therefore, the appropriate setting for the labyrinth which represented humanity's earthly

151

journey towards salvation, while the sanctuary symbolised the divine presence of God Himself.

It is hard to imagine today the power that was contained in this symbolic dimension of the sanctuary, but a description of the dedication of the new choir of Canterbury Cathedral in 1130 goes some way towards illustrating it:[5] 'The ceremony, which was attended by the king as well as the entire hierarchy of his realm, seemed to contemporaries more splendid than any other of its kind since the dedication of the Temple of Solomon.' The assembly chanted the liturgical 'Awesome is this place. Truly, this is the house of God and the gate of Heaven, and it will be called the court of the Lord.' Upon hearing these words, and beholding the new choir, at that moment ablaze with innumerable lights, King Henry I 'swore with his royal oath "by the death of God" that truly [the sanctuary] was awesome.' So the sanctuary floor of a great church like Westminster Abbey was already invested with cosmological significance by virtue of its position alone.

The four-fold symmetry of the Westminster pavement is the first confirmation of its design's cosmological intent. As the manuscript schemata have shown, the square was seen as a symbol of the multi-levelled quaternity of the material universe. Calcidius described quaternity as the primal structure of creation: 'The Godhead wanted to make the world as similar as possible to the Being which it really is. This Being contains four forms, therefore there should be four kinds of living being in the universe: the heavenly race of gods (Fire) and the earthly beings, subdivided into the flying (Air), the swimming (Water) and those living on the ground (Earth)'.[6] These were the categories of living creatures allied with such artistic skill to the four Elements by the illuminator of the Genesis initial of the St Hubert Bible. Furthermore, the standard layout of horoscopes during the middle ages took the form of a square with another square inset at 45 degrees, just as in the pavement. With the diagonals of the larger square added, the figure was divided into twelve equal parts, representing the astrologers' twelve houses of the heavens.

Within this generalised cosmological image, it is possible to begin to determine which particular aspects of the cosmos are implied in the pavement's design by reference to comparable schemata. The quaternary dimension of the pavement is emphasised not only by the four sides of the two squares that form the broad structure of the design, but also by the four roundels orbiting the central roundel and the four larger outer roundels on the sides of the inner square. In any such arrangement of four, the four Elements are bound to be the first candidates to be considered. Calcidius uses them to categorise his four groups of living beings, and the majority of manuscript schemata build upon the four Elements as their conceptual framework.

As a starting point of this hypothesis then, the four outer roundels of the central quincunx may be taken as representing the four Elements; Fire, Air, Water and Earth. Which roundel stands for which Element becomes clearer later. The immediate problem is to allocate a meaning to the focus of the whole design, the central roundel. In his annotation of Flete's text, Richard Sporley explains that the central roundel represented the archetype mentioned in the inscription ('Here is the perfectly rounded sphere which reveals the eternal pattern of the universe') because 'it contains within itself the colours of the four Elements'.[7] Different colours may certainly be distinguished in this single onyx marble roundel but there is no discernible order to the random swirling patterns of its coloured bands. Sporley must surely have had in mind the Elements in their undifferentiated state of primal chaos. In his *Commentary on the Timaeus*, Calcidius provides a more detailed picture of this confused state of matter, identifying it with the 'earth' created by God in the first sentence of Genesis, 'In the beginning God created the heaven and the earth.'[8]

Now we should see which heaven and which earth the Bible is speaking about. Those who are satisfied with a confused concept think that the heaven we see and the earth which carries us are meant, but those with a deeper insight say that this heaven was not made in the beginning but on the second day. For in the beginning light was made and called 'day', and after it this heaven which God called 'firmament'. On the third day, after the removal of the waters, the dry land appeared and this was called 'earth'. From this it is clear that in the passage quoted it is not our heaven and earth that are meant but other things which are older and should rather be perceived by the intellect than by the senses. Thus the Bible testifies that the true heaven is something different from the firmament, and, further that the earth meant here is something different from the dry earth which appeared on the third day.

Calcidius prefers to see this creation of 'heaven and earth' as the primal division between spirit and matter. He uses the next phrase of Genesis, 'And the earth was without form, and void', to confirm his opinion that the 'earth' 'must refer to corporeal matter, the primary substance of the world before it assumed various forms shaped by the skill of the divine Maker. During this phase it was still without colour or quality, and that which is in such a condition is certainly invisible and shapeless. It is called "empty and nothing", because, although a recipient of all qualities, it possesses no quality of itself.'[9]

Calcidius calls this undifferentiated stage of matter *silva*. Bernardus Silvestris, writing his *Cosmographia* in the twelfth century, uses the veil of *integumentum* to describe essentially the same process of creation by mythological *dramatis personae*. He opens his story with the personification of Silva 'yearning to emerge from her ancient confusion' and demanding 'the shaping influence of number and the bonds of harmony'.[10] Hyle, a kind of alter-ego of Silva, appeals on her behalf to Noys, a character derived from the biblical Sapientia, whose wisdom, consisting of the archetypes of creation, is contained in a mirror. 'It is Silva's plight', Hyle complains, 'to be whirled about in flux and thrown back again into her original confusion by random eddies; peace, love, law, and order are unknown to her. Because she is lacking in all these Silva may scarcely lay claim to her true title as the work of God . . . Apply your hand, divide the mass, refine its elements and set them in their stations; for they will appear more pleasing when thus disposed. Quicken what is inert, govern what moves at random, impose shape and bestow splendour. Let the work confess the author who has made it.'[11]

The image of turbulent waters to illustrate primal matter in its undifferentiated state was already well established in Greek philosophy, probably by Heraclitus, and has its echoes in the Hebrew Scriptures. In Genesis, 'the Spirit of God [usually identified with the *logos* of St John's Gospel] moved on the face of the waters', or as it appears in the New English Bible of 1970, 'a mighty wind swept over the surface of the waters'. The *logos* is the biblical equivalent of Plato's archetype. Its intervention causes the random movement of the *silva* to become directed to the formation of the forms of the four Elements – not yet the Elements in their material existence, but in their ideal archetypal form. In Calcidius' description, this second stage of creation is caused by 'vestiges of bodies' or 'qualities' falling into the *silva*. He quotes Plato as saying, 'In this way these first four bodies are swayed to and fro, as in an eddying strait, and finally separated according to kinds.'[12]

Returning to the pavement, we may now see the central roundel and its random streaks of colour as Calcidius' *silva*, or the 'earth' of the first sentence of Genesis – primal matter in its undifferentiated state about to receive the qualities that will cause its random eddies to separate out the forms of the four Elements. Around the central *silva* roundel are the four roundels of the Elements, linked to the centre by interweaving band patterns that are directly analogous to the eddies that swirl round to separate out the forms of the Elements 'according to kinds'. These kinds are the four primary qualities which govern the natures of the Elements: Hot and Cold, Dry and

Moist. The band patterns of the central quincunx can therefore be read as these qualities since each roundel is touched by two bands, just as each Element has two qualities. The bands also link one roundel to the next, as a single common quality links neighbouring Elements. The central quincunx, therefore, represents both the genesis of the four Elements from undifferentiated matter, and the qualities that link them together into Plato's image of an unbroken circle of Elements each giving birth to the other.[13]

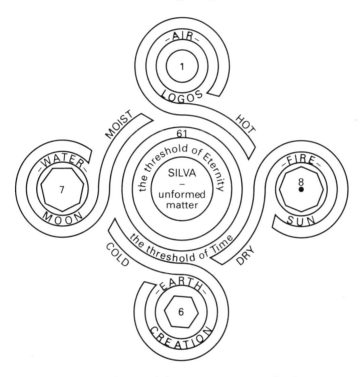

120 Symbolic schema of the pavement's central quincunx

The bringing forth of silva and its differentiation into the forms of the Elements happened before the advent of time, in a place somewhere between divinity and creation. Having created matter and given it the forms of the primal Elements, the next stage in bringing the world into existence was to begin Time. According to both Plato and Genesis, God accomplished this by the creation of the sun and moon. 'With a view to the generation of time, the sun and moon and the five other stars, which bear the appellation of "planets", came into existence for the determining and preserving of the numbers of Time',[14] and 'God said, Let there be lights in the firmament of the heaven to divide the day from the night; and let them be for signs, and for seasons, and for days, and years . . .'[15]

The roundel to the south of the central roundel has a feature that is unique in the pavement. At its centre is a small disc of black marble. A circle with a dot in the centre had long been the astrological and alchemical symbol for the sun. Since the sun plays such an important role in this second stage of creation, there is every reason to suggest that this southern roundel with its central black 'dot' stood for both an Element and the sun. The polygon it contains has eight sides, the number eight standing for Sunday and for the regeneration and resurrection symbolised daily by the rising sun. In this view, the week was analogous to the musical scale. Just as 'doh' is the first and eighth note of the scale, so Sunday was seen as the first and eighth day of the week.

The sun's celestial partner may also be found here. The roundel on the opposite side of the quincunx, that to the north, is set with a seven-sided polygon. The number seven was associated with the moon because of the seven phases of the moon and the convenient fact that the sum of the first seven numbers is twenty-eight, the number of days in the lunar month. Seven was also directly associated with the four Elements because it represented the number of transmutations between them: formless matter to Fire, Fire to Air, Air to Water, Water to Earth, Earth to Water, Water to Air, and Air to Fire.[16]

When the sun and moon appear as a pair, for example in the iconography of the Crucifixion, the sun normally appears to the left and the moon to the right. The Westminster pavement reverses these positions. Examples of Crucifixion scenes with the same arrangement as the pavement can be found,[17] but possibly more relevant than the iconography of the Crucifixion in this context is the *In principio* monogram of the St Hubert Bible. Here the figure who personifies the Element of Fire carries the sun and the moon to right and to left, just as at Westminster (*see 109*).

It is logical in the Westminster design to associate the sun with the Element of Fire, and the moon, because of its tidal influence, with Water. In any square or circular schema of the four Elements, Fire and Water have to be on opposing sides since they have no quality in common: Fire is Hot and Dry, and Water, Cold and Moist. This enables the Elements of Fire and Water to be assigned to the south roundel (the sun) and the north roundel (the moon) respectively.

Both Air and Earth, which mediate between the two Elements already fixed, may then be allocated either to the east and or to the west roundels. Here there are no obvious clues to the appropriate correspondences between roundels and Elements. On balance, it seems most likely that Air should be assigned to the eastern roundel. The east was traditionally the origin of the spirit of enlightenment, and spirit partook of the Element of Air: 'spirit' is synonymous with 'breath' in all three of the Bible's languages (*ruah* in Hebrew, *pneuma* in Greek, and *spiritus* in Latin). The eastern roundel is also the only one of the four not containing a polygon. As a simple disc it must be considered closer to the Divine than the other three, which contain polygons. It may be interpreted as the 'Spirit of God' or the 'mighty wind' which moved across the face of the waters to begin the process of differentiation in unformed matter, and can, therefore, be identified with the *logos*. The western roundel then becomes Earth. Its hexagon may be taken as a reference to the perfection of the archetype, six being the first perfect number, or to the six faces of the cube which was the geometric solid assigned to the Element of Earth. In either case, a fitting opposition is made between the western and eastern roundels, the created facing the Creator, or the form of perfection facing the source of all perfection.

The first pieces of the jigsaw may now be fitted together to encapsulate the first three stages of creation: the generation of unformed matter, its differentiation into the forms of the four Elements, and the beginning of Time signalled by the creation of the sun and moon. To recapitulate, the central roundel of the pavement represents Calcidius' *silva*, unformed matter in a state of random motion. By the action of the *logos*, the spirit with the knowledge of the archetypes symbolised by the eastern roundel of the quincunx, blowing across the face of the waters their random motion is redirected into eddies which define the positions of the forms of the Elements by their qualities. The south roundel is attributed to Fire; the west to Earth; the north to Water; and the east to Air. Air is connected to Fire by a band pattern that represents the quality Hot; Fire to Earth by Dry; Earth to Water by Cold; and Water to Air by Moist.

The completion of this divinely perfect arrangement is signified by the six-sided figure contained in the west roundel. Next the creation of the sun, the south roundel identified by the astrological symbol of a circle with a central dot, and the moon, the north roundel with its seven-sided polygon, heralds the beginning of Time.

The two levels of time presented in this schema, astronomical time and the timelessness of eternity, are paralleled in the sections of the pavement's inscription set in this area. The verse around the central *silva* roundel speaks of the archetype, a concept which exists in eternity. This timeless setting of the *silva* is underlined by the outer band around the central roundel. Its pattern consists of a circle of sixty-one lozenges. Since Babylonian days, sixty had been recognised as the number of time, the hour being divided into sixty minutes. In terms of numerology, adding one to sixty expressed the passage beyond time into eternity. It is surely more than coincidence that the cosmological rose window at Lausanne Cathedral is made up of sixty-one figurative panels of stained glass. The lines of the inscription which calculated the duration of the world by the multiplied life-spans of various creatures, clearly set in the dimension of astronomical time, were written around the outer edge of the quincunx, thus containing the forms of the Elements as they had been extended into temporal existence by the creation of the heavenly bodies.

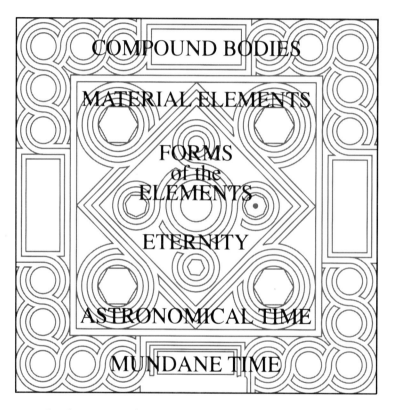

121 The three stages of matter and three timescales of the pavement

At this point we should be reminded by Calcidius that so far only the forms of the four Elements have been created. The 'first motion does not contribute to the coming to existence of anything; its purpose is the separation of the Elements'.[18] The Elements have yet to achieve material and spatial existence so that they may become the building blocks of the natural world. The purely circular composition of the central quincunx emphasises the idea that it stands for those things existing only in the intelligible world.

It is in the next level of the pavement's design that the sensible world makes its appearance.

The quincunx is enclosed by a square whose corners point to the four corners of the compass, a clear reference to the tangible world in which we live. The square had long been regarded as a symbol of the four Elements in their physical and temporal manifestation. John of Seville frequently used the term *angula* to describe the four Elements, the reason for his preference being that 'the Chaldean philosophers have compared these four matters of the world to the four corners of a quadrangle.'[19] In the Westminster pavement the four Elements are not found at the corners of the square, but budding off the sides as circles with richly-patterned hexagons. These six-sided figures continue the theme of the perfection of the Elements, even though they have crossed the barrier into the tangible and corruptible world.

The central motif of the quincunx has now to be seen as a 'seed' from which the outer roundels grow, acting as an intermediary between the eternal archetypes and the Elements created in their image – a kind of buffer between the spiritual and the material. (The problem of how God achieved creation without Himself being 'contaminated' by materiality had long exercised the ingenuity of Christian philosophers. The result was various concepts of sequential and hierarchical emanations which served to progressively distance the Creator from creation.) The area within the diagonal square, therefore, remains in the intelligible world, while that around it belongs to the sensible world. These two areas are differentiated by their main background infill patterns: those patterns within the square of medieval origin (the two late seventeenth-century insertions must be disregarded) have six-fold symmetries, six, once again, being the number of perfection. The area around the square has, by contrast, four-fold symmetries, emphasising the material nature of the sensible world.

The square outer border of the pavement consists of four panels and a great variety of roundels, representing in totally abstract form the infinite diversity of the world built up from the material manifestation of the four Elements. Furthest from the eternal centre of the pavement, it represents the lowest of the three levels of time, the mundane and transitory world of human life and achievement.

At this stage, the exposition of the pavement's design must be slightly redirected because the inscription makes it perfectly clear that the design concerns the end of the world, not its beginning. The pavement must also be seen in the context of the whole sanctuary. A large painted wooden panel, now in the south ambulatory of the Abbey, is believed to have

122 The Four Elements in the globe of the world from the Westminster retable

formed the retable of the medieval high altar (*see 118*). This panel, made to stand at the back of the altar, would almost certainly have been designed to fit into the same iconographic scheme as the pavement, and may be contemporary. Its central panel shows Christ holding in His hand the globe of the world with figurative representations of the four Elements (*see 122*). Traditionally this has been considered to represent the image of Christ as the Creator of the world, but the iconography of the scene is unusual in that the figures attending Christ, the Virgin Mary and St John, are both shown holding palm leaves. It has recently been pointed out[20] that palm imagery was sometimes associated in England with the *Agnus Dei*, Christ as the Sacrificial Lamb by whose death humankind will be redeemed. One of the central episodes of the apocalyptic vision of St John the Divine is the worship of the *Agnus Dei*. In holding the globe of the four Elements of the world in His hand it is probably more likely, therefore, that Christ is portrayed here not as the Creator of the world, but as its Saviour, the *Salvator Mundi*. This interpretation obviously brings the figurative iconography of the retable close to the abstract imagery of the pavement.

The depiction of the Apocalypse in art was at its peak during the thirteenth century. The illuminated manuscript known as the *Douce Apocalypse*[21] (*see 119*), dates from this time and has been compared in its style of painting to the Westminster retable.[22] Interest in all aspects of the awesome event had been stimulated by the major controversy over the prediction of the end of the world which had been aroused by the writings of Joachim di Fiore. Joachim di Fiore was a Calabrian abbot who claimed, in the early 1180s, to have had the meaning of The Revelation of St John the Divine revealed to him by God. He produced the first detailed reading of the Revelation in which its symbolism was not only correlated with the major events of the past history of the Church but also used to predict what was to come. The most controversial aspect of Joachim's work was his conclusion that the history of the world is divided into three great ages, each marked out by its degree of spiritual awareness (echoes of the crypt frescos of Anagni Cathedral may be softly heard here). The third age, which would bring the Antichrist and his defeat, seemed close at hand. These ideas were taken up by his followers and pursued to heretical lengths. The formula for the end of the world in the Westminster pavement may be seen as a rebuttal of these Joachite beliefs.

The end of the world was imagined as a reversal of the process of creation. The human body, along with the rest of creation, will be resolved into the four Elements. The four Elements will return into the primal chaos – hence the apocalyptic vision of the stars (Fire) falling to the earth – and finally matter will be reabsorbed into the Divine Mind and eternity. As all things proceed from God, so in God they find their final completion – the *finem* of the pavement's inscription in all its meanings. This concept had been explored by John Scotus Erigena writing in the ninth century. He constructed a system of four stages or divisions of nature. The fourth division is, paradoxically, the return of nature to primal unity: 'the body of man is restored to the Elements; these Elements coalesce in the resurrection into a new body; and this turns to spirit, the spirit reverts to its original causes, the causes to God.'[23] 'I am Alpha and Omega, the beginning and the ending, saith the Lord.'[24]

Since the Apocalypse reversed creation, the design of the pavement reads from the outside inwards, unlike the Lausanne window but just like a labyrinth. The starting place is the mundane dimension of time, populated by the teeming diversity of life, represented in the pavement by the variety of the roundels of its border. These are resolved into the four material Elements shown as the larger roundels budding from the sides of the inner square. There is a total of nine roundels in the main part of the design, reflecting again the *primum mobile*, the ninth sphere of the universe. In numerological terms nine also stands for the ultimate completion of creation (being three times three) at the moment when it is poised for the move to the decad and thus for the return to unity. Therefore, in the central quincunx we may see the sun and moon falling into chaos rather than resolving it, destroying Time rather than initiating it. The roundel with the seven-sided polygon becomes a symbol of the dominating number in the Apocalyptic vision of St John: the seven churches of Asia, the seven candlesticks, the book with seven seals, and the seven-headed monster. The hexagon of the western roundel now represents not the six days of creation, but the analogous six ages of the world leading up to the Last Judgement. The sixth age will be followed by the cosmic Sunday, a great Sabbath of eternal rest, symbolised by the eight-sided polygon of the southern 'sun' roundel. Finally, at the centre of the pavement, creation steps through the ring of sixty-one out of time and into eternity where it is reunited with its divine archetype. The *finem* of the *primum mobile* is thereby fulfilled, both in terms of its temporal destruction and its goal, the return to God.

Unlike most schemata the pavement is, in this sense, an 'inside-out' cosmology, deo-centric rather than the more familiar geo-centric or homocentric models. This standpoint agrees well with the emanative theories of the divinity which had been propounded by Dionysius, the pseudo-Areopagite, and given a new lease of life at the time of the making of the Westminster pavement through the writings of Robert Grosseteste, whose synthesis of St Augustine's neo-Platonism and the works of Aristotle set the philosophical tone for the rest of the medieval period. His *De Luce*, a description of light as the tool of creation, has been described as the only notable scientific cosmogony written between the *Timaeus* and early modern times.[25] Grosseteste accepted the identity of Dionysius as the disciple and companion of St Paul, describing him as 'a neo-Platonic Christian harmoniser of philosophy and religion' but 'more a neo-Platonist than a Christian'.[26] In *De Luce*,[27] 'taking as his starting point the light produced by the command of Yahweh, and amorphous matter, Grosseteste set himself to "think God's thoughts after him" and to imagine how the omnipotent mathematician planned the process which gave as its result a world-machine that is plainly Aristotelian in its essential features.'

This interpretation of the pavement's significance invests great symbolic power in the central roundel (something of the mystic associations of the centre between four roundels has already been illustrated by the story of Galla Placidia at Ravenna). At Westminster, the central roundel marks the place upon which the monarch is anointed with holy oil during the ceremony of Coronation. It is this act which symbolically confers Divine

123 *opposite* 15th-century manuscript showing the Coronation of Charlemagne on a pavement set with ceremonial roundels

tant comme il tenu pleui̇ si le sy croiuoit
e leur donna de ses richesses . Cy fine le
premier liure de histozien charlemaine

Cy comence le second liure des histoires char
lemaine premierement coment il fut cou
ronne a empereur en leglise saint pierre
de homme / Apres coment il condampna
par eulx ceulx qui auoient saudi la apostolle
lyon . Et puis des roules des terres qui
furent par le monde / e des messages e pns
aaron le roy de perse
e iour de la natiuite en
tra lempereur en leglise
saint pierre de homme
droit en ce point que on
deuoit celebrer la grant messe La apostolle
lyon lui assist la couronne imperial ansi

Right upon the monarch. The coronation dimension of the pavement is also expressed in the use of purple porphyry. This marble had long carried imperial overtones. Roundels of porphyry were used to mark out ceremonial positions in the Palace of Constantine. The Holy Roman Emperor, Henry V, stood on the central roundel of Old St Peter's when he received the Imperial Crown from the Pope in 1106. A manuscript illustration of the Coronation of Charlemagne by Jean Foucquet,[28] dating from the second half of the fifteenth century, shows roundels set out on the pavement (*see 123*), with Charlemagne kneeling towards the centre of a group of four roundels. Smaller roundels form a border, somewhat in the manner of Westminster. When political circumstances forced Charles V to be crowned at Bologne rather than Rome, it is said that porphyry discs were laid down temporarily to represent the roundels at St Peter's.[29]

It is not clear whether Henry III had intended the Westminster pavement to serve as a coronation floor, but since the French coronation church of Reims had provided one of the models for the rebuilding of Westminster, it would seem likely that this would have been conceived as a part at least of the pavement's symbolic function. The central onyx marble roundel representing the chaos of unformed matter might well be seen as a metaphor for the secular chaos of an ungoverned state that is to be resolved by the power of the Crown, a situation all too familiar to Henry III. Even Robert Grosseteste, who resented Henry's attempt to put himself on a level with the anointed clergy, conceded that the anointing of the King with holy oil 'bestowed upon the recipient the sevenfold gifts of the Holy Ghost, which gave the King insight into the ordering of things temporal and spiritual'.[30] It comes as a disappointment to find that the earliest records of the coronation ceremony describe the pavement as being covered with rich fabric. If the design of the pavement was covered over, is it likely that there was any recognition of a special significance for the pavement in the context of the English Coronation? Or did hiding it from public view mean that its significance was too great to be an open secret?

The primary religious function of the design of the Westminster pavement was to present a schema that enabled the observer to reflect upon the divine order of the universe, how it had come into being from eternity and how it would return to eternity. The process is not illustrated literally, but by presenting the required ingredients and principles in a meaningful relationship to one another. The three main elements of the design represent the three stages of both the birth and the death of the universe. Like the three-fold division of the verses of the inscription, these three design elements also signify three levels of time: the mundane scale of human activity, the astronomical scale of world ages, and the timeless scale of eternity. Together, design and inscription express the division of the universe into three levels of existence: the archetypal, the spiritual and the material. The triple dimension Grosseteste expressed as the 'reason of the creature in the Eternal World', the 'understanding of the thing imprinted in the angelic intellect', and the 'coming-to-be of the creature in reality'.[31]

The relationship between a symbol and its meaning is a complex one, with no simple genesis. A geometric pattern and its symbolic significance gravitate together by a mutual attraction, sanctioned by the prevailing cultural consensus which, in its turn, is further enriched by the new alliance. This intricate process has been aptly described as being 'determined by a network of reciprocal half-distinct connotations'.[32]

We have picked one pathway through the labyrinth of meanings and the web of 'reciprocal half-distinct connotations' that may be ascribed to the Westminster sanctuary pavement. No doubt there are other paths which may be equally valid. The purpose here has been to demonstrate in some detail just one way in which the pavement's design provided a contemplative tool for the monks who looked upon it.

Robert Grosseteste believed that 'God brings about an order that is always good order, and that consists in a beauty that imitates His own nature'.[33] Revelation of the beauty of divine order was the goal of all medieval ecclesiastical art and architecture. It was both the reason for art and the yardstick by which it was judged. The Westminster Abbey sanctuary pavement provides a sublime example of the realisation of this goal. When we begin to understand something of its esoteric language, the eloquence of its design and meaning may be seen to equal the best philosophical writing of the medieval period.[34]

> From the intellectual universe the sensible universe was born, perfect from perfect. The creative model exists in the flawlessness of its flawless model and waxes beautiful by its beauty, so by its external exemplar it is made to endure eternally. Setting out from eternity, time returns again to the bosom of eternity, wearied by its long journey.

Ultimately all human understanding can achieve is a metaphor of reality. At the close of the twentieth century, science itself is no longer confident, or arrogant, enough to claim absolute objectivity. This limitation was readily accepted by the medieval thinker, but is more disturbing to the modern intellect accustomed to a secure and concrete reality, and seduced by the mastery of technology. But as our minds become progressively tuned to ecological and to global concerns, so the Platonic image of the world as a living creature is re-awakened from its sleep.

The metaphor of reality in which we live is gained by dredging the chaos of perceptual input with a mental net, humanity's universal patterns of thought. Could it be that through cosmological speculation we discover neither the secrets of the universe nor the nature of some supernatural Being, but of ourselves? The further we go, the closer we come to home.

Acknowledgments

A cross-disciplinary work like this would have been much impoverished without the generous assistance of experts in several different fields and without access to the records and libraries of various institutions. My first acknowledgment, however, must be a personal one to Pamela Tudor-Craig, Lady Wedgwood, who first introduced me to the Westminster pavement, and subsequently provided unflagging encouragement. I have also to give special thanks to Keith Critchlow of the Royal College of Art for inspiration and guidance through the minefields of sacred geometry and number symbolism.

Without the co-operation of the Dean and Chapter of Westminster, the project would have been literally impossible. I have to thank two successive Deans for their support: the Very Reverend Edward Carpenter and the Very Reverend Michael Mayne. The period of my work at Westminster saw the retirement of Peter Foster, Surveyor to the Fabric for many years, whose own interest in the pavement provided a practical springboard for this study. His friendly interest was continued by his successor, Donald Buttress. Also at the Abbey, I would like to extend special thanks to Richard Mortimer, Keeper of the Muniments, and Enid Nixon, Assistant Librarian, for providing research facilities and much useful advice, and to Emma St John-Smith, Public Relations Officer, for smoothing out the serious organisational difficulties involved in working on a pavement in the middle of the country's busiest church.

For providing research facilities outside of the Abbey, I am grateful to the staffs of the library of the Warburg Institute, the Department of Manuscripts at the British Library, the National Art Library and Department of Prints and Drawings at the Victoria and Albert Museum, the Society of Antiquaries, the Local History Department of the Westminster Library, and the College of Arms. I am also grateful to Robin Sanderson of the Geological Museum for generously sharing his expert knowledge of stone building materials. At the British Museum my thanks are due to Venetia Porter and Judith Kolbas, for expert advice, and to Ian Freestone, Michael Hughes and D. R. Hook of the Museum's Research Laboratory for their scientific analysis of samples from the pavement.

I am grateful to Dom Sylvester Houédard of Prinknash Abbey for casting a theological eye over my text, though I fear he might still find it irredeemably pagan in parts. Gillian Paterson and Christopher Norton also provided much helpful advice. Finally, my thanks to Bob Sharples of University College for checking my Latin translations, to Irene Clarke and Daniella Dangoor for translating German and Italian respectively, and to Janet Marc and Jill Butler for help in the production of the typescript.

Richard Foster
Twickenham, 1991

Bibliography

Note: Some works on the Abbey are referred to frequently in the text. The following are often identified by the author's name alone:

Rudolph Ackermann, *The Monuments of the Abbey Church of St Peter's, Westminster, Its Antiquities and Monuments*, London 1812.

Edward Wedlake Brayley and John P. Neale, *The History and Antiquities of the Abbey Church of St Peter, Westminster*, vol. 1, London 1818, vol. 2, London 1823.

William Camden, *Reges, reginae, nobiles & alii in Ecclesia Collegiata B. Petrus Westmonasterii sepulti*, London 1600.

Jodocus Crull, *The Antiquities of St Peter's, or the Abbey Church of Westminster*, London 1711.

John Dart, *Westmonasterium, or the History and Antiquities of the Abbey Church of St Peter's, Westminster*, London 1742.

William Dugdale, *Monasticon Anglicanum*, vol. 1, trans., Hugh Bredin, Yale University 1986.

John Flete, *De Fundatione Ecclesiae Westmonasteriensis*, 1443, (Westminster Abbey MS 29), ed., J. A. Robinson, Cambridge 1909.

Henry Keepe, *Monumenta Westmonasteriensia*, London 1683.

James Peller Malcolm, *Londinium redivivum: or, An Ancient History and Modern Description of London*, London 1802.

Jocelyn Perkins, *Westminster Abbey, Its Worship and Ornaments*, Alcuin Club Collection, vol. 33, Oxford & London 1938.

Richard Sporley, *A History of the Abbots, Priors, etc., of Westminster Abbey*, 1450, (British Library MS Cotton Claudius A.8.).

Stephen Wander, *The Westminster Sanctuary Pavement*, in *Traditio*, vol. 34, New York 1978.

John Weever, *Ancient Funerall Monuments within the United Monarchie of Great Britaine, Ireland, and the Islands adjacent etc.*, London 1631.

Herbert Francis Westlake, *Westminster Abbey*, London 1923.

Richard Widmore, *An History of the Church of St Peter, Westminster, commonly called Westminster Abbey*, London 1751.

PRIMARY SOURCES

ANGLICUS, Robertus, *Commentary on the Sphere of Sacrobosco*, ed. & trans. Lynn Thorndike, Chicago 1949.

Annales Prioratus de Dunstaplia (British Library MS Cotton Tiberius A. 10.) in *Annales Monastici*, Vol. 3, ed. Henry Richards Luard, London 1866.

ARISTOTLE, *De Caelo*, trans. J. L. Stocks in *The Works of Aristotle*, vol. 2, Oxford 1930.

ARISTOTLE, *De Mundo*, trans. D. J. Furley, Loeb Classical Library, Cambridge 1955.

Bibliography

ARISTOTLE, *Physica*, trans. R. P. Hardie & R. K. Gaye in *The Works of Aristotle*, vol. 2, Oxford 1930.

Calendar of Patent Rolls in the Public Record Office, vol. 6, 1266–1272, ed. J. G. Black, H.M.S.O., London 1913.

CALCIDIUS, *Timaeus a Calcidio Translatus Commentaioque Instructus*, ed. J. H. Waszink, *Corpus Platonicum Medii Aevi*, vol. 4, London 1962.

CAPELLA, Martianus, *Works*, ed. Adolphus Dick, 1925.

CICERO, *Timaeus*, ed. Franciscus Pini, Rome 1965.

DANTE ALIGHIERI, *The Divine Comedy: Purgatory*, trans. Dorothy L. Sayers, Penguin Classics, London 1955.

EVERISDEN, John de, *Miscellany of John de Everisden*, College of Arms MS Arundel 30.

FICINO, Marsilio, *The Book of Life*, trans. Charles Boer, University of Dallas 1980.

FLETE, John, *De Fundatione Ecclesiae Westmonasteriensis*, 1443, Westminster Abbey MS 29, ed. J. A. Robinson, Cambridge 1909.

HESIOD, *The Homeric Hymns and Homerica*, ed. and trans. H. G. Evelyn-White, New York 1914.

LISMORE, *Lives of the Saints from the Book of*, ed. & trans. Whitley Stokes, Oxford 1890.

MACROBIUS, *Commentary on the Dream of Scipio*, trans. William Harris Stahl, Columbia University, New York 1952.

NENNIUS, *British History and the Welsh Annals*, ed. & trans. John Morris, London 1980.

NICOMACHUS OF GERASA, *Introduction to Arithmetic*, in *Great Books of the Western World*, ed., Robert Maynard Hutchinson, Chicago, London & Toronto, 1952.

PARIS, Matthew, *Historia Anglorum* and *Abbreviatio Chronicorum Angliae*, ed. Frederick Madden, London 1869.

PARIS, Matthew, *Chronica Majora*, ed. Henry Richards Luard, London 1880.

PLATO, *Meno*, trans. W. K. C. Guthrie, Penguin Classics, London 1956.

PLATO, *Timaeus*, trans. R. G. Bury, Loeb Classical Library, London & Harvard 1929.

RISHANGER, William de, *The Chronicle of William de Rishanger*, British Library MS Cotton Claudius D. 6., ed. James Orchard Halliwell, Camden Society Publications, series 1, vol. 15, London 1840.

RORICZER, Matthias, *Büchlein von der Fialen Gerechtiget*, Regensburg 1486, facsimile edition with an introduction by K. Schottenloher, Regensburg 1923.

SACROBOSCO, Johannis de, *The Sphere*, ed. & trans. Lynn Thorndike, Chicago 1949.

SILVESTRIS, Bernardus, *Cosmographia*, trans. Winthorp Wetherbee, New York and London 1973.

SPORLEY, Richard, *A History of the Abbots, Priors, etc. of Westminster Abbey*, British Library MS Cotton Claudius A. 8., 1450.

VILLANI, Giovanni, *Chronica*, ed. Francesco Gherardi Dragomanni, Florence 1845.

VITRUVIUS, M. Pollio, *De Architectura*, trans. W. Newton as *The Architecture of M. Vitruvius Pollio*, London 1791.

SECONDARY SOURCES

ACKERMANN, Rudolph, *The History of the Abbey Church of St Peter's, Westminster, Its Antiquities and Monuments*, London 1812.

AITCHINSON, Leslie, *A History of Metals*, vol. 2, London 1960.

ALLEN, Richard Hinckley, *Star Names: their Lore and Meaning*, New York 1963, first published 1899.

ANDRIEU, Michel, *La Rota Porphyretica de la Basilique Vaticane*, in *Mélanges d'Archéologie et d'Histoire*, vol. 66, 1954, pp. 189–218.

ANGLO, Sydney, *Spectacle, Pageantry and Early Tudor Policy*, Oxford 1969.

ARDALAN, Nader and BAKHTIAR, Laleh, *The Sense of Unity*, Chicago and London 1973.

ARNALDI, Francisci, ed., *Latinitatis Italicae Medii Aevi*, Brussels 1939.

AUERBACH, E., *Tudor Artists*, London 1954.

BADAWY, Alexander, *Coptic Art and Archaeology: the Art of the Christian Egyptian Church from the Late Antique to the Middle Ages*, Boston, Mass. 1978.

BADHAM, Sally, BLAIR, John & EMMERSON, Robin, *Specimens of Lettering from English Monumental Brasses*, London 1976.

BARRAL I ALTET, Xavier, *Les Mosaïques de Pavements Médiévales de la Ville de Reims*, in *Congrès Archéologique de France*, vol. 135, 1977, pp. 79–108.

BARNES, Carl F., Jnr., *Villard de Honnecourt, the Artist and his Drawings: a Critical Bibliography*, Boston, Mass. 1982.

BEER, Ellen J., *Die Rose der Kathedrale von Lausanne*, Bern 1952.

BELOE, E. M., *Photo-Lithographs of Monumental Brasses in Westminster Abbey*, London 1898.

BIDDLE, Martin, *Nonsuch Palace, 1959–60*, Surrey Archaeological Society, Guildford 1961, (reprinted from *Surrey Archaeological Society Collections*, vol. 58).

BINSKI, Paul, *The Painted Chamber at Westminster*, Society of Antiquaries of London 1986.

BINSKI, Paul, *What was the Westminster Retable?* in the *Journal of the British Archaeological Association*, vol. 140, 1987, pp. 152–174.

BINSKI, Paul, *The Cosmati at Westminster and the English Court Style* in *Art Bulletin*, vol. 77, no. 1, New York 1990, pp. 6–34.

BLACK, W. H., *Catalogue of the Arundel Manuscripts in the Library of the College of Arms*, London 1829.

BLACK, W. H., *Catalogue of Patent Rolls: 1266–1272*, vol. 6, London 1913.

BLAIR, John, *English Monumental Brasses before the Black Death*, in *Collecteana Historica: Essays in Memory of Stuart Rigold*, Kent Archaeological Society, No. 30, 1981.

BLAIR, Revd. John, *The Chronology and History of the World*, London 1768.

BOBER, Harry, *In Principio: Creation before Time*, in *De Artibus Opuscula*, vol. 60, 1961, pp. 13–28.

BOLTON, Arthur T., & Hendry, H. Duncan, eds., *John Talman*, Wren Society, vol. 17, Oxford 1940.

BOND, Francis, *Westminster Abbey*, London 1909.

BORENIUS, Tancred, *The Cycle of Images in the Palaces and Castles of Henry III*, Journal of the Warburg and Courtauld Institutes, vol. 6, 1943, pp. 40–50.

BOVINI, Giuseppe, *Ravenna Mosaics*, English edition, London 1957.

BRANMER, Robert, *Historical Aspects of the Reconstruction of Reims Cathedral, 1210–1241*, in *Speculum*, vol. 26, Cambridge, Mass. 1961, pp. 23–37.

BRAYLEY, Edward Wedlake & NEALE, John P., *The History and Antiquities of the Abbey Church of St Peter, Westminster*, vol. 1, London 1818, vol. 2, 1823.

BRENDEL, Otto J., *Symbolism of the Sphere: a Contribution to the History of Earlier Greek Philosophy*, Leiden 1977.

BROWNSWORD, R., & PITT, E. E. H., *A Technical Study of Some Medieval Steelyard Weights*, in *The Proceedings of the Dorset Natural History and Archaeological Society*, vol. 105, 1983, pp. 83–88.

BRUZELIUS, Caroline Astrid, *The Thirteenth-century Church at St-Denis*, Yale University Press, New Haven & London 1985.

BUCHER, François, *The Lodge Books and Sketch Books of Medieval Artists* in *Architector*, vol. 1, New York 1979.

BURGES, William, *The Mosaic Pavements*, in *Gleanings from Westminster Abbey*, by George Gilbert Scott, Oxford & London 1863, pp. 97–105.

BURLAND, C. A., *The Arts of the Alchemists*, London 1967.

Bibliography

BUTLER, Christopher, *Number Symbolism*, London 1970.

CARLEY, James, *Glastonbury Abbey*, London 1988.

CARNAN, T., *An Historical Description of Westminster Abbey, its Monuments and Curiosities*, London 1783.

CARPENTER, Edward, ed., *A House of Kings*, London 1966.

CHEETHAM, Nicolas, *Keepers of the Keys: the Pope in History*, London & Sydney 1982.

CLAUSSEN, Peter Cornelius, *Magistri Doctissimi Romani*, Stuttgart 1987.

COLVIN, Howard, ed., *Building Accounts of King Henry III*, Oxford 1971.

COLVIN, Howard, *A Biographical Dictionary of British Architects 1600–1840*, London 1978.

COLVIN, Howard, *History of the King's Works*, HMSO, vol. 1, 1963, vol. 4, 1982.

CONNOR, R. D., *The Weights and Measures of England*, H.M.S.O. 1987.

COTTINGHAM, Lewis, *The Tile Pavement of the Chapter House at Westminster*, in *Archaeologia*, vol. 29, 1842, pp. 390–391.

COWEN, Painton, *Rose Windows*, London 1979.

CROMBIE, A. C., *From Augustine to Galileo: The History of Science*, 1952.

CROMBIE, A. C., *Science*, in *Medieval England*, ed. Austin Lane Poole, Oxford 1958.

CROSBY, Sumner McKnight, *The Royal Abbey of Saint-Denis from its Beginnings to the death of Suger, 475–1151*, edited & completed by Pamcla Z. Blum, Yale University Press, New Haven & London 1987.

CRULL, Jodocus, *The Antiquities of St Peter's, or the Abbey Church of Westminster*, London 1711.

DART, John, *Westmonasterium or the History and Antiquities of the Abbey Church of St Peter's, Westminster... a survey of the Church and Cloisters taken in the Year 1723*, London 1742.

DICKES, William F., *Holbein's Ambassadors Unriddled*, London 1903.

DOLLINGER, Philippe, *The German Hansa*, trans. D. S. Ault and S. H. Steinberg, London 1970.

DUGDALE, William, *Monasticon Anglicanum*, vol. 1, ed. John Caley, Henry Ellis & Bulkeley Bandinel, London 1817.

ECO, Umberto, *Art and Beauty in the Middle Ages*, trans. Hugh Bredin, Yale University 1986.

ECOCHARD, Michel, *Filiation de Monuments Grecs, Byzantins et Islamiques: une question de géométrie*, Paris 1977.

ESMEIJER, Anna, C., *Divina Quaternitas*, Amsterdam 1978.

EVANS, M. W., *Medieval Drawings*, London 1969.

FERRERO, Vittorio Viale & Mercedes Viale, *Aosta, Romana e Medievale*, Turin 1967.

FORMILLI, C., *The Monumental Work of the Cosmati at Westminster Abbey* in *Journal of the Royal Institute of British Architects*, Series 3, vol. 18, no. 3, December 1910, pp. 69–83.

FROTHINGHAM, Arthur, *The Monuments of Christian Rome*, New York 1908.

GILSON, Etienne, *The Philosophy of St Thomas Aquinas*, trans. Edward Bullough, New York 1948.

GIMPEL, Jean, *The Cathedral Builders*, trans. Teresa Waughlondon 1988.

GLASS, Dorothy, *Studies on Cosmatesque Pavements*, BAR International Series 82, Oxford 1980.

GLASS, Dorothy, *Papal Patronage in the Early 12th century: Notes on the Iconography of Cosmatesque Pavements*, Journal of the Warburg and Courtauld Institutes, vol. 32, 1969, pp. 386–390.

GNOLI, Rancero, *I Marmori di Roma*, Rome 1971.

GRAVES, Robert, *The White Goddess*, London 1961.

GUIDOBALDI, Alessandra Guiglia, *Tradizione Locale e Influenze Bizantine nei Pavimenti Cosmateschi*, in *Bolletino d'Arte*, series 6, no. 26, 1984, pp. 57–72.

GUIDOBALDI, Frederico, *Pavimenti in Opus Sectile di Roma e dell'Area Romana: Proposte per una Classificazione e Criteri di Datazione*, in *Studi Miscellani 26, Seminario di Archeologia e Storia dell'Arte Greca e Romana dell'Università di Roma*, Rome 1985, pp. 171 255.

HAGENDAHL, Harald, *Augustine and the Latin Classics*, vol. 1, Gothenburg 1967.

HARRINGTON, John, *The Abbey and Palace of Westminster*, London 1869.

HARRISON, Walter, *A New and Universal History, Description and Survey of the Cities of London and Westminster*, London 1776.

HARVEY, John, *The Plantagenets*, London 1948.

HENINGER, S. K., Jr., *The Cosmographical Glass*, San Marino, California 1977.

HERMAND, A., *La Mosaïque de St-Bertin*, in *Mémoires de la Société des Antiquaires de la Marinie*, vol. 1 St Omer 1834, pp. 147–166.

HERVEY, Mary F. S., *Holbein's Ambassadors: the Picture and the Men*, London 1900.

HOPE, W. H. St John, *On the Early Working of Alabaster in England*, Catalogue of English Alabaster Work, Society of Antiquaries, London 1910, pp. 1–15.

HOPE, W. H. St John, *The Obituary Roll of John Islip*, in *Vetusta Monumenta*, vol. 7, part 4, London 1906, pp. 39–51.

HOPPER, Vincent Foster, *Medieval Number Symbolism: its Sources, Meaning, and Influences on Thought and Expression*, Columbia University Press 1938.

HUTTON, Edward, *The Cosmati: the Roman Marble Workers of the XIIth and XIIIth Centuries*, London 1950.

INGRAM HILL, D., *New Bell's Cathedral Guides: Canterbury Cathedral*, London 1986.

JAIRAZBHOY, R. A., *Oriental Influences in Western Art*, Bombay, London, New York & Calcutta 1965.

JAMES, Montague Rhodes, *The Apocalypse in Art*, Oxford 1931.

JAMES, Montague Rhodes, *The Apocalypse in Latin: MS 10 in the collection of Dyson Perrins*, Oxford 1927.

JAMES, Montague Rhodes, *The Drawings of Matthew Paris*, Walpole Society, vol. 14, Oxford 1926.

JENSEN, Hans, *Sign, Symbol and Script*, trans. George Unwin, London 1970.

KAMPFER, Fritz, and BEYER, Klaus, *Glass: A World History*, Dresden 1966.

KEEPE, Henry, *Monumenta Westmonasteriensia*, London 1683.

KIDSON, Peter, *Systems of Measurement and Proportion in Early Medieval Architecture*, Ph.D. Thesis, Courtauld Institute 1956.

KIRBY, J. W., *Transcriptions of the Accounts of the King's Works at Greenwich*, in the *Journal of the Transactions of the Greenwich and Lewisham Antiquarian Society*, vol. 5, 1954, pp. 22–50.

KNOWLES, David, *The Evolution of Medieval Thought*, London 1962.

KOLBAS, Judith G., *A Colour Chronology of Islamic Glass*, in the *Journal of Glass Studies*, vol. 25, 1983.

KRAUTHEIMER, Richard, *Introduction to an Iconography of Medieval Architecture*, in the *Journal of the Warburg and Courtauld Institutes*, vol. 5, 1941, pp. 1–33.

LANCASTER, R. Kent, *Artists, Suppliers and Clerks: the Human Factors in the Art Patronage of King Henry III*, in the *Journal of the Warburg and Courtauld Institutes*, vol. 35, 1972, pp. 81–107.

LATHAM, R. E., ed., *Revised Medieval Latin Word List from British and Irish Sources*, Oxford 1965.

LEMAY, Richard, *Abu Ma'shar and Latin Aristotelianism in the Twelfth Century*, Beirut 1962.

LETHABY, William R., *Westminster Abbey and the King's Craftsmen*, London 1906.

LETHABY, William R., *Westminster Abbey Re-examined*, London 1925.

LEWIS, Suzanne, *The Art of Matthew Paris in the 'Chronica Majora'*, University of California and Scolar Press, London 1987.

Bibliography

MACEK, P. M., *The Westminster Retable: A study in English Gothic Panel Painting*, University of Michigan 1986.

McEVOY, James, *The Philosophy of Robert Grosseteste*, Oxford 1982.

MAGNI, Mariaclotilde, *Un remarquable témoignage du premier art Roman en Italie du Nord: la Cathédrale d'Aoste*, in *Cahiers Archéologiques*, vol. 24, 1975, pp. 163–172.

MALCOLM, James Peller, *Londinium redivivum: or, An Ancient History and Modern Description of London*, London 1802.

MARLE, Raimond van, *The Development of the Italian Schools of Painting*, The Hague 1923.

MORTON, A. L., *A People's History of England*, London 1979.

NEWMAN, A. K., *A Description of Westminster Abbey, its Monuments and Curiosities*, London 1809.

NICOLAS, Harris, *The Chronology of History*, London 1835.

NORTHROP, F. S. C., *The Meeting of East and West*, New York 1946.

NOORTHOUCK, John, *History of London*, London 1773.

OGG, Oscar, *The Twenty-Six Letters*, New York 1948.

PACHT, Otto, *Book Illumination in the Middle Ages*, trans. Harvey Miller, London 1986.

PANOFSKY, Erwin, *Abbot Suger on the Abbey Church of St-Denis and its Art Treasures*, Princeton University, 1946.

PARIS, M. Louis, *Le Dedale ou Labyrinthe de l'église de Reims*, in *Bulletin Monumental*, vol. 22, Paris 1856, pp. 540–551.

PEARCE, E. H., *The Monks of Westminster: Notes and Documents Relating to Westminster Abbey, No. 5*, Cambridge 1916.

PERKINS, Jocelyn, *Westminster Abbey, Its Worship and Ornaments*, Alcuin Club Collection, vol. 33, Oxford & London 1938.

PHYSICK, John, et al., *New Bell's Cathedral Guides: Westminster Abbey*, London 1986.

POLAK, Ada, *Glass: its Makers and its Public*, London 1975.

POOLE, Reginald Lane, *Illustrations on the History of Medieval Thought and Learning*, New York 1920.

PORTER, Arthur Kingsley, *Lombard Architecture*, vol. 1, Yale University Press, New Haven, Oxford & London 1917.

POWICKE, Maurice, *The Thirteenth Century*, Oxford 1962.

PRESSOUYRE, Léon, *Le Cosmos Platonicien de la Cathédrale d'Anagni*, in *Mélanges d'Archéologie et d'Histoire*, vol. 78, Paris 1966, pp. 551–593.

PRIOR, Edward, *The Sculpture of Alabaster Tables*, Catalogue of English Alabaster Work, Society of Antiquaries, London 1910, pp. 16–25.

QUERIDO, René, *The Golden Age of Chartres*, Edinburgh and New York 1987.

RAGLAN, Lord, *The Temple and the House*, London 1964.

RICHARDSON, Henry Gerald, *Early Coronation Records* in the *Bulletin of the Institute of Historical Research*, vol. 16, 1938, pp. 1–11.

RICHARDSON, Henry Gerald, *The Coronation in Medieval England* in *Traditio* vol. 16, New York 1960, pp. 111–202.

RILEY, Harry Thomas, ed., *The Chronicle and Memorials of Great Britain and Ireland during the Middle Ages*, Rolls Series 28, vol. 2, London 1865.

ROBINSON, J. A. & JAMES, M. R., *The Manuscripts of Westminster Abbey*, Cambridge 1909.

ROUTLEDGE, C. F., *Excavations at St Augustine's Abbey, Canterbury*, in *Archaeologia Cantiana* the *Transactions of the Kent Archaeological Society*, vol. 25, 1902, pp. 238–243.

R.C.H.M., *An Inventory of the Historical Monuments of London, 1. Westminster Abbey*, London 1924.

RUNIA, David T., *Philo of Alexandria and the Timaeus of Plato*, Leiden 1986.

SANDFORD, Francis, *The History of the Coronation of James II*, London 1687.

SAXL, Fritz, *A Heritage of Images*, London 1957.

SCHILLER, Gertrud, *Iconography of Christian Art*, trans. Janet Seligman, London 1971.

SCHRAMM, Percy Ernst, *A History of the English Coronation*, trans. L. G. Wickham Legg, Oxford 1937.

SCOTT, George Gilbert, *The Westminster Chapter House*, in the *Transactions of the London and Middlesex Archaeological Society*, vol. 1, 1860, pp. 141–142.

SCOTT, George Gilbert, *Gleanings from Westminster Abbey*, Oxford & London 1863.

SCOTT, George Gilbert, *Personal and Professional Recollections*, ed. G. G. Scott, London 1879.

SHELBY, Lon R., *The Geometric Knowledge of the Medieval Master Masons* in *Speculum*, vol. 67, no. 4, Cambridge, Mass. 1972, pp. 295–421.

SHERLOCK, D. & WOODS, H., *St Augustine's Abbey: Report on Excavations 1960–78*, Kent Archaeological Society for the *Historic Buildings and Monuments Commission for England*, Maidstone 1989.

SIBILIA, Salvatore, *Storia di Anagni*, Anagni 1967.

SIMSON, Otto von, *The Gothic Cathedral*, Bollingen Series, vol. 48, 1962.

SOUTHERN, R. W., *Robert Grosseteste: The Growth of an English Mind in Medieval Europe*, Oxford 1986.

STAHL, W. H. & JOHNSON, R., *Martianus Capella and the Seven Liberal Arts*, New York & London 1971.

STERN, Henri, *La Mosaïque de la Cathédrale de Reims*, in *Cahiers Archéologiques*, vol. 9, Paris 1957, pp. 147–54.

STOKES, Whitley & Stracham, John, *Thesaurus Paleohibernicus: A Collection of Old Irish Glosses Scholia Prose and Verse*, Cambridge 1901.

SUMMERSON, John, *Architecture in Britain 1530–1830*, London 1953.

THOMAS, Ivor, *Selections Illustrating the History of Greek Mathematics*, vol. 1, Loeb Classical Library, London 1939.

THORNDIKE, Lynn, *The Sphere of Sacrobosco and its Commentators*, Chicago 1949.

TSCHICHOLD, Jan, *An Illustrated History of Writing and Lettering*, published in German 1946, English edition 1947.

TUDOR-CRAIG, Pamela, et al., *New Bell's Cathedral Guides: Westminster Abbey*, London 1986.

VAUGHAN, Richard, *Matthew Paris*, Cambridge 1958.

WANDER, Stephen, *The Westminster Abbey Sanctuary Pavement*, in *Traditio*, vol. 34, New York 1978, pp. 137–156.

WEBB, G., *The Decorative Character of Westminster Abbey*, Journal of the Warburg and Courtauld Institutes, vol. 12, 1949, pp. 16–20.

WEEVER, John, *Ancient Funerall Monuments within the United Monarchie of Great Britaine, Ireland, and the Islands adjacent etc.*, London 1631.

WESTLAKE, Herbert Francis, *Westminster Abbey*, London 1923.

WIDMORE, Richard, *An History of the Church of St Peter, Westminster, commonly called Westminster Abbey*, London 1751.

WILKINSON, B., *The Later Middle Ages in England, 1216–1485*, London 1969.

WILSON, Christopher, et al., *New Bell's Cathedral Guides: Westminster Abbey*, London 1986.

WINDEN, J. C. M. van, *Calcidius on Matter, his Doctrine and Sources*, Leiden 1959.

WOLTMAN, Alfred, *Holbein and his Time*, London 1872.

WOODS, William, *England in the Age of Chaucer*, London 1976.

WORMALD, Francis, *Painting in Westminster Abbey and Contemporary Painting*, in the *Proceedings of the British Academy*, vol. 35, London 1949, pp. 166–175.

WOSIEN, Maria-Gabriele, *Sacred Dance*, New York 1974.

WRIGHT, Thomas, ed. & trans., *The Political Songs of Europe*, Camden Society, vol. 6, London 1939.

Notes

1 These Porphyry Stones

1 Malcolm, 1802, vol. 2, p. 89 (see Bibliography).

2 '*sed quia per senarium est operum significato perfectio*', Aurellii Augustini, *De Civitate Dei*, ed., J. E. C. Welldon, London 1924, p. 502.

3 *The Apocrypha and Pseudepigraphia of the Old Testament in English*, ed., R. H. Charles, vol. 1, Oxford 1913, *The Wisdom of Solomon*, trans., Samuel Holmes, p. 553, chap. 11, v. 20.

4 J-P Migne, *Patrologia Latina*, vol. 77, 1862, cols. 1027–8.

5 Erwin Panofsky, *Abbot Suger on the Abbey Church of St-Denis and its Art Treasures*, Princeton University 1946, p. 162.

6 *New Scientist*, 11 July, 1985, p. 24, quoting Arvind Borde in *Classical and Quantum Gravity*, vol. 2, p. 589.

2 King, Pope, Craftsman and Priest

1 Maurice Powicke, *The Thirteenth Century*, Oxford 1962, p. 19.

2 Dante, *The Divine Comedy: Purgatory*, 1314, canto VII:
'Look! there the king of simple life is set
Alone – Harry of England, far more blest •
In those fair branches he did beget.'

(verse translation by Dorothy L. Sayers, Penguin Classics Series, London 1955, p. 121).

3 Giovanni Villani, *Chronica*, ed. Francesco Gherardi Dragomanni, Florence 1845, vol. 1, pp. 192–3 (Book 5 chap. 4: '*Arrigo...fu semplice uomo e di buona fe e di poco valore*.')

4 R. Kent Lancaster, *Artists, Suppliers & Clerks: the Human Factors in the Art Patronage of King Henry III*, in the *Journal of the Warburg and Courtauld Institutes*, vol. 35, 1972, pp. 81–107.

5 H. M. Colvin, *The History of the King's Works*, vol. 1, HMSO 1963, pp. 131 & 132.

6 Matthew Paris, *Historia Anglorum*, ed. Frederic Madden, London 1869, vol. 2, pp. 454–5: '*...unum nobilissimum feretrum ex auro puro primo et purissimo et gemmis pretiosissimis*'.

7 Thomas Wright ed., *The Political Songs of England*, Camden Society vol. 6, London 1939, p. 67:
'*(P)ar la v. plais a Diex, Parris fout vil mult grant
Il i a .i. chapel dont je fi coetant;
Je le ferra portier, a .i. charrier vollant,
A Saint Amont a Londres toute droite en estant.*'

8 See Pamela Tudor-Craig, in *The New Bell's Cathedral Guides: Westminster Abbey*, London 1986, p. 118.

9 Westminster Abbey Muniment no. 6318B records the delivery of Henry's heart to the Abbess of Fontevraud.

10 J. G. Black ed., *Calendar of Patent Rolls*, vol. 6 1266–1272, London 1913. p. 338, Membrane 17 dated 8 May, Windsor.

11 Flete, p. 113: '*repatriando tamen adduxit mercatores et operarios, ducentes secum lapides illos porphyriticos, jaspides, et marmora de Thaso, quos sumptibus suis propriis emerat ibidem. ex quibus ipsi operarii coram magno altari Westmonasterii mirandi operis fecerunt pavementum.*'

12 Matthew Paris, *Chronica Majora*, ed. Henry Richards Luard, London 1880, vol. 5, p. 701: '*...gravis simam vehementer formidans constitutionem...*'

13 E. H. Pearce, *The Monks of Westminster*, Cambridge 1916, p. 50.

14 Westminster Abbey Muniment no. 12800.

15 The surviving volume is in the British Library, MS Cotton Ortho C 11. A printed version was edited by E. M. Thompson, *Customary of St Augustine's Canterbury and St Peter's Westminster*, Henry Bradshaw Society, vol. 38, 1904.

16 H. M. Colvin, *op. cit.*, p. 147, n. 2, quoting *Calendar of Patent Rolls 1266–72*, p. 338.

17 Westminster Abbey Muniment no. 28811.

18 British Library MS Cotton Tiberius A.10. Printed edition in *Annales Monastici*, ed. Henry

Richards Luard, London 1866, vol. 3, p. 305: '*Abbas de Westmonasterio Londiniae, tunc domini regis thesaurarius, obiit, quasi repente; propter austeritatem parum planctus a convento suo.*'

19 Flete, ed., J. A. Robinson, Cambridge 1909, p. 115.

20 A. L. Morton, *A People's History of England*, London 1979, p. 96.

21 e.g. Arthur L. Frothingham, *The Monuments of Christian Rome*, New York 1908, pp. 383–4, who maintains that the same craftsman was responsible for all the cosmati work at Westminster Abbey and the pavement at Canterbury Cathedral, and most recently by Peter Claussen (see below).

22 Peter Cornelius Claussen, *Magistri Doctissimi Romani*, Stuttgart 1987, pp. 174–86.

23 Dorothy Glass, *Studies on Cosmatesque Pavements*, BAR International Series 82, Oxford 1980, p. 93.

3 The Physical Evidence

1 Keepe, 1683, p. 32.

2 Malcolm, 1802, pp. 89–90.

3 The catalogue of materials is the result of surveys with Robin Sanderson of the Geological Museum and Ian Freestone of the British Museum, and of comparison with the most authoritative work on Roman marbles, *I Marmori di Roma* by Rancero Gnoli, Rome 1971.

4 Pipe Roll 53, Henry III, rot. 18d., quoted by H. M. Colvin, *The History of the King's Works, vol. 1*, HMSO 1963, p. 147, n. 2.

5 The research and analysis of the results were carried out by Dr Ian Freestone using a JEOL JSM 840 scanning electron microscope with attached Links Systems energy dispersive X-ray spectrometer.

6 Judith G. Kolbas, *A Colour Chronology of Islamic Glass*, in the *Journal of Glass Studies*, vol. 25, 1983, pp. 95–100, and in conversation.

7 Brayley, 1823, p. 42.

8 Book VII, chap. 1, trans W Newton, *The Architecture of M. Vitruvius Pollio*, vol. 2, London 1791, p. 156.

4 The Historical Record

1 John Flete, *De Fundatione Ecclesiae Westmonasteriensis*, 1443, Westminster Abbey MS 29 f. 41v.

2 Richard Sporley, *History of the Abbots of Westminster*, 1450, British Library MS Cotton Claudius A. 8., f. 59r.

3 W. H. St John Hope, *The Obituary Roll of John Islip, Abbot of Westminster*, in *Vetusta Monumenta*, vol. 7, London 1906, plate 22.

4 John Harrington, *The Abbey and Palace of Westminster*, 1869, plate 8.

5 Westminster Abbey Muniments, drawer 4.I.B.

6 W. R. Lethaby, *Westminster Abbey and the King's Craftsmen*, London 1906, p. 132 & appendix pp. 370–1.

7 Mary F. S. Hervey, *Holbein's Ambassadors: The Picture and the Men*, London 1900, pp. 225–7.

8 Bodleian Library, Western MS Rawlinson D 775.

9 E. Auerbach, *Tudor Artists*, London 1954, p. 9.

10 J. W. Kirby, *Transcriptions of the Accounts of the King's Works at Greenwich*, in the *Journal of the Transactions of the Greenwich and Lewisham Antiquarian Society*, vol. 5, 1954, p. 45.

11 Victoria and Albert Museum, Prints Collection, pressmark 92.D.60.

12 E157–1940, E166–1940, E173–1940, E174–1940, E177–1940 and E182–1940. The existence of these drawings was first pointed out by Stephen Wander, *The Westminster Abbey Sanctuary Pavement* in *Traditio*, New York 1978, vol. 34, p. 139, n. 4.

13 This is confirmed by his letter book for the years 1708–12,

Bodleian Library MS English Letters, e 34, according to Howard Colvin, *A Biographical Dictionary of British Architects 1600–1840*, London 1978, p. 800.

14 British Library MS. Add. 23070 is dated to 1706 and before with additions up to 1723. Published by the *Walpole Society*, vol. 22, Oxford 1932, pp. 26–7. My thanks to Hugh Macandrew of the National Gallery of Scotland for bringing my attention to the existence of this manuscript.

15 Details of the Queen Anne altarpiece also appear in the volume of John Talman's sketches in the Victoria and Albert Museum, 92.D.60, E177–1940r. and E152–1940v.

16 George Gilbert Scott, *Personal and Professional Recollections*, edited by Scott's son, London 1879, p. 391.

17 Edward Carpenter, ed., *A House of Kings*, London 1966, p. 308.

18 Quoted in Edward Carpenter, *op. cit.*, p. 143.

19 Edward Carpenter, *op. cit.*, p. 168.

20 Westminster Abbey Muniment No. 44030A.

21 Westminster Abbey Muniment No. 44032.

22 Westminster Abbey Muniment No. 44030A.

23 Westminster Abbey Muniment No. 44746.

24 Westminster Abbey Muniment No. 44798.

25 Westminster Abbey Muniment No. 45130.

26 Westminster Abbey Muniment No. 45244.

27 H. M. Colvin, *History of the King's Works*, vol. 1, H.M.S.O. 1963, p. 149.

28 Dorothy Glass, *Papal Patronage in the Early 12th Century*, Journal of the Warburg and Courtauld Institutes, vol. 32, 1969, p. 387.

29 Pavino, quoted by Michel Andrieu, *La Rota Porphyretica de la Basilique Vaticane*, Mélanges d'Archéologie et d'Histoire, vol. 66, 1954, pp. 191–2.

5   The Inscription

1   Leslie Aitchison, *A History of Metals*, vol. 2, London 1960, pp. 322 & 324.

2   The research and analysis of the brass letter from the Westminster pavement inscription was carried out by Dr M. Hughes and Dr D. R. Hook.

3   R. Brownsword and E. E. H. Pitt, *A Technical Study of some Medieval Steelyard Weights*, in *The Proceedings of the Dorset Natural History and Archaeological Society*, vol. 105, 1983, pp. 83–8.

4   Philippe Dollinger, *The German Hansa*, trans., D. S. Ault & S. H. Steinberg, London 1970, p. 245.

5   Sally Badham, John Blair, Robin Emmerson, *Specimens of Lettering from English Monumental Brasses*, London 1976, p. 1.

6   Sally Badham, John Blair, Robin Emmerson, *op. cit.*, p. 1., and John Blair, *English Monumental Brasses before the Black Death*, in *Collected Historica: Essays in Memory of Stuart Rigold*, ed. Alec Detsicas, Kent Archaeological Society 1981, p. 257.

7   E. M. Beloe, *Photolithographs of Monumental Brasses in Westminster Abbey*, London 1898, plate 1.

8   Trinity College, Dublin, MS E.2.32. (584). See J. A. Robinson & M. R. James, *The Manuscripts of Westminster Abbey*, Cambridge 1909, p. 25.

9   Westminster Abbey MS 29, f. 41v.

10   British Library MS Cotton Claudius A. 8.

11   Victoria & Albert Museum, E.157–1940 and E.166–1940.

12   Victoria & Albert Museum, E.182–1940.

13   Camden, 1600, f. E2r., '.*in quo circulis marmoreis aenis literis maiusculus inscribuntur hic versus...*'

14   Keepe, 1683, splits *duodeno* into two words: *duo deno*. Crull, 1711, compounds the two

words *bis centeno* into one. Dart, 1723, does the same but splits *subductis* into *sub ductis*. Widmore, 1751, spells *quatuor* without its second '*u*'. Malcolm, 1802, offers *sexago* in place of *sexageno*. Lethaby, 1906, compounds and contracts *bis centeno* to *bicenteno*.

15   D. J. Furley, trans., *Aristotle, On the Cosmos*, Loeb Classical Library, Cambridge 1955, p. 387, *De Mundo*, 397b.

16   The existence of both was pointed out by Lethaby, *Westminster Abbey and the King's Craftsmen*, London 1906, p. 111.

17   British Library MS Cotton Claudius D. 6. f. 191v.

18   College of Arms MS Arundel 30. f. 9r. This is a fascinating collection of material including chronologies, theories of musical harmony and even an esoteric system of dot notation that W. H. Black supposes to be a secret writing or 'shorthand'.

19   W. H. Black, *Catalogue of the Arundel Manuscripts in the Library of the College of Arms*, London 1829, p. 47.

20   *Subaddas* is given by Widmore (1751), Malcolm (1802), Ackermann (1812), Brayley (1823), Lethaby (1906), Robinson (1909), Perkins (1938) and Stephen Wander (1978); *superaddas* is given by Camden (1600), Weever (1631), Keepe (1683), Crull (1711), Dart (1723), Dugdale (1817) and Burgess (1863).

21   Theon of Smyrna, ed. Hiller 45. 9–46.19 in Loeb Classical Library, *Greek Mathematics*, trans. Ivor Thomas, London 1939, vol. 1.

22   Aristotle, *De Caelo*, book I, 1, 12–13, in *The Works of Aristotle*, trans. W. D. Ross, vol. 2, Oxford 1930.

23   Charles Boer trans., *Marsilio Ficino: The Book of Life*, University of Dallas 1980, p. viii.

24   British Library MSS. Egerton 118. f. 51r. and Egerton 133 f. 229r.

25   William Lethaby, *Westminster Abbey and the King's Craftsmen*, London 1906, p. 311.

26   John Morris ed. & trans., *Nennius: British History and the Welsh Annals*, London 1980, p. 18.

27   H. G. Evelyn-White ed., *Hesiod: The Homeric Hymns and Homerica*, London & New York 1914, p. 75, *The Precepts of Chiron*, Fragment 3.

28   Lynn Thorndike, *The Sphere of Sacrobosco and its Commentators*, Chicago 1949, p. 208.

29   *Sphaericus* is given by Camden (1600), Keepe (1683), Crull (1711), Dart (1723), Widmore (1751), Malcolm (1802), Ackermann (1817), Brayley (1823), Burges (1863), Lethaby (1906) and Perkins (1938), while Weever (1631) and Robinson (1909) give *sphericus*. Sporley (c. 1450) and Wander (1978) maintain Flete's spelling.

30   Victoria & Albert Museum, E166–1940.

31   W. M. Lindsay ed., *Isiddori Hispalensis: Etymologiarum sive originum Libri XX*, Oxford 1911, cited by Richard Krautheimer, *Introduction to an Iconography of Medieval Architecture*, Journal of the Warburg Institute V (1941), p. 7.

32   Plato, *Timaeus*, 320 to 338, trans. R. G. Bury, The Loeb Classical Library, *Plato VII*, pp. 61–2.

33   J. H. Waszink ed., *Timaeus a Calcidio Translatus Commentaioque Instructus*, London 1962, p. 25.

34   Cicero, *Republic*, book 4, verse 15.

35   Franciscus Pini, *M. Tulli Ciceronis Timaeus*, Rome 1965, p. 41.

36   trans. Lynn Thorndike in *The Sphere of Sacrobosco and its Commentators*, Chicago 1949, p. 201.

37   J. H. Waszink, *op. cit.*, p. 138.

38   Adolphus Dicke, ed., *Martianus Capella*, p. 430, book VIII, line 814.

6 *The Art of Geometry*

1 Lon R. Shelby, *The Geometric Knowledge of the Medieval Master Masons*, in *Speculum*, vol. 47, no. 4, 1972, p. 395.

2 Dorothy Glass, *Papal Patronage in the Early 12th Century*, Journal of the Warburg and Courtauld Institutes, vol. 32, 1969, p. 386.

3 F. Guidobaldi & A. Guiglia Guidobaldi, *Pavimenti Marmorei di Roma dal IV al IX secolo*, in *Studi di Antichita Cristiana*, vol. 36, Vatican 1983, pp. 315–19 & 418–35.

4 A. Guiglia Guidobaldi, *Tradizione Locale e Influenze Bizantine nei Pavimenti Cosmateschi*, Bolletino d'Arte, series 6, no. 26, 1984, pp. 57–72.

5 Plato, *Meno*, 85D, trans. by W. K. C. Guthrie in *Protagoras and Meno*, Penguin Classics, 1956.

6 Marcus Vitruvius Pollio, *Ten Books on Architecture*, Book IX, chap. 1, trans. W. Newton under the title *The Architecture of M. Vitruvius Pollio*, London 1791, pp. 198–9.

7 Paris, Bibliothèque Nationale, MS fr.19.093.

8 Carl F. Barnes, *Villard de Honnecourt, the Artist and his Drawings: a critical bibliography*, Boston, Mass. 1982, p. xx.

9 'Wilars de Honecort v(os) salue (et) si proie a los ceus qui de ces engiens ouverant, c'on trovera en cest livres q(u)'il proient por s'arme (et) qu'il lor soviengne de lui. Car en cest livre puet o(n) trover grant consel de la grant force de maconerie (et) des engiens de carpenterie, (et) si troveres le force de la portraiture, le trais, ensi come li ars de iometrie le (com)ma(n)d(e) (et) ensaigne', transcribed by Hans Robert Hahnloser in *Villard de Honnecourt*, Vienna 1935, p. 11.

10 Matthias Roriczer, *Büchlein von Fialen Gerechtigket*, 1923 facsimile of Regensburg edition originally published in 1486, with an introduction by K. Schottenloher.

11 Peter Kidson, *Systems of Measurement and Proportion in Early Medieval Architecture*, Ph.D. Thesis, Courtauld Institute, 1956, see especially vol. 1, pp. 116–126, and vol. 2 which presents an analysis of a selection of churches from different countries which display the 1:√2 ratio in their design.

12 Frederico Guidobaldi, *Pavimenti in Opus Sectile di Roma e dell'Area Romana: Proposte per una Classificazione e Criteri di Datazione*, in *Studi Miscellani 26, Seminario di Archeologia e Storia dell'Arte Greca e Romana dell'Università di Roma*, Rome 1985, p. 184.

13 O. Holder-Egger, ed., 'Monumenta Germanicae Historica: Scriptores rerum Langobardicanum et Italicanum saec.', 1878, p. 289, cited by Dorothy Glass, *op. cit.*, p. 388.

14 *De Lineis, Angulis et Figuris*, quoted by James McEvoy in *The Philosophy of Robert Grosseteste*, Oxford 1982, p. 168.

7 *Images of Divine Order*

1 'Divinorum humanorumque disparitatem unius et singularis summaeque rationis vis admirabilis contemperando coaequat; et quae originis inferioritate et naturae contrarietate invicem repugnare videntur, ipsa sola unius superioris moderatae armoniae convenientia grata concopulat', Suger, *Libellus Alter De Consecratione Ecclesiae Sancti Dionysii*, edited by Erwin Panofsky in *Abbot Suger on the Abbey Church of S. Denis and its Art Treasures*, Princeton 1946, p. 82.

2 Plato, *Timaeus*, 32B–C, trans. R. G. Bury, Loeb Classical Library, London & Harvard 1929, p. 59.

3 Theon of Smyrna, ed., Hiller, 45.9–46.19 in Loeb Classical Library, *Greek Mathematics*, trans., Ivor Thomas, London 1939, vol. 1.

4 Nicomachus of Gerasa, *Introduction to Arithmetic*, Book II, 28–35, in *Great Books of the Western World*, ed., Robert Maynard Hutchinson, vol. 11, Chicago, London & Toronto 1952, p. 847.

5 Plato, *Timaeus*, 32B–C, *op. cit.*, p. 59.

6 Caius College, Cambridge, MS 428, f. 21v., c. 1100.

7 St John's College, Oxford, MS 17, f. 7v., c. 1110.

8 Bayerische Staatsbibliothek, Munich, Clm. 13002, f. 7v., c. 1150.

9 Bibliothèque Royale, Brussels, MS II, 1639, f. 6v.

10 Harry Bober, *In Principio: Creation before Time*, in *De Artibus Opuscula*, vol. 40, 1961, pp. 14–26.

11 *Revelations* I, 8 & 11.

12 M. W. Evans, *Medieval Drawings*, London 1969, p. 9.

13 For example, the seventeenth-century *Sylva Philosophorum* by Cornelius Petraeus, Bibliotheek der Rijksuniversiteit, Leiden, Cod. Voss. chem. q. 61, see *Alchemy*, by Stanislas Klossowski de Rola, English edition, London 1973, pp. 120–2.

14 E. J. Beer, *Die Rose der Kathedrale von Lausanne*, Berne 1952.

15 Bibliothèque de l'Arsenal, Paris, MS 3516.c. f. 179r., c. 1240.

16 Keith Critchlow, *The Chartres Maze*, in *Architectural Association Quarterly*, vol. 5, no. 2, pp. 11–20.

17 N. Bergier, *Histoire des Grands Chemins de l'Empire Romain*, Paris 1622, and G. Marlot, *Histoire de la Ville, Cité et Université de Reims*, 1666, re-published Reims 1845. See Xavier Barral I Altet, *Les Mosaïques de Pavement Médiévales de la Ville de Reims* in *Congrès Archéologique de France*, vol. 135 1977, pp. 79–108.

18 Quoted by James Carley in *Glastonbury Abbey*, London 1988, p. 18.

8 Into the Labyrinth

1 *Quaestiones Quodlibetales*, VII, 6, 3, quoted by Umberto Eco in *Art and Beauty in the Middle Ages*, p. 60.

2 'This form of instruction is figurative. Figurative discourse is a mode of discourse which is called "a veil". Figurative discourse is twofold, for we divide it into allegory and *integumentum*. Allegory is a mode of discourse which is different from its surface meaning, as in the case of Jacob wrestling with the angel. An *integumentum*, however, is a mode of discourse which covers a true meaning under a fictitious narrative, as in the case of Orpheus. For in the case of the former history, and in the latter fiction, contains a profound hidden truth, which will be explained elsewhere. Allegory pertains to Holy Scripture, but *integumentum* to philosophical scripture', quoted in W. H. Stahl & R. Johnson, *Martianus Capella and the Seven Liberal Arts*, New York & London 1971, p. 24.

3 J. C. M. van Winden, *Calcidius on Matter, his doctrine and sources*, Leiden 1959, p. 2.

4 Lord Raglan, *The Temple and the House*, London 1964, p. 137, citing R. Bloch, *The Etruscans*, as his authority.

5 Otto von Simpson, *The Gothic Cathedral*, Bollingen Series, vol. 48, 1962, p. xviii, quoting *Annales Monastici*, IV, 19, ed., H. R. Luard, London 1869.

6 J. C. M. van Winden, *op. cit.*, p. 18.

7 '*sive lapis iste rotundus habens in se colores quattuor elementorum hujus mundi, videlicet ignis aeris aquae et terrae*', British Library MS Cotton Claudius A. 8. f. 59v.

8 J. C. M. van Winden, *op. cit.*, p. 60.

9 J. C. M. van Winden, op. cit., p. 61.

10 Bernardus Silvestris, *Cosmographia*, trans. Winthrop Wetherbee, New York & London 1973, p. 67.

11 Bernardus Silvestris, *op. cit.*, p. 68.

12 Bernardus Silvestris, *op.cit.*, p. 237.

13 Plato, *Timaeus*, 38C, trans., R. G. Bury, Loeb Classical Library, London & Harvard 1929, p. 115.

14 Plato, *Timaeus*, 38C, quoted by S. K. Heninger, Jr., in *The Cosmographical Glass*, San Marino 1977, p. 9.

15 *Genesis*, 1, 14.

16 W. H. Stahl & R. Johnson, *Martianus Capella and the Seven Liberal Arts*, New York & London 1971, pp. 152–3.

17 For example, on a fragment of a portable altar, c. 1160, in the Treasury of St Servatius, Seiburg, Lower Rhine, and in a pen-and-ink drawing, c. 1140, in the Gladbach Missal, Munchen-Gladbach Minster Archives, Cod. 1.f.2r. See, Gertrud Schiller, *Iconography of Christian Art*, vol. 2, trans. Janet Seligman, London 1972, plates 409 & 435.

18 Calcidius, *Commentary on the Timaeus*, trans. J. C. M. van Winden, *op. cit.*, p. 238.

19 '*Elementa vocant philosophi caldeorum angulos, et merito, quia sicut figura quadrangula quatuor habet angulos, ita et hic mundus quatuor constat elementis*', John of Seville's translation of the *Instructorium Mauis* by Abu Ma'shar', quoted by Richard Lemay in *Abu Ma'shar and Latin Aristotelianism in the Twelfth Century*, Beirut 1962, p. 76.

20 Paul Binski, *What was the Westminster Retable?* in the *Journal of the British Archaeological Association*, vol. 140, 1987, pp. 159–65.

21 Oxford, Bodleian MS Douce 180.

22 Paul Binski, *The Painted Chamber at Westminster*, Society of Antiquaries, London 1986, p. 50.

23 Reginald Lane Poole, *Illustrations of the History of Medieval Thought and Learning*, New York 1920, p. 61.

24 *Revelations* 1, 8.

25 James McEvoy, *The Philosophy of Robert Grosseteste*, Oxford 1982, pp. 119 & 120.

26 James McEvoy, *op. cit.*, p. 18.

27 James McEvoy, *op. cit.*, p. 151.

28 *Les Grandes Chroniques*, Bibliothèque Nationale, Paris, MS Fr. 6425, f. 89v.

29 Michel Andrieu, *La Rota Porphyretica de la Basilique Vaticane*, in *Mélanges d'Archéologie et d'Histoire*, vol. 66, 1954, p. 205.

30 Percy Ernst Schramm, *A History of the English Coronation*, trans., L. G. Wickham Legg, Oxford 1937, p. 129.

31 James McEvoy, *op. cit.*, pp. 63 & 64.

32 Richard Krautheimer, *Introduction to an Iconography of Medieval Architecture*, in the *Journal of the Courtauld and Warburg Institutes*, vol. 5, 1941.

33 James McEvoy, *op. cit.*, p. 129.

34 Bernardus Silvestris, *op. cit.*, p. 89.

Sources of Illustrations

The *Ancient Art and Architecture Collection*, 114, 115; by permission of the *Bayerische Staatsbibliothek*, Munich, 110 (MS Clm. 13002, f.7v.); the *Bodleian Library, University of Oxford*, 108 (St John's College, Oxford, MS 17, f.17v.), 119 (MS Douce 180, f.18r); courtesy of *BBC Television*, 13, 61, 64, 66; by permission of the *British Library*, 81 (MS Cotton Claudius A.8, f.59r.), 83 (MS Cotton Claudius D.6, f.191v.), 85 ('Historia Abbatiae Cassinensis' by Erasmus Gattola, 1733); by permission of the Syndics of *Cambridge University*, 4 (Cambridge University Library MS Ee.3.59, f.30.), 107 (Caius College, Cambridge, MS 428, f.21v.); by permission of the *College of Arms*, 84 (MS Arundel 30, f.9r.); courtesy of the Master and Fellows of *Corpus Christi College, Cambridge*, 3 (MS 16, f.56.); by permission of the *Royal Commission on the Historical Monuments of England*, 53; *Malcolm Crowthers*, 118, 122; *Richard Foster*, 6, 7, 8, 10, 70, 82, 86–91, 98, 104–6, 115, 116, 120, 121 (courtesy of the Dean and Chapter of Westminster) 1, 5 (W. A. M. 9465), 11, 15–50, 55, 56 & 57 (W.A.M. 4.1.B.11), 58, 62, 63, 69, 71–8, 80 (Westminster Abbey MS 29, f.41v.), 96, 99–103 (courtesy of the Board of Trustees of the Victoria and Albert Museum) 2, 12 (E.173–1940), 60 (E.157–1940), 65 (E,182–1940), 67 (E.182–1940 & E.177–1940), 95; courtesy of the *National Museum of Wales*, 79 (inv.38.765.); by permission of the *National Gallery*, 59; by permission of the *Bibliothèque Nationale*, Paris, 92–4 (MS Fr. 19.093.), 116 (MS Arsenal 3516.c, f.179r.), 123 (MS Fr. 6465, f.89v.); courtesy of the *Bibliothèque Royale Albert 1er*, Brussels, 109 (MS II, 1639, f.6v.); *Scala*, 9; the *Society of Antiquaries*, 68; by courtesy of the Board of Trustees of the *Victoria and Albert Museum*, 51 (facsimile from 'Vetusta Monumenta'), 111 (inv. 4757–1858); courtesy of the *Dean and Chapter of Westminster*, 52, 54; *Zodiaque*, 117.

Index

(illustration numbers are shown in bold type)

accounts, 12, 14, 15, 16, 20, 21, 39,
    65, 73–5
Ackermann, Rudolph, 49, 55–6, 62,
    68, 92
Ackermann's aquatint, **58**
Ages of Man, the four, 4, 19, 135, 136,
    145
ages, world, 96–8, 102, 161
Agnus Dei, 160
Air, 4, 5, 104, 132–5, 144, 152, 153,
    156, 157
alabaster, **38**, 33, 39
Albertus Magnus, St, 18
alchemy, 143, 156
Alexander IV, Pope, 17
altar-piece, the Queen Anne, **63**, 65–6,
    67, 68, 74–6
Ambassadors, The (Holbein), **59**,
    56–60
Amiens Cathedral, 12
Anagni,
    Cathedral, **6**, 17, 18, 20, 22, 24, 26,
    77
    crypt frescos, **7, 8, 105, 106**, 18–19,
    135, 136, 147, 149, 161
analysis,
    of glass, 40–1
    of brass letters, 83–4
Andrewes, Dean, 71
Anglicanus, Bartholomeus, 82
Anglicus, Robertus, 103, 107
Anjou, 10, 13
Anne, Queen, 65, 67, 74, 75
Annus, **114, 117**, 145, 147
Antiquaries, Society of, 56, 61, 63
Aosta Cathedral, **117**, 145, 147
Apocalypse, the, **119**, 160–1
Aquinas, St Thomas, 18, 20, 148, 149
archetype, 103, 104, 109, 110, 153,
    154, 157, 162, 165
Aristotle, 96, 97, 100, 109, 162

Armstrong, Neil, 5
atomic absorption spectrophotometry,
    84
Augustine, St, 4, 162

Barons' War, 9
Becket, Thomas à, 8
Beer, Ellen, 145
Bernasconi, Francis, 67
black coralite limestone, **32**, 38, 45
black limestone, **31**, 38
Blair, John, 86
Blythburgh, Church of the Holy
    Trinity, **115**, 143
Bober, Harry, 137
Boethius, 20
Bonaventure, St, 18
brass, 82–5
Brayley, Edward Wedlake, 45, 49, 85
breccia giallo, **35**, 38, 45
Bridewell Palace, 29
British Museum Research Laboratory,
    41, 83
Burges, William 76–7
Byzantine marbles, 112, 114

Calcidius, 106, 107–8, 149, 152–4, 158
Cambio, Arnolfi di, 27
Camden, William, 48, 89, 92, 94
Canterbury,
    Archbishop of, 13–14
    Cathedral, 7, 8, 147, 152
Capella, Martianus, 108, 109, 148
carboniferous limestone, **27**, 36–7, 44,
    45
Carnan, T., 70, 74
Carrara marble, 34, 38, 59
Cassian, 148
chaos, primal, 153–4, 161, 164
Charles II, 73, 74, 76
Charles V, Holy Roman Emperor, 164

Charlemagne, **123**, 164
Chartres Cathedral, 13, 145–6
Church, John, 65
Cicero, 106–7
cipollino, **37**, 38, 45
Civil War, 71
Civita Castellana, Church of S. Maria
    Maggiore, 22
Claussen, Peter, 26–7
Clement IV, Pope, 21, 93
    tomb of, **9, 10**, 22–4, 26, 27, 63
Colvin, Sidney, 58
Commonwealth, 72–3, 76
Compass, Points of the, 136
Constance, Solomon of, 136
Constantinople,
    Emperor's Palace, 35, 164
coronations, **3, 69, 123**, 7, 8, 162–4
Cornwall, Richard, Earl of, 84, 86
cosmati, **2**, 17, 21–2, 30, 34, 39, 42,
    44, 59, 111
Cosmatus family, 22
cosmogony, 133–4, 153–9, 162, 164
cosmology, **3**, 96, 100, 144, 146, 147,
    152
Cosmos, the, as a living being, 100,
    105–7, 166
counter-Reformation, 76
Court of Rome, **1**, 7, 13, 15–16, 93,
    109
Courtauld Institute, 63
Critchlow, Keith, 146
Crokesley, Abbot Richard, 15, 18
Crucifixion, cosmic iconography of,
    156
Crull, Jodocrus, 33, 73
cutting techniques, stone, **49, 50**, 45–6,
    64, 67

damage to pavement, 65–6, 74, 75–6
Dante, Alighieri, 10, 146

Dart, John, 33, 49, 56, 61–2, 63, 65 6

Desiderious, Abbot, 12

Devonian limestone, 33, 38

Dinteville, Jean de, 58

Dionysius the pseudo-Areopagite, 162

Dissolution, 70, 76

'doubling of the square', 91, 94–7, 116–18, 119–25

Douce Apocalypse, 119, 160

Dugdale, William, 49, 104

Dunstable Priory, 20

Earth, 4, 5, 104, 132–5, 147, 152, 153, 156, 157

Edward the Confessor, 9, 10, 12
  shrine of, 4, 68, 2, 8, 22, 27, 35, 69, 70, 71, 75–6, 92
  translation of, 8, 14, 27

Edward I, 10, 20, 74, 101

Edward V, 7

Edward VIII, 7

Egyptian gabbro, 38

Einstein, Albert, 6

Elements, the four, 4, 5, 6, 19, 104, 108, 132–5, 144, 145, 148–9, 152–61

Elizabeth I, 71

Empedocles, 132

End of the world, 96–8, 102, 159–62

Erigena, John Scotus, 161

eternity, 97, 109, 161, 162, 164–5

Euclid, 111, 128

Everisden, John de, 84, 99–100, 101

exegesis, 5, 79, 97, 148

Fathers of the Church, 4, 111, 133

Feckenham, Abbot, 71, 76

Ficino, Marsilio, 100–1

Fiore, Joachim di, 161

Fire, 4, 5, 104, 132–5, 144, 145, 152, 153, 156, 157, 161

Flete, John, 80, 14, 17, 18, 21, 48, 86–9, 90, 92–9, 101, 103, 153

Fontevraud Abbey, 13

Foucquet, Jean, 164

Four,
  Ages of Man, 4, 19, 135, 136, 145
  Cardinal Virtues, 147
  Elements, 4, 5, 6, 19, 104, 108, 132–5, 144, 145, 148–9, 152–61
  fundamental forces, 5–6
  Points of the Compass, 136
  Qualities, 132, 133, 135, 136, 145, 154–5, 156, 157

Rivers of Paradise, 145

Seasons, 4, 19, 135, 136, 144, 145, 147

Temperaments, 4, 135, 145

gabbro, 30, 38

Galen, 19, 135

Gebel Dorkham, 35

geometric solids, 104, 134

geometry,
  constructive, 111, 116–25, 128–9
  natural, 30
  of cosmati patterns, 87–90, 44, 45, 78, 114, 115–16, 125–8, 130
  practical, 11, 128
  speculative, 4, 5, 111, 128–9, 130, 131–2, 135–6, 144, 165

Genesis, 97, 133, 137, 152–5

Genoise serpentine, 28, 37, 44

George IV, 66

Gerasa, Nicomachus of, 133

giallo antico, 26, 36, 44, 47, 128

Gibbons, Grinling, 65

Gibbons, J. Harold, 56, 52

glasses,
  European, 39, 40–1
  Islamic, 39, 40–2
  Roman, 40–1
  weights, 42
  Westminster pavement, 39, 40, 41, 42, 39–42, 77

Glastonbury, 147

Gloucester Cathedral, 8

Gloucester, William of, 10

Gospel of St John, the, 154

Gradi, S. Maria, 23

Graves, Robert, 102

Greenwich Palace, 59–60

Gregory the Great, Pope, 5

Grosseteste, Robert, 130, 149, 162, 164, 165

Guidobaldi,
  Alessandra, 112, 115
  Frederico, 122

guilloche motif, 86, 112–5

Gwilym, Ap, 102

Hadfield, C., 57, 54, 68

Hampton Court, 65

Hanbury Church, 39

Hansa merchants, 84–5

Harley, Sir Robert, 71

Harrington, John, 52, 50, 54, 67

harmony, 4, 5, 30

Hawksmoor, Nicholas, 70

Henry I, 152

Henry II, 13

Henry III, 2, 7, 8–14, 20, 21, 65, 70, 74, 84, 93, 109, 147, 164
  tomb of, 2, 2, 35
  Great Seal of, 10

Henry V, Holy Roman Emperor, 164

Henry VII, 60, 70

Henry VIII, 59, 60, 70

Heraclitus, 154

Hervey, Mary F. S., 58–60

Hesiod, 102–3

Heythe, John, 60

Hippocrates, 19, 135

horoscopes, 152

Hosch, Eduoard, 145

Holbein, Hans, the Younger, 56–60

Holy Trinity, the, 143

Honnecourt, Villard de, 92–4, 118–21, 122, 128

Hyle, 154

illumination of
  manuscripts, 129, 135–44, 145, 152, 164

Innocent IV, Pope, 11

inscription, 71, 3, 7, 62, 80–110
  colons, 82, 94–5
  distribution of letters, 82, 88–9, 93, 94, 103
  letter composition, 82–5
  letter forms, 72–8, 82, 85–6
  mortar, 83, 94
  three time scales of, 110, 157–8, 164

integumentum, 148

Investiture Controversy, 112

Isabella, Queen, 13

Islip, Abbot, 51, 49, 65, 70

James I, 71, 75

James II, 69, 65, 74

jasper, 33

Jerome, St, 85

John, King, 8, 13

Jung, Carl, 129

Keepe, Henry, 31, 33, 48, 70, 73, 89, 104

Kidson, Peter, 122, 125

Kolbas, Judith, 42

labyrinth, 146–7, 151, 161

lapis lazuli, 33

latten, 82–5

Laurentius family, 17, 22

Lausanne Cathedral, **112, 113**, 141, 144, 146, 149, 158, 161
Lessington, William de, 86
Lethaby, William, 52, 56, 58, 59, 60, 63, 90, 101
Lewisham, Phillip de, 15, 17, 18
Liberal Arts, the Seven, 147
limestone,
   black, **31**, 38
   black coralite, **32**, 38, 45
   carboniferous, **27**, 36–7, 44, 45
   Devonian, **33**, 38
   Purbeck, **23**, 30, 34, 59, 76, 82, 84, 94, 122, 125
   red crinoidal, **34**, 38
Lincoln Cathedral, 86
Lismore, Book of, 101–2
logos, 154, 157
Louis IX, 12, 13
lydian, 33

Macrobius, 106
macrocosm, **19**, 103, 104, 108, 109
Maine, 10
Malcolm, James Peller, 3, 31–3, 49, 89, 92
Malmesbury, William of, 147
manuscript illumination, 129, 135–44, 145, 152, 164
Mary I, 70–1
matter, primal, 153–4, 157
memento mori, 58
memorial brasses, 82, 84
'Meno', the, (Plato) 116–17, 122
microcosm, **106, 110**, 19, 103–4, 136–7
Monte Cassino Abbey, **85**, 112, 115
Montfort, Simon de, 8
Months, Labours of the, 136, 144, 145, 147
moon, 145, 155, 156, 157, 162
mortars,
   lime, **49**, 36, 46
   cement, **50**, 46, 64
   resin, 83, 94
mosaic, 2, 63, 73, 112–14
Murano island of, Venice, 39
Myos Hormos, 35

Narbonne, Peter, Archbishop of, 24
Narni, S. Domenica, 43
nave, symbolism of, 151–2
Nennius, Bishop of Bangor, 102
Nicomachus of Gerasa, 133
Noys, 154

number,
   masculine and feminine, 148
   of the Four Elements, 133, 135, 141
   of Time, 92, 155, 157–8
   perfect, 4, 100, 148
   symbolism, 4, 101, 156, 157, 161, 162
neo-Platonism, 4, 100–1, 103, 105, 128, 132–3, 141, 147, 162
Normandy, 10
Norris, George, 74

Oderisius, Petrus,
   (Odoricus), 7, 21–7, 93, 109, 129, 148
old red sandstone, 38
Old Sarum, 7
opposites, reconciliation of, 132–3
opus sectile, 2, 30, 35, 111–15
onyx marble, **29**, 37–8, 76–7, 153, 164
Origen, 148
Orvieto, Badia di SS. Severo & Martirio, 44
Ossius, Bishop, 149

palm leaves, symbolism of, 160
Paris, Matthew, 10, 12, 13, 141
Paris, Treaty of, 10
Paulus family, 22
Peter, Archbishop of Narbonne, 24
phenocysts, 35, 46, 67
physics, modern 6–7
Pisano, Nicola, 27
Placidia, Galla, 129, 162
planets, 96, 108, 137, 155
Plato, 19, 103, 105, 108, 116, 122, 134, 149, 154, 155, 166
Plotinus, 105
Poitou, 10
porphyry, 33, 77, 93, 109
   green, **25**, 21, 35, 44, 45, 46, 47, 59, 67, 128
   purple, **24**, 2, 35–6, 44, 46, 47, 59, 67, 128, 129, 164
primal chaos, 153–4, 161, 164
primal matter, 153–4, 157
primal unity, 6, 161
primary mix materials, **43, 47**, 44–5, 47
primum mobile, 96–7, 100–1, 109, 110, 130, 161, 162
Purbeck marble, **23**, 30, 34, 59, 76, 82, 94, 122, 125
Pythagoras, 4, 100, 128, 133–4

quadrature **94–7**, 116–18, 119–25

Qualities,
   the four primary, 132–3, 135, 136, 145, 154–5, 156, 157
   the six secondary, 134, 135
Quellin, Arnold, 65
Queen Anne altar-piece, **63**, 65–6, 67, 68, 74–6

Rainerius family, 22
reconciliation of opposites, 132–3
red crinoidal limestone, **34**, 38
Reformation, 70, 71, 76
Regensburg, 137, 141
Reichenau, Wilhelm von, 129
Reims,
   Cathedral, 12, 13, 164
   St-Remi, 147
Relativity, Theory of, 6
relics, 12–13
restoration, **64–7, 70**, 43, 47, 52, 64, 66, 67, 69–70, 71, 73–6, 78–9
retable, the Westminster, **118, 122**, 159–60
Revelation of St John the Divine, 19, 160, 161, 162
Reyns, Henry of, 12
Richard I, 13
Richard, Earl of Cornwall, 84, 86
Rishanger, William de, **83**, 98–100, 101
Rivers of Paradise, the four, 145, 147
roman foot, 122–4
Rome,
   classical, 34
   Court of, 1, 7, 13, 15–16, 93, 109
   Old St Peter's, 77, 164
   SS, Quatro Coronati, 111
Roriczer, Matthias, 121, 122, 128–9
Royal Commission on Historical Monuments, **53**, 51, 54

Sacroboscus, the Sphere of, 103
St Albertus Magnus, 18
St Augustine, 4, 162
St-Bertin, Abbey of, 147
St Bonaventure, 18
Sainte-Chapelle, 12, 13, 14
S. Denis, Abbey of, 5, 14, 132, 147
St Hubert Bible, the, **109**, 137, 141, 152, 156
St Jerome, 85
St John, 160
St Paul, 13
St Thomas Aquinas, 18, 20, 148, 149
Salvator Mundi, Christ as, 160

sanctuary, symbolic significance, 151–2
Sandford, Francis, 74
Sapienta, 18–19, 154
schemata, 4, 19, 131–3, 135–41, 141, 148–9, 152, 162, 164
Scott, George Gilbert, 54, 64, 67–9, 76, 86
Seasons, the four, 4, 19, 135, 136, 144, 145, 147
secondary mix materials, **44, 48**, 44, 47, 73
Selve, Georges de, 58
serpentine, **28**, 33, 37, 44, 45
Seville, Isidore of, 105
shrine of Edward the Confessor, **4, 68**, 2, 8, 22, 27, 35, 69, 70, 71, 75–6, 92
Silva, 154, 157
Silvestris, Bernardus, 154
Smyrna, Theon of, 100, 133
Society of Antiquaries, 56, 61, 63
Socrates, 116–17
solids, regular geometric, **104**, 134, 157
Solomon of Constance, 136
Sporley, Richard, **81**, 48, 77, 88, 90–1, 93, 95, 97–101, 102, 104, 153
square root of 2, 122–5
Stanley, Dean, 67, 68
steelyard,
    the London, 84
    weights, **79**, 84–5, 86
Stokes, Whitley, 101–2
sub-atomic particles, 6
Suger, Abbot, 5, 132, 148
sun, 145, 155, 156, 157, 162

Talman, John, 56, 61–4, 68, 74, 77, 89, 103–4

Tarquinia, S. Maria di Castello, 43
Temperaments, the four human, 4, 135, 145
temple, origin of word, 151
tertiary mix materials, 45, 47, 74, 76, 78
Theodosius, Emperor, 129
Theon of Smyrna, 100, 133
three, number of completion, 100–1, 133
Timaeus, the, 19, 105–8, 133–4, 149, 153, 162
Time,
    creation of, 155, 157
    number of, 92, 155, 157–8
Torrigiano, Pietro, 60
touchstone, 33, 38
transmutation of the Elements, 156
trinities, **116**, 6, 143
Tutbury,
    Priory, 39
    quarries, 39
typology, Biblical, 141

unity,
    divine, 96, 110, 133, 161
    primal, 6, 161

Valence, John and Margaret of, 86
Vassallettus family, 17, 22
Vertue, George, 63–4
Victoria and Albert Museum, 62, 143
Victoria's Jubilee, Queen, **54**, 52
Villani, Giovanni, 10
Vincent, E. M., 86
Virgin Mary, 160
Virtues, four Cardinal, 147
Viterbo, Church of S. Francesco, 23

Vitruvius, 46, 117

Wander, Stephen, 104
Ware, Abbot Richard de, 1, 2, 7, 14–21, 48, 93, 109, 124, 129, 149
Water, 4, 5, 104, 132–5, 145, 147, 152, 153, 156, 157
Weever, John, 9, 89, 92
weights, steelyard, **79**, 84–5, 86
Wenlock, Abbot Walter de, 20
Westminster, Edward of, 10
Whitehall Palace, 65
Widmore, Richard, 49, 92, 103–4
William I, 7
William III and Mary II, 65, 74, 75
Winds, Earthly and Heavenly, 136, 145
Wisdom,
    Book of, 4
    Old Testament figure, 18–19, 154
Worcester Cathedral, 13
world,
    ages, 96–8, 102, 161
    end of, 96–8, 102, 159–62
Wren, Sir Christopher, 65, 66, 70, 74
Wright, Andrew, 60
Wyatt, Benjamin, 67

X-ray,
    energy dispersive techniques, 41
    fluorescence, 83

Year, the, **114, 117**, 145, 147

zodiac, signs of the, 6, 19, 136, 144, 145, 147